CW00531215

THEORIZING IN ⊔IAL SCIENCE

THEORIZING IN SOCIAL SCIENCE

The Context of Discovery

Edited by Richard Swedberg

Stanford Social Sciences
An Imprint of Stanford University Press
Stanford, California

Stanford University Press
Stanford, California

Printed in the United States of America on acid-free, archival-quality paper

Library of Congress Cataloging-in-Publication Data

Theorizing in social science : the context of discovery / edited by Richard
Swedberg.
    pages cm
Includes bibliographical references and index.
ISBN 978-0-8047-8941-7 (cloth : alk. paper)
ISBN 978-0-8047-9109-0 (pbk. : alk. paper)
    1. Social sciences—Philosophy. I. Swedberg, Richard, editor of compilation.
H61.T4646 2014
300.1—dc23

                                                        2013036393

For Mayer Zald (1931–2012),
our colleague and friend

Contents

Preface

Richard Swedberg

THE PURPOSE OF THIS BOOK IS TO START A DISCUSSION OF THE need for more creative theorizing in social science. We need better and bolder theory; and the key to producing it lies in the way that theory is being produced and how it is being taught to the next generation of social scientists. It primarily lies in the process of *theorizing*. In order to end up with better theory, in brief, we need to shift our main concern from theory to theorizing.

There is some reason to believe that the time is now ripe for this sea change from theory to theorizing. One important reason for this has to do with the emergence a few decades ago of cognitive science, especially cognitive psychology. Cognitive scientists have by now made good inroads into the mysteries of human thought processes; and the findings point in a very different direction from the kind of logical reasoning that for a long time has stood at the center of traditional theory in the social sciences. There exist many ways of thinking other than formal reasoning: with images, analogies, metaphors, and what in everyday language is called intuition.

In an earlier book a co-editor and I wanted to draw attention to the role of social mechanisms (Hedström and Swedberg 1997). We felt that much social science had become too focused on the analysis of variables and did not pay enough attention to the concrete ways in which social actions are linked together, via social mechanisms. In this volume the focus has been shifted to the general process through which theory, including social mechanisms, is produced in the first place.

Before you have a theory, you need to theorize—so how do you go about theorizing in a creative way? The authors of the chapters in this book represent different social sciences; and they all offer different answers to this question. This diversity is healthy in itself. It also testifies to the experimental nature of this volume, which does not have as its goal to summarize the current state of theory in social science, but to point in novel directions by focusing on the process of theorizing.

What unites the authors is a deeply felt desire to break with the present situation: a virtual standstill of theory in social science. The standstill over the past few decades is evident at least in comparison with the powerful development of methods over the same time period, not to mention the explosive rate of innovations in fields such as cognitive science, neuroscience, and genetics.

To change the course of theory in social science—how you produce it and how you teach it—is a huge task and necessarily collective in nature. It is our hope that the reader will want to join this enterprise and help to move it along. The project of creating a new wave of bold and interesting theorizing in social science is large enough, and at the moment also open enough, for a large number of people to participate. What some would regard as drawbacks—the early, sketchy, and unfinished nature of this project—innovators will see as opportunities and what makes it exciting and inviting.

The book is organized in the following manner. The first chapter, "From Theory to Theorizing," presents an overview of the project of theorizing. It discusses how theorizing differs from theory, what kind of theorizing is needed to innovate, and that one goes about theorizing (the different elements that make up the process of theorizing).

A somewhat longer version of this chapter was originally sent to all of the participants, who were asked to react to it in their own way (Swedberg 2012). The idea was not to comment on its content but to use its core argument as an inspiration to carry the project of theorizing forward, in the direction that each author thought best. The result is a plethora of ideas and suggestions, mixed with reflections on the authors' own experiences of theorizing in their research.

At first the reader may get the impression that the chapters are very far apart. But as Neil Gross discusses in the Afterword (Chapter 10), this is not the case. More precisely, there are two broad themes that all of the authors touch on. These are: what makes certain types of theorizing creative, and how to rein in and steer one's imagination in a creative direction when theorizing.

Several different factors can help to make theorizing creative. The general nature of human thought, especially as investigated by cognitive psychology and neuroscience, is one of these (see Chapters 1, 2). The reason for this is that the way human beings think comes much closer to what we have traditionally viewed as creative thought. We use, as earlier mentioned, analogies and metaphors, and we use intuition as a matter of course.

Opening up theorizing to the arts and to the general creativity of human beings is another way of making it more innovative (see Chapters 7, 9). Traditionally science and art have not been particularly close, but maybe the time has come to start pulling them closer together. Creative theorizing is furthermore a collective enterprise; and the focus should be on the community rather than on the talented but lonely individual. Creative theorizing fares best when many people theorize and when a creative attitude toward theorizing has become a public good (see Chapter 4).

The second major theme in this book is linked to the first, in the sense that it is concerned with creativity as well. The emphasis, however, is on the specific ways in which creative impulses can be turned into creative theorizing, and not just dissipate. You want to let loose the imagination but also steer it into interesting social science.

How to do this can be very difficult in practice. It is, for example, important to aim at the right level of theorizing (see Chapter 6). It is similarly crucial to choose the right topic and to deal with the empirical material in a special way (Chapters 5, 8). It is also important to understand the craft of theorizing: how to handle analogies, create an explanation, and the like (Chapters 1, 3). While it may not be possible to develop specific rules for how to theorize well, there nonetheless are certain steps that need to be taken, and these can be learned as well as taught.

But even if there do exist a few themes that tie the individual chapters together, each of them also brings something special to the project of creative theorizing. In the rest of this Preface I therefore say something about each chapter, so that the reader is able to easily find what he or she might be looking for or something that looks interesting.

In the first chapter—"From Theory to Theorizing," I outline and present the basic ideas behind the project of creative theorizing in social science. For example, I make an argument for why it is necessary to focus on what happens at the stage *before* the final formulation of theory, since this is where the key idea is conceived and then hammered out.

I also attempt to show how one goes about theorizing, what steps need to be taken before formulating a theory. I suggest that one should begin by observing, then name the phenomenon and create one or several concepts that capture it. After this, the theory needs to be built out, with the help of analogies, metaphors, typologies, and more. The final stage is when a tentative explanation is produced.

At the heart of Chapter 2—"Intuitionist Theorizing" by Karin Knorr Cetina—is the important shift that has taken place in our view of how thinking should be understood, thanks to cognitive psychology and neuroscience, and how this affects the view of what theorizing is. While we have previously looked mainly at and valued the logical and clear type of reasoning, we are today moving in a different direction. This different direction is still not set, but in the meantime Knorr Cetina suggests that we may want to look at the role of what she calls the inner processor in theorizing. This processor draws on long-term memory rather than the working memory, which has a much more limited capacity and only handles what we can recall consciously. The processor is implicit rather than explicit and intuitive rather than reflexive. It operates extremely quickly once it gets going—but it also pretty much comes and goes as it likes. To better understand theorizing in social science, the author concludes, we need to better understand our inner intuitive processor.

While Chapter 2 is mainly theoretical, Chapter 3—"Analogy, Cases, and Comparative Social Organization" by Diane Vaughan—is more practical in nature. Many of the other authors in this volume advocate the use of some special technique or tool when theorizing. According to Vaughan, analogies are especially useful for this purpose. They can be used, she says, not only to come up with an explanation, but also to choose a topic in the first place and to describe the topic.

To illustrate the usefulness of what she calls analogical theorizing, Vaughan uses her own well-known study of seemingly disparate topics, from how people end a relationship to the fate of the space shuttle *Challenger* in 1986 (Vaughan 1986, 1996). Vaughan's approach to the use of analogies, it should also be noted, is reminiscent of that of James Clerk Maxwell, who was an avid fan of analogies (Maxwell 1884). Like Maxwell, Vaughan does not advocate the simple use of analogies: comparing the phenomenon you are studying to some analogous phenomenon and theorizing the result. Instead she suggests that analogies should be seen as a tool for approaching a solution step by step.

Implicit in the arguments in the first three chapters is that the theorizer is an individual. The idea in Chapter 4, "The Unsettlement of Communities of Inquiry" by Isaac Ariail Reed and Mayer N. Zald, is different. These two authors emphasize that there is a necessary collective dimension to creative theorizing. Without acknowledging this collective dimension, they say, the theorizing project will fail, or it will surely be much less successful than it could have been.

It is particularly when a human community is going through important changes that the theorizing of social scientists can flourish, according to the authors. The community of scholars must as a consequence not be isolated from the larger community. It is only when the two are organically linked to each other that the full potential of theorizing in social science can be realized.

Although all of the contributors to this volume are deeply interested in how to raise the level of theorizing in social science, some are also very critical of the current attitude toward theory. Chapter 5—"Three Frank Questions to Discipline Your Theorizing" by Daniel B. Klein—is a case in point, with its critique of how theory is sometimes handled in economics.

According to Klein, theorizing does not mean that you can theorize in just about any way you want. Theorizing in social science will only be successful if it fulfills three conditions. First, theorizing has to deal with a real-world problem of some consequence ("*Theory of what?*"). Second, it has to provide a better explanation than the existing one ("*Why should we care?*"). And third, a good argument has to be presented why the new explanation is better than the existing one ("*What merit in your explanation?*").

Chapter 6, "Mundane Theorizing, *Bricolage*, and *Bildung*" by Stephen Turner, approaches the topic of how to theorize well in a different way from Klein. In Turner's view, there exist a few different ways of theorizing, depending on the ambition and skill of the social scientist. The first is what he calls mundane theorizing. This method, for example, might extend an existing theory to something that it did not originally cover. This may seem simple, but it can be hard to do.

The next level of difficulty occurs when one tries to bring two or more theories to bear on each other, in an effort to produce some kind of new synthesis. But creating a synthesis or *bricolage* of this type does not constitute the most creative and advanced type of theorizing, according to Turner. This is instead so-called high theory, or *Bildung*, which is characterized by three features. First, the theorizer must be able to look at other theories from the viewpoint of their producers. Second, he or she must be sensitive to the weaknesses of a theory. And third, a first-class theorizer must be ruthlessly honest when evaluating a theory.

People who engage in high theory derive a great deal of pleasure from what they do, says Turner. They also feel a distinct sense of community with other high theorizers, whether they agree with them or not. And they are absolutely passionate about what they do.

Chapter 7, "The Counterfactual Imagination" by Roland Paulsen, is written by a sociologist who shares the concern of many of the contributors to this book, namely that the current way of theorizing in the social sciences is often conducted in the wrong way. He is, however, alone in being interested primarily in counterfactuals and the creative role that these can play in theorizing.

The core of Paulsen's argument is that social scientists need to train their counterfactual imagination. If they do this, he says, they will be able to handle some important social science topics in a much better way than they currently do. We cannot, for example, fully understand power, if we do not understand the counterreaction—or counterfactual reaction—that power produces. Similarly, it is through the use of the counterfactual imagination that power can be transcended.

Chapter 8 is called "The Work of Theorizing," and its author, Karl E. Weick, is one of the few social scientists who has been intensely interested in theorizing throughout his career. More than twenty-five years ago he suggested the following: "Theory cannot be improved until we improve the theorizing process, and we cannot improve the theorizing process until we describe it more explicitly, operate it more self-consciously, and de-couple it from validation more deliberately" (Weick 1989: 516).

The part of the theorizing process that Weick discusses in this book has to do with how one makes the transition from the stage of observation to the formulation of concepts and a theory—or more precisely, how one goes from social reality to a really live kind of theory without producing the narrow knowledge-in-hindsight that social science so often seems to end up with.

Weick's answer is that we have to realize that the transition from observation to a theory is best understood as the result of a very delicate and tension-filled process in several steps. Weick also provides the potential theorizer with a useful list of fourteen items to keep in mind when theorizing.

James G. March, the author of the next chapter, "Susan Sontag and Heteroscedasticity," has also been concerned with theorizing for much of his career. And like Karl Weick, he shares the conviction that art can be of help in producing good social theory. In Chapter 9 he notes that while we today can produce students who are skilled in methods, we have failed to teach them how to handle the aspects that especially concern artists, authors, and poets. Both social science methods and artistic qualities, however, are needed to produce a truly creative social science. We therefore need to get a handle on the kind of techniques that artists use and adapt them for the purpose of social scientists.

Is this a realistic project? And if so, how can it be accomplished? March hesitates, but not when it comes to the urgency of these ideas. What he finds difficult is instead to outline what these new techniques should look like and how to teach them. In the meantime, however, he says there are some themes and focal points that are important for students of social science to understand. These include *ambiguity, contradiction, context* in meaning, and the role of *affirmation* in construction (or the quality of beauty).

This volume ends with an Afterword by Neil Gross, who raises some additional critical issues. He notes that the ideas of pragmatism, especially the work of Charles Peirce, have influenced many of the chapter authors. He also issues three warnings to those who want to get involved in the project of creative theorizing, and says that unless these are heeded the whole project may be endangered. These are as follows: you should focus on the way that social scientists have *actually* behaved when theorizing; you should not divert your energy to interdisciplinary efforts; and it is important to face the fact that so far theorizing has mainly been a male enterprise.

Finally, let me draw attention to the fact that one of the contributors to this book departed this world just after submitting his chapter. Mayer Zald (1931–2012), co-author of Chapter 4, will be sorely missed. Mayer was a brilliant social scientist, a beloved colleague, and extremely generous to his colleagues and students with praise as well as time and concern. It is fully in character, we think, that his last work contains a plea that, when we discuss theorizing, we should realize that true and humane theorizing in social science always has its roots in the larger community.

For encouragement, help, and suggestions I would like to first thank Mabel Berezin. I am also grateful to many other people who have helped to shape the project of creative theorizing in social science, including Andy Abbott, Margareta Bertilsson, Angie Boyce, Mikael Carleheden, Christoffer Carlsson, Nicolas Eilbaum, Laura Ford, Emily Goldman, Emily Hoagland, Darcy Pan, Lambros Roumbanis, and Hans Zetterberg. The comments of two anonymous reviewers were very helpful. I have, finally, learned much from the students in my classes on theorizing at Cornell University, Copenhagen University, and Stockholm University. For financial support I gratefully acknowledge my debt to Cornell's Department of Sociology and its Institute for the Social Sciences (ISS).

Contributors

Karin Knorr Cetina is George Wells Beadle Distinguished Service Professor of Sociology and Anthropology at the University of Chicago and principal investigator of the project "Scopic Media," University of Constance. Major publications include *Epistemic Cultures* (Harvard University Press, 2003), *Handbook of the Sociology of Financial Markets* (edited with Alex Preda, Oxford University Press 2012), and *Maverick Markets: The Global Currency Market as a Cultural Form* (forthcoming).

Neil Gross is professor of sociology at the University of British Columbia. His most recent books are *Why Are Professors Liberal and Why Do Conservatives Care?* (Harvard University Press, 2013), and *Social Knowledge in the Making* (University of Chicago Press, 2011, co-edited with Charles Camic and Michèle Lamont).

Daniel B. Klein is professor of economics at George Mason University, where he leads the graduate program in Adam Smith studies, and a fellow of the Ratio Institute in Stockholm. He is chief editor of *Econ Journal Watch*, author of *Knowledge and Coordination: A Liberal Interpretation* (Oxford University Press, 2012), and editor of *What Do Economists Contribute?* (NYU Press/Palgrave, 1999).

James G. March is professor emeritus at Stanford University where he has been on the faculty since 1970. Other of his books published by the Stanford University Press include: *Explorations in Organizations, The Dynamics of*

Rules (with Martin Schulz and Xueguang Zhou) and *The Roots, Rituals, and Rhetoric of Change* (with Mie Augier).

Roland Paulsen is a postdoctoral research fellow in the Department of Business Administration, Lund University. He received his PhD in sociology from Uppsala University; his main fields of study are the sociology of work and critical theory. He is the author of *Arbetssamhället: Hur arbetet överlevde teknologin* (2010) and *Empty Labor: Subjectivity and Idleness at Work* (2013).

Isaac Ariail Reed is assistant professor of sociology at the University of Colorado at Boulder. He is the author of *Interpretation and Social Knowledge: On the Use of Theory in the Human Sciences* (University of Chicago Press, 2011).

Richard Swedberg is professor of sociology at Cornell University. His two primary specialties are economic sociology and social theory. He is the author of several books, including *The Art of Social Theory* (forthcoming). He is also co-editor (with Neil Smelser) of *The Handbook of Economic Sociology* (Princeton University Press, 1st ed. 1994, 2nd ed. 2005) and (with Peter Hedström) of *Social Mechanisms* (Cambridge University Press 1998).

Stephen Turner is Distinguished University Professor in Philosophy at the University of South Florida. His books include *The Impossible Science*, with Jon Turner (1990) and *The Social Theory of Practices* (1994). His most recent book is *Explaining the Normative* (2010). Two collections of his essays are forthcoming: *The Politics of Expertise* and *Understanding the Tacit*.

Diane Vaughan is professor of sociology at Columbia University. In addition to the three books analyzed in her chapter, two are in progress: *Dead Reckoning: System Effects, Boundary Work, and Risk in Air Traffic Control* and *Theorizing: Analogy, Cases, and Comparative Social Organization*.

Karl E. Weick is Rensis Likert Distinguished University Professor of Organizational Behavior and Psychology, Emeritus, at the Stephen M. Ross School of Business at the University of Michigan. He is the author of many articles and books, including *Sensemaking in Organizations* (1995), *Managing the Unexpected* (with Kathleen M. Sutcliffe, 2001, 2006), and *Making Sense of the Organization* (vol. 1: 2001, vol. 2: 2009).

Mayer N. Zald (1931–2012) was professor emeritus, Department of Sociology and Schools of Business and Social Work, at the University of Michigan. His work focused on social movement theory, organizational theory, and sociology as human science. He wrote or edited twenty-one books, most recently *Social Movements and the American Health System*, with Jane Benaszak-Holl and Sandra Levitsky (Oxford University Press, 2010). In 2008 he received the John D. McCarthy Award for Lifetime Achievement in the Scholarship of Social Movements and Collective Behavior.

1   From Theory to Theorizing

Richard Swedberg

S INCE THE MID-TWENTIETH CENTURY THE SOCIAL SCIENCES HAVE
made great advances in the kind of methods that they use. In the
area of theory, however, the situation is quite different. The development since
World War II has been quite uneven in this respect; sociologists and other
social scientists are today very methodologically competent, but considerably
less skillful in the way they handle theory. The major journals contain many
solidly executed articles, though creative and theoretically sophisticated articles are less common.

Why is this the case? And can the situation be changed? Can the theory
part be brought up to par with the methods part in today's social science? One
answer that I suggest we may want to explore is the option of placing more
emphasis on *theorizing* than on *theory*; and in this way start to close the gap
between the two.

Roughly speaking, the expression "to theorize" refers to what one does to
produce a theory and to the thought process before one is ready to consider
it final. While theorizing is primarily a process, theory is the end product.
The two obviously belong together and complement each other. But to focus
mainly on theory, which is what is typically done today, means that the ways
in which a theory is actually produced are often neglected. This is true both
for the individual researcher and for social science as a whole.

Emphasizing the role of theorizing also has huge consequences for the way
that theory is taught, a topic that is of great importance and deserves a volume

of its own. For example, when sociological theory is often taught today, the student gets to know what Durkheim, Weber, Bourdieu, and others said—knowledge that will supposedly come in handy once the student undertakes future research projects. But teaching theorizing is very different; here the goal is for the student to learn to theorize on his or her own. The point is to learn to develop theories for one's own empirical work, not just use someone else's ideas.

The emphasis on each individual doing his or her own theorizing means that each individual must draw on his or her unique set of knowledge and experience. I refer to the central role of the individual in the theorizing process as *personalism*; the term refers to the fact that theorizing will only be successful if one delves deeply into one's own self and experiences. You have to know theory to theorize, but to theorize well you also need to relate to it in a personal way.

Also, just as the individual is always exposed to the risk of failing when he or she does anything authentic, the same is true for theorizing (Kierkegaard [1846] 1962). Repeating other people's theory entails little risk, unlike theorizing on one's own. This is part of the meaning of Weber's statement that "the scientific worker has to take into his bargain the risk that enters into all scientific work: Does an 'idea' occur or does it not?" (Weber 1946: 136).

There exist many ways of theorizing, including induction, deduction, generalizing, model-building, using analogies, and others. Some of these, I argue, are especially useful for theorizing in sociology and social science. In discussing and presenting the different types of theorizing I will often use the work of Charles S. Peirce as my guide. The writings by Peirce, especially "How to Theorize" and "Training in Reasoning," are extremely suggestive for theorizing (e.g., Peirce 1934, 1992d/1998). I have similarly found many relevant insights in cognitive science.

But it is also clear that much of what has been written on theorizing has been forgotten and that no one has tried to pull together the most important texts or tried to piece together the tradition of theorizing that I have attempted to describe in this introductory chapter. The writings that do exist are scattered throughout the enormous literature in social science, in autobiographical accounts by social scientists, and in their correspondence.[1]

Finally, throughout this chapter I point out the many obstacles that currently exist to creative theorizing. These epistemological obstacles, as I will call them (following Gaston Bachelard), are of different kinds (see, e.g.,

Bachelard [1934] 1984). Some of them make it hard to deal effectively with data in the process of theorizing. Others encourage the social scientist to rely far too much on existing theory and skip the element of theorizing or reduce it to a minimum.

The Distinction between the Context
of Discovery and the Context of Justification

In approaching the topic of theorizing in social science, it is convenient to take as one's point of departure the well-known distinction in the philosophy of science between the context of discovery and the context of justification. In doing so, it is possible to show that both the current neglect of theorizing and the related overemphasis on theory have much to do with the tendency in today's social science to largely ignore the context of discovery, and instead to focus most of the attention on the context of justification.

The distinction between the context of discovery and the context of justification received its most influential formulation in the 1930s through the work of Hans Reichenbach and Karl Popper. Today the distinction is still around, even if it has been criticized over the years and is far from generally accepted (Hoyningen-Huene 1987; Schickore and Steinle 2006). It should be pointed out that the argument in this chapter does not rest on the notion that these two concepts are each other's absolute opposites or that there exists a sharp conceptual line between the two. Nonetheless, the distinction represents a useful point of departure for the discussion.

Both Reichenbach and Popper worked on ways to improve empiricism as a philosophy of science. Reichenbach coined the terms "context of discovery" and "context of justification," while Popper helped to diffuse them by giving them a central place in his influential work *The Logic of Scientific Discovery* (Popper 1935: 4–6; Popper 1959: 31–32, 315; Reichenbach 1938: 6–7, 281; Reichenbach 1951: 231). Both used the distinction primarily with the natural sciences in mind, not the social sciences.

Reichenbach defined the context of discovery as "the form in which [thinking processes] are subjectively performed," and the context of justification as "the form in which thinking processes are communicated to other persons" (Reichenbach 1938: 6). While science can address issues in the context of justification in a satisfactory way, the same is not true for the context of discovery. "*The act of discovery escapes logical analysis*" (Reichenbach 1951: 231, emphasis added).

Popper similarly argued that everything that precedes the formulation of a theory is of no interest to science and logic. It belongs at best to "empirical psychology" (Popper 1935: 4–5; Popper 1959: 31–2). This meant in practice that what accounts for the emergence of new theories cannot be studied. In his influential work Popper kept hammering away at this message: it is impossible to study theoretical creativity; the only place for science is in the context of justification (Popper 1982: 47–48).[2]

In terms of theorizing in the social sciences, what is important in Reichenbach and Popper's distinction is that attention was now directed away from the context of discovery and toward the context of justification. A theory that cannot be verified (Reichenbach) or falsified (Popper) is not scientific; and it therefore becomes imperative to establish the link between theory and facts according to scientific logic.

Since the context of discovery was seen as impossible to study with scientific rigor, it fell to the side. If we for the moment view the scientific enterprise as consisting of three elements—one goes from (1) *theorizing*, to (2) *theory*, to (3) *the testing of theory*—only the second and third elements received sustained attention in social science. The first element was largely ignored. Since there exist good reasons for believing that one draws on different ways of thinking when theorizing and when testing and presenting ideas to an audience, this neglect has had serious consequences for social scientists' capacity to theorize.

The strong focus on verification and falsifiability in sociology after World War II is illustrated by Robert K. Merton's influential work in the 1950s and 1960s. Merton looked at theory mainly from the perspective of testability, as his well-known definition of theory illustrates. "The term *sociological theory* refers to logically interconnected sets of propositions from which empirical uniformities can be derived"; and these uniformities should be established via "empirically testable hypotheses" (Merton 1967: 39, 66, 70).

Because the emphasis on the methods part of social science continued after Merton, the first of our three elements—theorizing—has been largely ignored. In the rest of this chapter, I will therefore focus on theorizing. This should not be interpreted as an argument that theory and the testing of theory are not of crucial importance, only that theorizing is in need of extra attention today since it has been neglected for such a long time.

The General Structure of the Process of Theorizing

> Theory cannot be improved until we improve the theorizing process,
> and we cannot improve the theorizing process until we describe it more
> explicitly, operate it more self-consciously, and de-couple it from validation
> more deliberately. A more explicit description [of the process of theorizing]
> is necessary so we can see more clearly where the process can be modified
> and what the consequences of these modifications are.
>
> Karl Weick, *"Theory Construction as Disciplined Imagination" (1989)*[3]

Merton was well aware that good theory was the result of inspiration and creativity, as well as rigorous and systematic work with data. He noted that method books are full of "tidy normative patterns," but do not describe how sociologists actually "think, feel and act" (Merton 1967: 4). As a result of this, Merton continued, studies have "an immaculate appearance which reproduces nothing of the intuitive leaps, false starts, mistakes, loose ends and happy accidents that actually cluttered up the inquiry" (Merton 1967: 4).

But even if Merton was a very creative theorist himself, he does not seem to have felt that theory could be advanced very much by focusing directly on the context of discovery. His main contribution to an understanding of discovery underscores this very point, namely the idea that discoveries happen by sheer accident or "serendipity" (Merton 1967: 158–62; Merton and Barber 2004).

A similar attitude was present among the sociologists who were engaged in what became known as "theory construction" in the mid-1960s to the mid-1970s. According to a historian of this approach, theory construction essentially continued the "verification approach" of Merton and other Columbia University sociologists (Zhao 1996: 307; see also Hage 1994; Willer 1996; Markovsky 2008). Studies that did not develop a satisfactory way of testing theory were often labeled "verbal" or otherwise pushed to the side as pre-scientific and passé (Blalock 1969). The classics were sometimes mentioned as an example of a failure to properly "formalize" (see, e.g., Freese 1981: 63).

While one can learn much about theorizing from the advocates of theory construction, they were primarily interested in the context of justification, not the context of discovery. Their main concern was with the way you develop and test hypotheses, not with what precedes those two operations. They also focused primarily on formal and cognitive elements, and had little to say on such topics as intuition, imagination, and abduction. This also goes for the best works in the genre, which are of high quality, such as *Constructing Social Theories* by Arthur Stinchcombe, and *An Introduction to Models in the Social Sciences* by Charles Lave and Jim March (Willer 1967; Stinchcombe 1968; Lave and March [1975] 1993).

How then is one to proceed in order to bring what happens in the context of discovery into the theorizing process in an effective way? Can one, for example, produce practical rules for how to theorize, and can these rules then be used to produce a skill in theorizing that matches the skill in methods that exists today? This is the main question I try to address in the rest of this chapter. The first part of my answer, drawing on Peirce and others, is that some preliminary rules or guidelines of this type can be devised. The second part of my answer is that it is imperative to proceed beyond knowing rules or guidelines, and to develop a skill in theorizing.

It deserves to be repeated that in order to succeed in this enterprise we also need to get rid of some of the epistemological obstacles to theorizing. One of these is the idea that in order to theorize one has to proceed in a scientific or logical manner. This is not the case; and there exists today a large literature in cognitive science that shows this (for a discussion of this topic, see Chapter 2, by Karin Knorr Cetina).

To theorize well one needs inspiration, and to get inspiration one can proceed in whatever way leads to something interesting—and that means *any way*. This is permissible because the goal, at this stage of the process, is simply to produce something interesting and novel, and to develop a theory about it. It is only at a later stage, when the theory is being tested or otherwise confronted with data in a systematic manner, that scientific and rigorous rules must be followed. To use an analogy from the area of criminal justice: when you are trying to figure out who the murderer is, you are in the context of discovery; when you are in court and have to prove your case, you are in the context of justification.

In brief, creativity is primarily what matters when a theory is devised; and scientific logic and methodological rigor are primarily what matters in the context of justification. This, incidentally, is precisely what Reichenbach and Popper argued. But what to their followers in social science became a reason to ignore the context of discovery—it takes you away from rigor, logic, and proof—can also be seen as an opportunity, an opportunity to make full use of one's imagination, intuition, and capacity for abduction (see also, e.g., Weick 1989; Luker 2008).

A second epistemological obstacle to theorizing is the view, in sociology and many other social sciences, that empirical data should enter the research process first in the context of justification or when the hypotheses derived from a theory are tested. According to this view, the social scientist should start the study with a distinct research question or a distinct theoretical point in mind, then construct hypotheses, and finally confront the hypotheses with data.

This approach is implicit in much of mainstream sociology and also in some of the other social sciences. The researcher is encouraged to begin with a research question, and then try to answer it with the help of data (Merton 1959). Or the researcher selects some theoretically interesting idea, and then proceeds to the empirical phase, in the hope of being able to further explore and develop it in this way.

Like middle-range theory, theory-driven research represents a deliberate attempt to steer free of "mindless empiricism" or the production of facts with little or no reference to theory. In so-called mindless empiricism one begins by collecting data in an attempt to avoid any artificial or preconceived theoretical notions. One then summarizes the result without linking it to a theory.

The way in which theory was overtaken by the rapid development of methods after World War II is also reflected in the fact that quite a bit of theorizing is presented these days as being part of methods. This is, for example, the case with some qualitative methods, including participant observation and grounded theory. There is similarly a tendency among the proponents of theory construction to talk about "theoretical methods" (e.g., Willer 1967; Stinchcombe 1978; Freese 1980).

The problem with using this type of terminology is that it feeds into the tendency to focus primarily on the role of methods in social science research rather than on creativity and originality. The result, especially for qualitative methods, is a failure to realize that theorizing constitutes an independent element in the research process, and that theory is not the same as methods. Theory has its place in the research process, and it also needs its own space.

The types of research that so far have been discussed leave very little room for creative theorizing, except when carried out by those rare individuals who have a natural talent for it. They somehow succeed under any circumstances. But the average social scientist is different. As a graduate student, he or she will typically have been taught methods, but not theorizing, since the topic is rarely taught in theory classes (see, e.g., Markovsky 2008). As a result, all too

often an awkward attempt is made to force research findings into some existing theory or just stick a theoretical label on them. First you do the research,
and then you try to figure out if your findings fit some theory.

The dilemma for much of contemporary social science is consequently that
you are damned if you do and damned if you don't. It is hard to produce good
theory if you start from the facts; and it is hard to produce good theory if you
start from theory. In the former case, there will be no theory; and in the latter
case, the theory already exists.

How then to proceed? The strategy I advocate as a response to this dilemma
is to let empirical data drive the theorizing process. This is natural for empirical social science and should not be seen as advocacy of mindless empiricism.
On this point the classics are very instructive. Weber, Durkheim, and many
others of the pioneering generation in modern social science advocate *starting with the facts*. In *Rules of Sociological Method*, Durkheim says that the
researcher should proceed "from things to ideas," not "from ideas to things"
(Durkheim [1895] 1964: 15). And according to Weber, "theory must follow
the facts, not vice versa" (Weber 2001: 36).None of the authors of the classics,
however, has showed how to go from facts to theory in the creative manner in
which they themselves excelled. One way of doing this—and this is what sepa-
rates the approach I advocate from mindless empiricism, theory construction,
and theory-driven research—is to let the data enter the research process *at
two different stages*. One should start the research process by exploring data.
And at a later stage one should formulate hypotheses (or their equivalents)
and systematically confront these with data.

How is this done? Just as some researchers advocate the use of a pilot study
before the main study is carried out, an early empirical phase is necessary, in
my view. But its purpose is very different from that of a pilot study, namely
to develop creative research ideas through theorizing. The first part of the
research process can be called a *prestudy*; and it is characterized by theorizing
based on empirical material that has been generated with the aim of making
a (modest) discovery.

The reason to give it a special name is to draw attention to it as a distinct
element in the research process. While the term *prestudy* may suggest associations with the pilot study and the exploratory study, it has a different purpose,
namely to make it easier to develop a creative theoretical approach to a topic.[4]
At the first stage of the research process (during the prestudy), one should
deal with the data in whatever way is conducive to creativity—and *then* try to

theorize with the help of these data. Once an interesting theoretical idea has been formulated and developed into a tentative full theory, one can proceed to the second stage, which is the context of justification where the main study is carried out. This is where the research design is drawn up and executed. From this point on, rigor and logic are crucial since the data to be used have to be collected in reliable ways and also presented in this manner to the scholarly community.

Note that what is being discussed are not major discoveries by major social scientists, but the kind of modest discoveries that most social scientists can produce if they are well trained and passionate about their work.

Two other points should also be added to this account of the two stages of the research process, the prestudy and the main study. First, this is a very general description of how new ideas may be developed and later tested. It is well known, for example, that when hypotheses are tested unexpected findings might lead to the formulation of a new theory. Or to phrase it differently: creative theorizing may also take place in the context of justification.

There is furthermore the fact that many researchers will work for decades on a problem, hoping to solve it one day; and no prestudy is necessary in this case. In brief, the two stages are often mixed or merge with each other. The process also tends to be iterative.

The second point is that, for successful theorizing to take place in social science, the researcher needs to be thoroughly grounded in its core ideas and know many of its concepts. This is a version of Pasteur's dictum that "chance only favors the prepared mind," or, to use a more recent and popular version of the same idea, the 10,000-Hour Rule of Malcolm Gladwell (you need to do something for 10,000 hours to become really good at it; Gladwell 2008: 35–68). Creative theorizing may be laissez-faire in its general approach, but it can only be done well if the theorizer is firmly grounded in theory.

This does not mean that the researcher has to master all the works of Weber, Durkheim, Simmel, Parsons, Merton, Goffman, Coleman, Bourdieu, and everyone else who has made a substantial contribution to social science. What it does mean is that the researcher should have penetrated to the very core of the social science enterprise and learned the ABCs of theorizing. A sociologist should, for example, understand intimately some of the major theories and also be familiar with many concepts in his or her field.

To summarize: one way to improve theorizing is to theorize on the basis of facts *before* the research design has been drawn up and executed. Theorizing also often takes place when the research design is drawn up and when it is executed, but it is dangerous to wait until these stages to theorize.

In addition to theorizing in the prestudy and when the research design is drawn up and executed, there is a third form of theorizing—what may be called fundamental theorizing. This type of theorizing addresses questions like, What is a fact? What does causation mean? What constitutes an explanation?

The Different Types of Theorizing in Social Science

Theorizing during the Prestudy
The most important place for theorizing is in the context of discovery and in close connection with data (the prestudy). While one should proceed according to the accepted methods of the social science community when the main study is carried out, things are much freer at this stage since the main point is to come up with good ideas.

Theorizing during the Main Study
Even if the most important place for theorizing is in the context of discovery, theorizing also takes place in the context of justification or when the main study is being carried out. Examples of this include the kind of theorizing that must take place if the theory that was developed in the context of discovery turns out to be wrong, or if it cannot be turned into useful hypotheses (or the equivalent), or if these hypotheses turn out to be wrong. Very difficult and/or laborious problems also tend to take a long time to solve.

Fundamental Theorizing
In order to theorize and carry out social science research more generally, certain things must be taken for granted. These include answers to questions such as, What constitutes a fact? What is a concept? What constitutes causation? These presuppositions are nonempirical in nature; and when one questions and improves on them one is engaged in fundamental theorizing.

Those who put in the 10,000 hours in sociology or another social science often do so because they are obsessed with what they are doing. In "Science as a Vocation" Weber speaks of the "strange intoxication" that drives the serious scholar and says that this way of acting is "ridiculed by every outsider" (Weber 1946: 135).

Weber elevates his point about the scholar's strange intoxication to a general rule and also notes that "nothing is worthy of man as man unless he can pursue it with passionate devotion." There is clearly an existential dimension to this argument; and one can also find similar statements about the role of passion in the works of many scientists and philosophers. Kierkegaard, for example, argues that passion should be part of everything one does in life, including thinking and theorizing (Kierkegaard [1846] 1992). If something should be done, it should be done with passion.

The research process, to summarize the argument so far, consists of two phases: an early and imaginative phase of theorizing (*the prestudy*), and a later phase in which the major research task is carried out according to the rules of the profession (*the main study*). In the next two sections I suggest that to develop a competence in theorizing, one does well to initially follow some basic rules and then go from there. I also try to outline what some of these rules or steps may look like.

The Full Research Process (The Prestudy and the Main Study)

Phase 1: The Prestudy or The Theorizing and Early Discovery Phase

—Observe and Then Choose Something Interesting or Surprising to Study

—Name the Phenomenon and Formulate the Central Concept

—Build Out the Theory

—Complete the Tentative Theory, Including the Explanation

Phase 2: The Main Study or The Phase of Major Research and Justification

—Draw up the Research Design

—Execute the Research Design

—Write Up the Results

Observation

> DR. WATSON: "This is indeed a mystery," I remarked. "What do you imagine that it means?"
>
> SHERLOCK HOLMES: "I have no data yet. It is a capital mistake to theorize before one has data. Insensibly one begins to twist facts to suit theories, instead of theories to suit facts."
>
> —*Sir Arthur Conan Doyle, "A Scandal in Bohemia" (1891)*[5]

Theorizing is often seen as an activity that is very different from observation, but this is not the way that the term was originally understood. The word "theorize" comes from the Greek and means *to see, to observe*, and *to contemplate*. It is a mixture, in other words, of several activities: observing something, thinking something through, and finding something out. A philosopher has suggested that theorizing according to the Greeks means that you concentrate on a phenomenon and stay with it, in this way trying to understand it (Heidegger 1977: 163).

Theorizing, it is also important to realize, is not conducted in the same way as reasoning according to formal logic. Theorizing draws on a very different way of thinking, or more accurately, on several different ways of thinking. This is an important point that I will return to later, but for now I will stay with the role of observation in theorizing. If observation should be part of theorizing, how can this be accomplished? The short answer to this question is that you cannot theorize without having something to theorize about. And this something you have to acquire through observation. Building a theory and observation are in this sense closely and organically related. From this perspective, observation is an integral part of theorizing.

Charles Peirce's discussion of this issue is instructive. Observation, he said in a lecture course in 1898, is one of the three "mental operations" that make up "reasoning" (the others are "experimentation" and "habituation"; Peirce 1992b: 182). He also specified that there is a logical part to the mental operation of making observations, as well as a more intuitive part. One is part of "the upper consciousness" and the other of "the subconscious." The conscious part of observation should be used to get a structural sense of a phenomenon; one proceeds with this purpose in mind until one's idea corresponds to the phenomenon. This type of observation is described by Peirce as an act "moulding . . . a more or less skeletonized idea until it is felt to respond to the object of observation" (Peirce 1992b: 182).

The less conscious part means that you take off from some phenomenon in order to get a better grip on it. What matters here is "associational potency" or "a magnified tendency to call up ideas," rather than logical thought (Peirce 1992b: 182). As an illustration Peirce gives the example of himself looking very closely at an impressionist painting of the sea. "As I gaze upon it I detect myself sniffing the salt-air and holding up my cheek to the sea breeze" (Peirce 1992b: 182).

The two types of observation do not mix well, according to Peirce. He is also adamant that the theorizer must be careful not to let the conscious part suffocate the unconscious part.

Effective theorizing is closely linked to observation; and observation should here be interpreted in the very broad sense that it has been understood throughout the history of science (see, e.g., Daston and Lunbeck 2011). It should not only include, for example, Peirce's conscious type of observation but also his subconscious version. It should include what we ordinarily mean by observation as well as experiments. It should include observations of others as well as observation of oneself (introspection). It should include meaning and not just view behavior from the outside (thick description vs. thin description). Since the main idea is to say something *new* when one theorizes, however modest this novelty may be, it is crucial to get as much and as varied information as possible.

Sources should and can be numerous and of all types. This means newspapers, archives, books, dreams, daydreams, illusions, speculations, interviews, details, statistical tables, big data, anecdotes, conversations, what is on the Web, what one has overheard, and much, much, much more. Ideally, one should use all of one's senses: sight, hearing, smell, touch, and taste (Simmel [1907] 1997). Anything that provides knowledge, information, associations, and ideas for what something is like is acceptable at this stage of the inquiry. The first rule for observation at the stage of discovery is: *Anything goes!*

As James G. March points out in this book, social scientists have much to learn from artists, especially about observation (see also March 1970). Not only painters and sculptors but also poets and novelists have much sharper eyes than the average social scientist. And with a slight twist of hand, insights from the arts can become ideas to be tried out by social scientists. For this reason, good theorists will naturally want to gravitate toward art and learn from artists (March 1970).

Similarly, any objects that can be of help in making interesting observations should be used, from tape recorders and cameras to equipment for different types of neuro-imaging (Law 2004). There is, to repeat, no need to be overly scientific and methodical at this stage. The main point is to get to know a phenomenon as thoroughly as possible—and for this imagination is often more important than logic.

The best information is the information that one acquires oneself. Primary material is untheorized material and much to be preferred over what other social scientists have produced, even if it can be very hard to acquire. Tocqueville once said that he would much rather create his own data than use those of others, even if doing so was much harder and more time consuming. "I take incredible pains to find the facts for myself [and] I thus obtain, with immense labor, what I could have found easily by following another route" (Tocqueville 2003: 1200). Observation, in Everett C. Hughes's precise formulation, is first of all about the importance *"to see for oneself"* (Hughes 1984: 497, emphasis added).

It is imperative to hold off on theorizing one's observations until one knows quite a bit about the topic to be theorized. Unless this is done, one will theorize on the basis of scant information or on the basis of ideas that float around in society but do not capture what actually goes on. Another helpful rule at this stage comes from Wittgenstein: *"Don't think but look!"* (Wittgenstein 1953: 66e).

The classical place where this attitude toward observation is explained is *The Rules of Sociological Method* by Durkheim. He calls the popular notions that we all have of what things are like "preconceptions" (*prénotions*); and he contrasts these with the "social facts" that the sociologist wants to find, map out and explain (Durkheim [1895] 1964: 17).

One of Durkheim's most important rules for how to conduct research is the following: *"All preconceptions [prénotions] have to be eradicated"* (Durkheim [1895] 1964, 31; emphasis in text). To accomplish this, the researcher has to enter the research with an understanding of his or her *"complete ignorance"* about the situation (Durkheim [1895] 1982: 246, emphasis added).

Durkheim states firmly that one should avoid introspection and focus on external facts since only these can be observed in a reliable manner. But this instruction, I argue, mixes up what is appropriate in the context of discovery with what is appropriate in the context of justification. At the initial stage of the research—the theorizing and creative stage— it may be useful to do precisely the opposite of what Durkheim recommends, namely to penetrate as deeply as possible into the social facts, including the way those affect ourselves. You not only want to know what happens at the surface of some phenomenon, but also need to get to know it in its most fluid and intangible parts—and one way to do this is through introspection or self-observation. To repeat, the reason for proceeding in this manner is to get information that is as detailed and precise as possible about a phenomenon before beginning to theorize it.

Another argument for self-observation is the existence of secrets and private experiences. Some of the things one lives through are next to impossible to communicate, including certain religious experiences and some types of mental illness. Neither do people divulge their innermost secrets. But having insight into yourself makes it easier to get a sense for what people want to keep hidden.

The researcher should be aware that in observing something one also acquires quite a bit of information unconsciously. This means that one should try to train one's cognitive skills of observation as well as one's general sensibility, and in this way pick up as much as possible of what is going on in the environment. By opening oneself up in this manner to phenomena, one becomes aware of some of the tacit knowledge and insignificant details that come with all observation (Collins 2010). C. Wright Mills, who was very interested in the process of theorizing, wrote in *The Sociological Imagination* that "social observation requires high skill and acute sensibility" (Mills 1959: 70).

It can finally be noted that if one wants to be a creative observer, it may be useful to avoid reading too many secondary works early on. Most sociologists smile when they recall Auguste Comte's doctrine of "mental hygiene" or his decision to not read any works on the topic he was studying, on the ground that doing so would block his creativity. While this is no doubt the wrong strategy to follow, a good argument can be made for trying to formulate one's own view, based on primary material, well ahead of reading what other social scientists have written on the topic.

More Rules and Steps

theorizer n. one who theorizes
- Oxford English Dictionary[6]

Theorizing includes observation as well as the activities discussed in this section, such as naming, conceptualizing, constructing typologies, and providing an explanation. When these activities are carried out as part of the prestudy, this should be done primarily *for heuristic reasons.* This means that they are to be used first and foremost for purposes of discovery and not to summarize the results of systematic empirical research.

C. Wright Mills speaks inspiringly in *The Sociological Imagination* about the craft of sociology consisting of two parts: method and theory (Mills 1959: 228). A sociologist, he says, should be his or her own theorist as well as methodologist. I am very sympathetic to Mills's idea that theorizing is a craft (or part of a craft), rather than, say, a job or a profession. One reason for this has to do with the important role that learning by doing plays in executing a craft. The type of knowledge that one needs to craft as well as to theorize, is *practical knowledge.* Another important point is that tacit knowledge is crucial in crafting. It is well understood that the hand of the craftsman knows more than his or her mind; and being aware of this is essential for the craftsman to do a good job.

But even if the expression "the craft of theorizing" is appealing, one should be warned against the idea that theorizing can be reduced to a set of explicit rules, especially cognitive rules that should always be followed. Rules are typically helpful for the beginner, but they can also block a person's development once a certain stage of competence has been reached. The reason for this is that rules do not take into account the context or the concrete situation (Wittgenstein 1953; Dreyfus and Dreyfus 1986). If rules are always followed, they will lead in the wrong direction and become one of those epistemological obstacles that Bachelard talks about.

But rules that are followed only until a skill has been developed are a different story. The ones I propose as basic to theorizing in social science at the stage of the prestudy and elsewhere are the following: *naming, conceptualizing, broadening the concept into a theory*, and *completing the tentative theory through an explanation.* I have roughly enumerated these activities in the order in which they tend to be carried out, even if the actual process at a later stage is typically iterative and also more complex.

The Basic Steps of Theorizing in Social Science

Step 1: Observe, and Choose Something Interesting to Investigate
You can only theorize on the basis of observation. Anything that can stimulate an extensive view of the phenomenon should be used, from sturdy scientific facts to art in various forms. *"Don't think but look!"* (Wittgenstein)

Step 2: Name and Formulate the Central Concept
Give a name to what you observe and try to formulate a central concept based on it. Here as elsewhere abduction (Peirce) is the key.

Step 3: Build Out the Theory
Give body to the central concept by outlining the structure, pattern, or organization of the phenomenon. Use analogies, metaphors, and comparisons—and all in a heuristic way to get a better grip on the phenomenon under study.

Step 4: Complete the Tentative Theory, Including the Explanation
Formulate or model a full tentative theory of the phenomenon, with special emphasis on the explanation that constitutes the natural end of the theorizing process.

One becomes good at theorizing through practice. At first one may be nervous about it, but after a while one becomes more confident. To theorize is also a reflexive activity, and one gradually teaches oneself how to theorize by doing it repeatedly and thinking about what one does. One theorizes and reflects on what one does right and what one does wrong. Engaging in a kind of auto-ethnographic analysis helps to develop a skill in theorizing.

While the full cycle of theorizing goes from observation to explanation, it is not uncommon to stop at some stage in the middle and use already existing concepts, categories, and explanations. Although it clearly constitutes a contribution to establish a new and interesting phenomenon or concept, the natural end point in the theorizing process should be to provide an explanation for the phenomenon.

Naming, to turn to what comes after observation, is a difficult philosophical concept (Kripke 1980). Here, however, I simply use the word to refer to the following two related elements of theorizing: locating and separating out a novel phenomenon, and giving it a name. It is clear that one may also want to name items other than new phenomena, such as new concepts or new models of explanation. To cite Montesquieu in *The Spirit of the Laws*, "I have had new ideas; new words have had to be found or new meanings given to old ones" (Montesquieu [1748] 1989: xi).

Discovering a new phenomenon constitutes one of the most important tasks in social science, and finding the right word(s) to describe it, and in this way really capture its essence, is difficult. But if this is not done, the phenomenon can slip through one's fingers. It can similarly be hard to find a name that fits the new phenomenon and provides it with a distinct identity.

The prevalent view in any society is that most phenomena are well understood. To the sharp-eyed observer, however, phenomena are typically different from their common perception (Durkheim's "preconceptions"). Things in modern society also often change. To see something novel and to go beyond habitual categories is very difficult. It can also take considerable courage and be unsettling. Good observation, like good theorizing, is a lonely business.

It sometimes happens that one locates a totally new phenomenon, but this is not common. What one observes is typically something that already is covered by some concept, but not completely so. In this situation it is important not to dismiss the difference and to squeeze one's observations into an existing category or theory. Instead one should zoom in on the difference, magnify it, and explore if the new phenomenon does not merit a new name or at least a new description or definition.

There are different approaches to naming a new phenomenon. One can, for example, use a term that already exists in everyday language and just introduce it into the social science vocabulary. According to Durkheim, this is the best way to proceed. But he also mentions one exception: when a lay term covers "a plurality of distinct ideas" (Durkheim [1895] 1964: 37n12), then it is preferable to create "new and distinctive terms."

In my view, Durkheim's exception may well be the rule. A word used in everyday language may refer to very different phenomena in social science. A new word may therefore be warranted.

New names can be existing words or words that most people do not know. Choosing a common word, and in this way drawing attention to a phenomenon and marking it off from other phenomena, can be helpful in some cases. Another way of proceeding is to choose a forgotten or rarely used name, such as anomie (Durkheim), habitus (Bourdieu) or serendipity (Merton). One can also create a totally new name, such as sociodicy (Aron), catnet (Harrison White) or gloriometer (Tarde).

Weber argues that it does not matter very much if one uses a new term or an existing one, as long as its meaning is clear (Weber 2001: 63, 77). He also notes that some academics become irritated when a new term is introduced unless they have coined it themselves. His own preference, when no term already exists, was to use "the nearest and most descriptive words from traditional language" (Weber 2001: 63). As an example he mentioned "innerworldly asceticism."

My own view is that one should avoid introducing too many new names or giving a new phenomenon an odd name. It is rare to discover something really novel; and forcing the reader to remember new terms that don't add much to the discussion only creates irritation. The rule should be that if one has something important to say, a new name is warranted. And just as we think highly of Marx and Weber, we have a high regard for such plain concepts as "capital" and "social action." In brief, in the end it is usually the idea and force behind the name that counts, not the name itself.

In discussing naming I have a few times crossed the line between a name and a concept. There are several differences between the two; in particular, a scientific concept is more analytical and abstract than a name. Peirce defines a concept as "the rational purport of a word or a conception"; and the reference to rationality is important (Peirce 1992d/1998: 332). It is precisely this quality, one can argue, that has made the concept into "one of the great tools of all scientific knowledge" (Weber 1946: 141).

An important rational quality of a scientific concept is that it makes it possible for some phenomena to be clearly identified as belonging to a general category. Another has to do with its role in the scientific enterprise as a whole. A good concept is one that can be linked to a typology or to an explanation in a natural way, and one that is generally easy to work with.

Linking the central concept in the prestudy to a classification, a typology, or an explanation is what I refer to as "building out the theory." It can be described as going beyond the definition of a concept and outlining the full structure of how a phenomenon operates. What causes a phenomenon, and what consequences it has, also belong to this phase of theorizing.

One can either develop a new concept or use an already existing one. It is also possible to improve on an existing concept by adding to it. In developing a new concept one can either create a totally new concept or, more commonly, turn a rudimentary concept into a full-fledged one. The former is sometimes called a proto-concept, and the transition from a proto-concept to a full-fledged concept has been discussed by Robert K. Merton (1984) in a very instructive way (see also Fleck [1935] 1979).

"A proto-concept," Merton says, "is an early, rudimentary, particularized and largely unexplicated idea." "A concept," in contrast, "is a general idea which, once having been tagged, substantially generalized, and explicated can effectively guide inquiry into seemingly diverse phenomena." While proto-concepts "make for early discontinuities in scientific development," fully developed concepts "make for continuities by directing our attention to similarities among substantively quite unconnected phenomena" (Merton 1984: 267).

The term "theorizing," as currently used in sociology, is an example of a proto-concept. Ever since its first appearance in a sociological journal (in 1896), this term has been much less popular among sociologists than "theory" (Small 1896: 306). Through a search on JSTOR one can follow its sporadic appearance in sociology journals from the 1890s to today. Such a search also shows that although the term "theorizing" has been used now and then, it has never been properly defined, discussed, and expounded upon. As a result—and as Merton later predicted— little progress has been made in understanding the process of theorizing.

It is also possible, as mentioned earlier, to improve on an existing concept. This can be done in several different ways. Weber, for example, sometimes split one concept into two, in this way making it more useful for a particular purpose (e.g., interests became ideal interests and material interests; rationality became formal rationality and substantive rationality. According to Weber, the value of a concept should also be judged by how useful it is for the concrete task at hand. In itself a concept cannot be said to be good or bad (Weber [1922] 1978: 26).

It is sometimes necessary to clarify an existing concept; and this usually means that it is also changed in some respect. Merton regarded conceptual clarification as a particularly important task in social science. "A good part of the work called 'theorizing,'" he once wrote, "is taken up with the clarification of concepts—and rightly so" (Merton 1948: 513). It has also been suggested that the most important scientific concepts are not suddenly invented, but evolve over time (Nersessian 2008). In sociology, status and class are examples of this.

A discussion of concepts would be incomplete without a mention of Wittgenstein's work. It was Wittgenstein who first questioned the age-old notion that a concept can be clearly and unambiguously defined, and that the items it covers all have something in common. He concluded that at the most there may exist a certain resemblance between some of the items that a concept covers ("family resemblance"; Wittgenstein 1953). This critique of the classical notion of a concept is today commonplace in cognitive psychology.

Wittgenstein also warned that words and concepts in philosophy can lead you astray; and his ideas on this score can be extended to the social sciences. One solution when there exists a concept that blocks insight, Wittgenstein suggested, is simply to restate the phenomenon without using the concept. This is what Heinrich Hertz did, according to Wittgenstein, when he suggested that Newtonian physics should be recast without using "force" as the central concept (Monk 1990: 446).

Another example of how to proceed in this type of situation comes from World War II, when Wittgenstein worked as a volunteer at a hospital in London. Since World War I it had been known among medical doctors that many soldiers and civilians who had suffered acute traumatic injuries experienced so-called wound shock (Monk 1990: 445–53). The doctors Wittgenstein worked with, however, were unable to clinically establish the symptoms associated with wound shock. Finally, and to Wittgenstein's great satisfaction, they decided to simply abolish the concept and instead focus on studying what happens when traumatic injuries take place. Wittgenstein suggested that the word "shock" should be printed upside down every time it was used, to indicate how useless it was.

One can also build a theory out in other ways, with the help of metaphors and analogies, types and typologies, and more. Metaphors are especially useful as heuristic devices (Silber 1995). The key idea is to compare what is being researched with something else, and in doing so open up the topic to new perspectives. Well-known examples of master metaphors in social science include society as a contract (Rousseau), society as an organism (Durkheim), and the mind as a computer (cognitive psychology).

Despite the advances that can be made with the help of metaphors, some social scientists fear that they are too "literary" or otherwise unscientific, and therefore try to avoid them. This seems to be especially common in modern economics (see, e.g., McCloskey 1985). The result of eliminating metaphors, some political scientists have argued, is to severely impoverish the analysis (Zashin and Chapman 1974).

Exactly how metaphors operate is not clear, even if there are a number of studies on the topic. Philosopher Max Black has, for example, developed an influential theory of metaphors that is worth mentioning, the so-called inter-action view of metaphors. According to Black,

> A memorable metaphor has the power to bring two separate domains into cognitive and emotional relation by using language directly appropriate to the one as a lens for seeing the other; the implications, suggestions, and sup-porting values entwined with the literal use of the metaphorical expression enable us to see a new subject matter in a new way. The extended meaning that results, the relations between initially disparate realms created, can neither be antecedently predicted nor subsequently paraphrased in prose . . . Metaphori-cal thought is a distinctive mode of achieving insight, not to be construed as an ornamental substitute for plain thought. (Black 1962: 236–37; cf. 28–47)

An analogy is similar to a metaphor, but the distance between what you want to better understand and some other phenomenon that can be helpful in this is not so large. Some helpful attempts to explore the use of analogies in theorizing have also been made by sociologists (see, e.g., Abbott 2004: 113–18; Vaughan 2004, this volume). Analogies play an important role in legal reasoning as well, especially in legal systems based on custom. The key idea is that you subsume a new case under an old case, often following the logic of syllogism (Weber [1922] 1978: 407, 787; see also Levi 1949; Sunstein 1993).

The study of analogies has advanced the furthest in cognitive science (e.g., Gentner 2003; Nercessian 2008). According to cognitive scientists, human beings use analogies in a variety of situations, especially when they need to understand something new. While reasoning by logic is traditionally seen in Western thought as the best way to advance to a solution, the use of analogies is another and many times superior way of dealing with a problem. Analogies, cognitive scientists also argue, are often used together with other nontradi-tional aids, such as images and simulation.

Research in cognitive science on the use of analogies, patterns, and other nontraditional ways of reasoning is of much interest to the project of theoriz-ing in social science, for several reasons. For one thing, it is clear that analo-gies and similar non-logical ways of thinking play much a bigger role in the context of discovery than in the context of justification. For another, always following the rules of logic will block progress.

According to various experiments in cognitive science, it would appear that one can train oneself to become better at nontraditional ways of reasoning. So far cognitive science has focused mainly on the use of these types of reasoning in everyday life. But once the research turns to how these are being used by scientists, the result may also be relevant for social science theorizing.

To repeat, creating types and categories is another way of building out a theory. While categories may be created for heuristic purposes, they are essentially used to differentiate facts from each other, and in this way to order them. A taxonomy or a classification can be very useful, but should not be mistaken for an explanation or seen as the substitute for one. Ever since the heyday of Linnean botany, it has been realized that a classification can also block research. Ideally, there should be a natural link between a classification and an explanation.

Types may be developed further than categories, but are usually less comprehensive. A type may be part of a conceptual pair (such as *Gemeinschaft-Gesellschaft*) or of a full typology (such as Weber's three types of authority). Some argue that a typology can only be justified on empirical grounds (e.g., Lazarsfeld 1962; Bailey 1973). This, however, is only true at the stage of justification. At the stage of discovery a type can be used for heuristic purposes, as a way of discovering something new.

Arguments in favor of using the type as a heuristic tool go far back in sociology. They can be found in what Weber says on the ideal type and in what Durkheim says on typology in *The Rules of Sociological Method*. Indeed, Weber uses the word *heuristic* (*heuristisch*) to describe one of the reasons why we may want to use an ideal type in the first place (Weber [1922] 1972: 10; 1988: 190; cf. Bruun 2007: 225–31).

At a general level, Weber's ideal type can be described as a special type of concept; more precisely, it is a concept that has been specifically constructed for social science purposes. It is created through an "analytical accentuation" of certain elements in a phenomenon and can as a consequence be described as a "conceptual construct" (*Gedankenbild*) (Weber 1949: 90, 93). Weber also makes clear that an ideal type is not a hypothesis to be verified, but serves a different purpose. "It [the ideal type] is no 'hypothesis' but it offers guidance to the construction of hypotheses" (Weber 1949: 90).

An ideal type can also be heuristic in several ways according to Weber. It may, for example, be helpful to begin an analysis by constructing an ideal type because having an ideal type makes it easier to handle a bewildering number of facts. The ideal type, Weber writes, "serves as a harbor before you have learned to navigate safely in the vast sea of empirical facts" (Weber 1949: 104).

An ideal type can also be of heuristic assistance in other ways. You can, for example, construct an ideal type and then compare it with the empirical situation. In this way you may find out that you are either on the right track or that there is too much of a gap between the two, in which case you have to account for the difference (Weber [1922] 1978: 21). This is, for example, how rational action should be used, according to Weber.

A handy tool for theorizing, which is related to the idea of typology, is the 2 x 2 table. By constructing a 2 x 2 one can sometimes go from an intuition to a more precise idea (see, e.g., Collier et al., 2008). Stinchcombe describes the fourfold table as "a standard tool of sociological theorizing"; and it is clear that quite a few sociologists view it as a handy way to work out their ideas (Stinchcombe 1968: 46).

Thomas Schelling, an economist who excels in theorizing, has pointed out that if one uses a 2 x 2 for two actors, one has the rudiments of a simple game of strategy. The example he uses to show this is two persons who are traveling on a train and want to meet up in the dining car (or who alternatively want to avoid each other when it is time to eat). Since there are two dining cars on the train, one in first class and one in second class, a choice has to be made. This choice can be depicted in 2 x 2 matrices, which are similar to the ones used in game theory (see also, e.g., Rapoport et al. 1976).

Schelling's argument can be found in his article "What Is Game Theory?," where his analysis is a far cry from the complex models that are common in today's game theory. According to Schelling, however, "what may be of most interest to a social scientist is these rudiments . . . The rudiments can help him to make his own theory, and make it in relation to the particular problems that interest him . . . Whether the theory that he builds with [these rudiments] is then called game theory, sociology, economics, conflict theory, strategy or anything else is a jurisdictional question of minor importance" (Schelling 1984: 221–22).

If Step 1 in theorizing is to observe; if Step 2 is to name the phenomenon and develop a central concept; and if Step 3 is to build the theory out; then

Step 4 is to complete the tentative theory, including an explanation (see insert on page 17 again).

A fully built out theory can take the form of a model but does not have to do so. Words are used for many explanations, and mathematics for many models. Diagrams may be used at several stages in the discovery process and also as a heuristic tool for explanation (Peirce 1933; Larkin and Simon 1987; Podolny 2003). Similarly, decision trees and network figures can be used to make ideas flow and help the analyst come up with explanations. In all of these cases, it deserves to be mentioned once more, what is involved is a non-traditional kind of thinking, say thinking in some form of pattern.

Can material objects be used for heuristic-explanatory purposes in social science, a bit like Linus Pauling's wooden model of a triple-strained DNA helped Francis Crick and James Watson to discover the correct molecular structure of DNA? Or, to use another example, can they be used in the way that a miniature model of a car accident supposedly triggered Wittgenstein's so-called picture theory of meaning? No examples for social science immediately come to mind, even if the idea of using objects to construct an explanation in social science seems plausible enough.

If one on the other hand takes a broad view of how an explanation comes into being at the stage of discovery, there are many examples of how objects can be of help. The paper files and index cards that were used by an earlier generation of social scientists for taking notes, and which today have been replaced by computer files and special programs for note-taking, are one example.

Robert K. Merton and Niklas Luhmann both had enormous card files and their own ways of interacting with them. Merton seems to have used his files mainly as an extended memory, while Luhmann said that his files helped him to enter into a dialogue with himself (M. Evans 1961: 39–40; Luhmann 1981). Readers of *The Sociological Imagination* may also recall Mills's playful suggestion for how to discover new connections in the material you have collected: "You simply dump out heretofore disconnected folders, mixing up their contents, and then re-sort them" (Mills 1959: 212).

In a similarly extended manner, one can perhaps say that objects are used for explanation also in experiments. After the concept, Weber considered the experiment to be "the second great tool of scientific work" (Weber 1946: 141). The types of experiments conducted by social scientists are very different from those that are common in the natural sciences (see, e.g., Knorr Cetina

2002). They also exist in a bewildering amount of variation (Morton and Williams 2008). Still, objects of different kinds are often part of what produces the explanation; and this also goes for so-called thought experiments.

Explanation is one of the most difficult topics in the philosophy of science; and I will limit myself to some elementary remarks on its role at the stage of discovery. There exist many different types of explanations, and each science usually draws on several of them. A good knowledge of this plethora of explanations—in law, medicine, the social sciences, and other fields—is very helpful when one tries to come up with an explanation of one's own.

Some of these explanations may at first seem curious, but they can still be useful for heuristic purposes. Take, for example, functionalist explanations. These are currently not considered legitimate in social science, but can nonetheless help to generate new ideas. Weber makes precisely this point in *Economy and Society*. While emphasizing that a functionalist analysis can be "highly dangerous," he also argues that it is not only helpful but "indispensable" at an early stage of the analysis (Weber [1922] 1978: 15).

Models are crucial to certain types of explanations; and they are often formulated in mathematical language (Schelling 1978; Simon 1991; Varian 1998). Models are more intuitive and less worked out at the stage of discovery than at the stage of justification. Still, one advantage of using a model when theorizing is that all assumptions are explicit and open for inspection. Another is that models are economical; and a third is that they show all the consequences of making certain assumptions, including novel and unexpected ones.

Models essentially reconstruct something *as if* it had happened in a specific way (see, e.g., Vaihinger [1911] 2009). According to one philosopher, they are "speculative instruments." Like a wedding, they bring together "disparate subjects." They also "reveal new relationships" and, "as with other weddings, their outcomes are unpredictable" (Black 1962: 237).

Stephen Toulmin, another philosopher, describes the virtues of a model as follows: "It is in fact a great virtue of a good model that it does suggest further questions, taking us beyond the phenomenon from which we began, and tempts us to formulate hypotheses which turn out to be experimentally fertile. . . . Certainly it is this suggestiveness, and systematic deployability, that makes a good model something more than a simple metaphor" (cited in Black 1962: 239).

Recently the metaphor of social mechanisms has become popular in sociology (e.g., Hedström and Swedberg 1998). Although it is hard to explain exactly what a social mechanism is, one does not have to be overly concerned with this issue at the stage of discovery. What is more important is to try to come up with new social mechanisms—that is, new ways of explaining what takes place in a highly transparent manner. With the help of a mechanism one should be able to see *exactly* how C leads to D leads to E. The general goal in science of creating *clarity* is closely related to the idea of social mechanisms (Peirce 1992a: 124–41; Weber 1946: 151).

Conclusions

> Above all, seek to develop and to use the sociological imagination . . . Let every man be his own methodologist; let every man be his own theorist; let theory and method again become part of the practice of a craft. Stand for the primacy of the individual scholar.
> —C. Wright Mills, *The Sociological Imagination* (1959: 224)

The main message of this chapter is that, given the current lopsided development in social science, with methods being highly developed and theory much less so, we may want to focus our energy on theorizing rather than on theory. One way to do this, I also suggest, is to turn to the context of discovery and then proceed to the context of justification. Or to phrase the same idea in different words, in order not to get bogged down in a description of the terms "context of discovery" and "context of justification," the natural place for creative theorizing is *before* the research design is drawn up and executed, and in close collaboration with observation.

If carried through with consistency, the enterprise of theorizing might help to usher in a new period of interesting and creative theory in social science. One reason for hoping this is that there is no reason to believe that only a small number of gifted scholars can produce theory. Everyone who can think can ultimately also theorize; and the project of theorizing is inherently democratic (Kant [1784] 1970). The general goal of developing the project of theorizing is to create a lively and friendly culture of theorizing in the social sciences that will help the average social scientist to be more creative.

In order to make the project of theorizing into a coherent whole, much more needs to be said and done than what can be found in this chapter. Imagination, intuition, and improvisation are three important topics that deserve long and thorough discussions. One would also want to get a better understanding of how to move from the prestudy to the main study. The notion that one can just introduce the prestudy and hook it up to the main study, hoping that the two will neatly fit together, is probably illusory. Changes in the one presumably entail changes in the other. There may also exist a gray zone between the prestudy and the major study that needs to be better understood.

One should also be aware that, before a theory has been properly tested, the data gathered at the stage of observation in the prestudy may lead one astray. While it is possible to speak positively of "theoretical sampling" and "the testing of ideas" at the stage of discovery, it is also clear that there is a good chance of making huge errors at this stage (see Glaser and Strauss 1967; Coslor 2011). Behavioral scientists have discussed some of these errors, such as anchoring error, availability error, and attribution error (see Tversky and Kahneman 1982; Groopman 2008; see also Peirce 1992b: 193–96). There may be other errors as well, which are specific to this type of theorizing.

And last, the project of theorizing can truly flourish only if theorizing becomes a communal and cooperative enterprise among all kinds of social scientists, linked to each other as well as to people around the world. Peirce liked to point out that scientific inquiry is profoundly communal in nature, and that new ways of theorizing and analyzing will succeed only if they are deeply rooted in a universal community of scholars (on this see also the chapter by Reed and Zald in this book). Inquiry and community, Peirce said, must come together in a true community of inquiry—or into *a general culture of theorizing*, as I prefer to put it.

2   Intuitionist Theorizing

Karin Knorr Cetina

NTUITIONIST THEORIZING IS NOT A NEW BRAND OF THINKING. SCI-
entists, for instance, are well aware that they have something called
intuition on which they draw in their work, as are doctors and actors. "It is
always with excitement that I wake up in the morning wondering what my
intuition will toss up to me, like gifts from the sea . . . " the biologist Jonas Salk
said.[1] And "You must train your intuition," Ingrid Bergman demanded—less
interested, perhaps, in creativity than in wanting to tell us something about
good acting. The traders I observed in my study of financial markets were
doing things "by the seat of their pants"—or so they claimed when I tried to
question them about how they were selecting information and trading. The
answer, of course, left me as much in the dark as I had been before I interviewed them. But it tells us that intuition matters in many walks of life—and
seemingly that all people are able to say about it that it exists and they find it
worth using.

This chapter is an attempt to dig deeper in one narrow area, that of theorizing. It is also an attempt to dissociate theorizing somewhat from method.
In the social sciences, theories and theory construction are strongly associated with method. We make determined attempts to come up with protocols
and prescriptions that instruct the inexperienced in how to make coherent,
defensible sense out of the chaos of data. But when I consider my own research
I find that, while I always needed my empirical methods to come up with
good evidence, I never found the recipes for theory building, or the logics of

inference we teach, particularly helpful when theorizing this evidence. What I say in this chapter is an attempt to formulate what we may be doing when we don't follow procedures and yet come up with theoretical knowledge. I draw on my own experience in this, but also on the knowledge of disciplines that have made some advances in understanding cognition and emotion. My own research is mostly observational, ethnographic, and communication- and discourse-oriented. Intuitionist theorizing is not limited to such areas, as the anecdotal evidence scientists give us about how intuition matters to them suggests. I talk about theorizing as part of the context of discovery, rather than as something to do with validation (see Swedberg 2012b; and Swedberg, this volume). The context of justification, as validation is technically called, is intended to capture what goes on (philosophically speaking) after scientists reach the finish line and publish their research—communication, critique, and replication that all lead to the formation of a consensus. In this chapter I am interested in what happens before publication.[2] It is plain that attention needs to be paid to the so-called context of discovery and its processes. The logical reconstructions we have given it (e.g., induction, abduction) are not incompatible with what I have to say, but they are sparse in nature. They can be supplemented by saying more about the cognitive and other processes that theorizing involves.

What, then, is intuitionist theorizing? And what is it not? Why separate it from method, and, worse yet, even shift it away from reason, as I propose to do? In the first section of this chapter, I begin with what the intuitionism I propose is not, but is likely to be confused with. I then define intuitionist theorizing in a positive if somewhat technical way, by linking it to particular processing circuits in the brain that I explain and illustrate. The following section is a brief excursion into ontology. I argue that the empirical is inherently theoretical and draw attention to the distinction between two types of theorizing, "approach-based" and "theoretically adequate." There is a stronger case to be made for bringing intuition into play when we seek theoretically adequate knowledge. The proceeding section brings up various processing requirements and effects of intuitionist theorizing, particularly the regime of attention it requires. Some of these necessities and effects may be irritating for the theorizer's environment. Intuitionist theorizing can limit sociability and may also be threatened by it. I then I ask whether theorizing involves emotions and illustrate how this might be the case. The last paragraphs summarize my argument and put it into the context of further research.

Intuitionist Theorizing Defined

There is by now a small body of nontechnical expositions of how intuition matters to behavior that draw on brain research (Gladwell 2005; Gigerenzer 2007; Haidt 2001; Haidt and Kesebir 2010; Kahneman 2011). The drawback of this literature for the present purpose is that it has a particular goal that I do not share in this chapter. It wants to clarify decision making and appraisals of things that are based on "gut feelings," "hunches," and "snap judgments," or in other words, on intuitions that help people make decisions unthinkingly, rapidly, and without argument. It happens that a surprising number of these judgments turn out to be correct, the literature says. People do get things right when they anchor them in some unconscious process. Gladwell, for instance, starts his book with the example of an art historian who, when she was taken to the Getty's museum's restoration studio to see a well-preserved sixth-century BC sculpture of a nude male the museum was acquiring, had the immediate hunch that something was amiss. Another expert felt an "intuitive repulsion" when he saw the statue, and a third thought it was "fresh," knowing that "fresh" was not the word that ought to pop into one's head when looking at a two-thousand-year-old statue. The sculpture turned out to be a fake (Gladwell 2005: 5). Gladwell's book offers many more examples of such rapid intuitive judgments, as does Gigerenzer's. The advantage of the latter book is that it also details the experimental setups and outcomes through which Gigerenzer and his team concluded that human decisions are based less on rational choice than on something else—a something he associates with intuition. Haidt, who proposes a social intuitionist model, also tries to understand judgments—particularly moral judgments. His point is similar: "Moral intuition is a kind of cognition," he says, "but it is not a kind of reasoning" (Haidt 2001: 814). We may know instantly that some behavior is morally wrong, for instance, without being able to give good reasons for why we think it is when pressed. The reasoning system may construct post hoc justifications for the instant judgment, and that may give us the illusion of having reasoned things out objectively, even when we did not. Gladwell, whose book is an attempt to sum up much of the literature, says about judgments that "we really only trust conscious decision making," but that there are moments "when our snap judgments and first impressions can offer a much better means of making sense of the world." The first task of his book is to convince us that "decisions made very quickly can be every bit as good as decisions made cautiously and deliberately" (Gladwell 2005: 4). Kahneman, drawing on his and his collaborators decades-long work on the heuristics of decision making, deems these accurate intuitional responses as unsurprising, linking them to the recognition of situational cues that trigger information stored in memory by someone with experience. "Good intuitive judgments come to mind with the same immediacy" as when a 2-year old looks at a dog and says "doggie." (Kahneman 2011: 11–13).[3] The book illustrates and updates his earlier work on the fallibility of decision making by attempting to explain the heuristics of judgment in terms of the automatic processes of the intuitive system.

The task I have set myself in this chapter is to give an account of theorizing, and this presents us with a problem that is different from the one these authors address. When we theorize we are not acting in the capacity of deciders or appraisers, judges or managers. We are trying to make some theoretically adequate sense out of an empirical reality we study, and this tends to be a slow process in which nothing is instantly clear. In fact, the predicament we feel we are in, and that often wears us out when trying to analyze data, may well be that we don't have good hunches. In the decision-making scenario, things happen in a blink. Intuition, in this case, is the "celebration of the power of the glance," as Gladwell puts it (2005: 4). Human traders in liquid markets truly exhibit this power when they act on incoming market data in split seconds. Such domains surely privilege "thinking fast" over "thinking slow," to use Kahneman's distinction (2011)—although terms like "thinking" or "decision making" are somewhat misleading when things are done in nanoseconds, and none of the common decision-making elements (e.g., deliberation, negotiation, information comparisons or searches, conscious reflection) appear to be in place. In the decision-making scenario it is seemingly also the case that "less information and computation can be more," a point Gigerenzer elaborates in his work (e.g., 2007: 20–39). The computational part of this argument is applicable to theorizing. But it is less clear that the theorizing scenario would be well served by the instruction to be frugal in the intake of information—following the "less information is more" principle. My point is that the theorizing scenario requires as much emphasis on "gut" as the decision-making scenario, but without the emphasis on speed—we want to shift things away from the blink, the "snap," the "instant," and the "glance." Intuitionist theorizing has as much of a stretched-out temporal life as deliberative theorizing—although time is not used for reasoning and deliberations. At least until we know more about it, intuitionist theorizing could also do with more information than Gigerenzer recommends. Unlimited memory and information surely has its downside if it means that we are flooded by irrelevant images and details that we cannot organize. But most non-diseased humans tend not to operate with open floodgates, or to lack the somatic markers that help us sort the relevant from the irrelevant information. As a researcher, I would always have liked a better memory and fewer limits on the information I was able to collect.

Having said where I depart from these writings on intuition, let me now try to spell out my positive model. I draw on the neurophysiological and cognitive psychology literature for this purpose, since these are areas that can go further with intuition than we can in the social sciences with our action-level data. When the traders I study told me they were doing things by the seat of their pants, this was an immediate conversation stopper. They obviously could not tell me more, and I had no really useful means to probe their intuitions further with the methods I had—interviews and observation. Neurophysiology opens up a field of inquiry at precisely the point where social scientists get stuck—although sociology and similar fields have long been aware of the existence of this same area. Polanyi, who wrote one of the first much-cited books on intuition, calling it "tacit knowledge," said he wanted "to reconsider human knowledge by starting from the fact that we can know more than we can tell" (Polanyi 1966: 4). Neurophysiology is in the process of demonstrating how we know more than we can tell.[4]

The neurophysiological literature is vast, and it is not clear that a consensus view has emerged on relevant topics. Damasio's (2012) claims about certain aspects of human consciousness, for instance, which are based on decades of experimental research, have been criticized by others who also have rich research records, and it is likely that such debates will continue for a while. There appears to be no clear answer to questions about the brain's construction either—whether it is organized in relatively independently functioning units stacked in a hierarchy in response to evolutionary pressures; or whether a more holistic network model, in which reason, thought, and emotion are linked in loops, is accurate.[5] Nonetheless, shared understandings currently exist concerning certain brain functions and mechanisms, and we can build on these if we use them as suggestive hypotheses rather than facts. I present these functions and mechanisms in some detail, since the literature may be unfamiliar and is at times complex.

First, the two types of mental processing. Neurophysiologist and cognitive psychologists distinguish between different neural structures and types of information extracted from the environment: emotional and cognitive (e.g., Damasio 2003, 2012). They also distinguish between "two distinct information processing systems to acquire, memorize and represent knowledge" (Dietrich 2004: 749). Such distinctions are not new, and they have lived a variegated life in different periods of history (Kaufman and Singer 2012: 1). But new techniques of brain imaging and new experimental research have revived and recast them, and they abound now in some areas under different names. Haidt (2001) provides an early review, as does Evans (2008; 2012). According to these reviewers, almost all authors agree on a distinction between processes that are unconscious, rapid, automatic, and high capacity, and those that are conscious, slow, and deliberative (Evans 2008: 256). Haidt (2001) and others distinguish between two processing systems and refer to the models as dual process models. Haidt attributes the following features to the first system, which he calls intuitive: it is fast and effortless, the process is unintentional, it runs automatically and demands no attentional resources; it is inaccessible— what enters awareness are only results; the process is parallel and distributed; pattern matching occurs, and thought is metaphorical and holistic; it is context dependent and platform dependent (it depends on the organism in which it occurs); and it is not unique to humans but common to all mammals. The reasoning system, in contrast, is slow and requires effort; the process is intentional and controllable; it is consciously accessible and viewable; it demands attentional resources that are limited; processing is sequential; symbol manipulation occurs and thought is truth preserving and analytical; it is context and platform independent (the process can be transported to other organisms and machines as long as they are rule following); and it is unique to humans after age 2 and perhaps to some language-trained apes. Evans extracts similar characteristics from the literature,[6] but he brings out one characteristic more clearly that I find important. This is that the implicit or intuitionist system (which Evans calls system 1; see also Kahneman 2011) is not only universal (common to all mammals) and independent of general intelligence measures, but also independent of our working memory. The reasoning system, in contrast, would be heritable, linked to general intelligence, and limited by the capacity of our working memory (see Table 2.1).

Why is working memory of particular importance? What we are aware of at a given time is represented in our working memory—it preserves in our

TABLE 2.1 Dual Process Model of Cognition

Implicit Processing System	Explicit Processing System
default process	reflective
high capacity	low capacity
unconscious (preconscious)	conscious
implicit	explicit
automatic	controlled
low effort	high effort
rapid	slow
holistic	analytic
associative (by some accounts) or rule based	rule based
evolutionarily old	evolutionarily recent
evolutionary rationality	individual rationality
shared with animals	uniquely human
nonverbal	linked to language

(Adapted from Carruthers 2009: 109 and Evans 2008: 257)

minds information that is relevant to the situation and that we can work with. But this working memory appears to be severely limited, either in storage or processing or both, to four items, plus or minus one (see Dietrich 2004: 752–53, for a summary; De Neys 2006). These are the number of items we can hold in working memory at one time, and/or the number of dimensions we can manipulate concurrently. The reasoning system requires access to a central working memory, whereas the implicit intuitionist system does not; hence the notion that the explicit reasoning system is capacity restricted. The capacity limitation of the explicit reasoning system is crucial, since it implies that complex tasks are more likely to be implicitly embedded. The amount of information that must be held concurrently in the focus of attention to hit a perfect golf shot, for instance, far exceeds a person's capacity. My traders were surely correct in describing trading as intuition-based. A rapidly changing market and context presented on several large screens where numerous new windows can be opened includes many more variables and items of information (the prices of various financial instruments, news items, graphs, stories, news headlines, alerts, incoming dealing requests, bulletin board updates, etc.) than the four we can deal with. Contrary to what we might expect, complex tasks will not be processed most efficiently by the explicit reasoning system, but by its implicit, intuitionist counterpart.

Let me look at one additional aspect of implicit processing in some detail, its emotional side. The list of attributes of the two modes of cognition did not include emotion, but both reviewers (and everyone else whose work I have read) deem emotions to be highly relevant. One widely cited experimental result that points to the role emotions play is based on the analysis of patients with damage to a particular area of the prefrontal cortex (Damasio 1994). As summarized by Damasio "The patients with ventromedial prefrontal lesions had remarkably preserved intellect, as measured by conventional neuropsychological instruments, and an equally remarkable defect of emotional behavior." These patients who had had normal social behavior and had not had difficulties in making sound decisions before the onset of their brain dysfunction, had notable impairments in social emotions (compassion, embarrassment), and made poor decisions after its onset. This was happening despite of the fact that the patients had "no detectable impairments of logical reasoning, no defects of learning and recall of the kind of knowledge required to make sound decisions, and no defects of language or perception." Damasio concluded that the disturbed emotional signaling might explain the decision defect (Damasio 2009: 210–11). What this means is that the emotional brain is designed "to attach a value tag to the incoming information that allows the person to evaluate the biological significance of a given event" (Dietrich 2004; see also LeDoux 1996). In Damasio's terms, the marker is a "memory trace." In past experiences one learned that certain phenomena, say "the premises of a problem, the options of actions, the factual outcome" were associated with certain emotional outcomes, and the marker signals the conjunction "of certain categories of situation or outcome with certain categories of emotional response." And when situations of a certain kind present themselves again, the marker is reactivated. That recall, it is important to note, may or may not become conscious. In either case, it replicates partially or completely the emotional state associated with the particular category of situation. To relate this back to the experimental investigations, the marker "weighs in on the decision process" in normal individuals, but fails to do so when brain damage in the ventromedial prefrontal cortex occurs (Damasio 2009: 211).

There is more to the emotional brain than emotional value tags. In Damasio's work, the notion of emotion is a stand-in for a whole "emotional machinery" that includes neural subprocesses of automated life regulation such as reward and punishment programs, drives and motivations, and the distinction between emotions and "feelings" as "the neural substrates of the perceptual read-outs of emotion action programs." But regardless of the complexities on the level of mechanisms and (sub)processes, an important outcome of the existing studies appears to be that the brain "can know the emotional quality of an object or event before cognition and consciousness enter the scene" (Franks 2010: 105). One can prompt subjects to scrutinize a task they are cognitively and emotionally involved in more deeply—one can instruct them to be more self-reflexive and they will become so. But if one doesn't, or if subjects are so completely focused on a task that they can't reflect on it, the automatic, implicit, intuitive process introduced earlier takes the emotional value tags (called somatic markers) into account as it sets the agenda and dictates responses, before the conscious, reasoning brain "knows" and steps in. And when it steps in, it appears to offer post hoc rationales that are not the actual causes of the responses. This is why Haidt (2001) offers us the analogy of the (emotional) dog and its (rational) tail: the tail is not the cause of what the dog does, and wagging the dog's tail with our hand will not make it happy.

Traditionally, we see reason and emotions as antithetical to each other, but neurophysiological research suggests that they are not, and that some emotions are necessary for effective thought. The above research also suggests that "most of our behavior and judgments are in fact made automatically (i.e., without intention, effort or awareness of the process):" they emerge first from the intuitive brain process, rather than from the reasoning process. And since emotional processing appears connected with the intuitive system rather than with the explicit reasoning system (see also Evans 2008: 256–58; Hassin et al. 2005; Wang 2006), we are the emotional dog walking, so to speak, although we also like to wag our tail afterward, making others and ourselves believe that we reasoned things out and were in control of the walk (Haidt 2001: 819).[7] The prefrontal cortex is seen as representing the neural basis of cognitive functions that we associate with such things as thinking, reasoning, and planning—that is, the reasoning system. It is possible that the "lower-level structures" that lie behind the prefrontal lobes "readily overpower and regulate" the higher-level structures, as Franks, who surveys this literature, reports. According to Carter (1999, cited in Franks 2010: 112), "the wiring from this lower part of the brain is robust and thick going up the cognitive systems, but the reverse is not true. Cognition going down the emotional systems has to fight a tough battle to make an impact, but emotion going upwards may be a much smoother movement." All this implies that intuitionist theorizing will also be emotional theorizing, as we may call it in analogy to emotional intelligence, and we can speculate what this may mean. Is an emotion-including theoretical take on the world a more adequate take? Do early positive experiences with particular theoretical explanations prompt us to pursue a progressive research program that is based on these experiences, and allow us to maintain it in the face of intermittent counter-evidence?[8] Do we need an emotional attraction to an area in order to develop and enhance our capacities as intuitionist theorizers?

According to Carruthers (2009: 109), "dual-system theories of human reasoning are now quite widely accepted, at least in outline." Many questions remain, not the least about the conditions and mechanisms of interaction between the two systems—note that the two systems typically run in parallel, and they are capable of "reaching different conclusion" (Haidt 2001: 819). Research suggests, for example, that the "most creative insights typically involve some sort of surprising interaction" between the current contents of the working memory, which is part of the reasoning system, and the long-term memories stored in the intuitive system (Kaufman and Singer 2012: 4).[9] Despite such questions, I find the dual process model appropriate for a theory of intuitionist theorizing, if only because it provides strong multidisciplinary evidence (neurological and behavioral-experimental) for the existence of an intuitionist information processing system that operates in us, is not controlled by or dependent on prefrontal cortex reasoning, and is more efficient (though also less flexible) than the former in dealing with complex information inputs. Building on this literature, intuitionist theorizing can be defined as unconscious mental activity that consists of transforming information absorbed in the empirical reality we study as researchers into theoretical concepts, relationships, and accounts that clarify the research area and help us understand the questions and problems posed. The concepts and relationships that emerge from intuitionist theorizing should be abstract, in the sense that their reach and interest transcend the incidents and events that gave rise to them. The process of transformation is not likely to be fast, and it is certainly not instant. It may take years to "discover" the language and connections that theorize a field. Intuitionist theorizing is a type of automatic learning by a system that takes care of other learning tasks too. Classical conditioning (of reflex behavior) has been linked to that system, as has instrumental learning in which one learns to modify one's behavior depending on its consequences, and, finally, observational learning (Norris and Epstein 2011: 1044). One would assume that theoretically adequate description in the social sciences is learned mostly through observation, and perhaps through some instrumental instruction. In humans, the automatic learning system not only influences their overt behavior (as it would in other higher-order animals), but also biases their conscious reasoning, these authors add. For the theorizer, this is good news. When we theorize, conscious reasoning comes into the picture intermittently and frequently. We call upon it, so to speak, when we step back and ask ourselves where we stand, and how we should go further, when we jot down our observations, questions, and partial insights, and when at the end of the research process theoretical claims need to be written up and defended. These are the times when reasoning profits from having become "biased"— adapted, that is, to what the implicit system has learned.

At the core of the notion of intuitionist theorizing lies a shift in perspective. It proposes that we move away from understanding theorizing as basically a bureaucratic activity of data administration and management—of compiling, filing, categorizing, coding, and digitalizing these data, and of searching, computing, and calculating their systematic features—and toward taking the human theorizer seriously for what he or she is: a skilled processor. The most interesting tool of this processor would appear to be the implicit and intuitive information processing system introduced earlier. It may well do some administrative work on the incoming data, but it is likely to have additional skills that it brings to the task and that are worth using and exploring. Our theory construction protocols and regulatory logics may have the same post hoc status as our explicit reasoning—they may be wagging the dog's tail, while the dog has been walking away on its own and making good progress.

The Theoretical Construction of Reality and Two Types of Theorizing

Up to now, I have laid out what underpins and explains the claim that theorizing can be an "intuitive," or implicit, automatic information processing activity by reference to our current neurological and cognitive understanding of the brain. I now want to start saying more about what this activity entails, and what supports it. It may be helpful for this purpose to continue to think of the implicit system as if it were an independent entity, rather than a process and circuitry in the brain connected to other processes and circuits. What could possibly enhance this entity's operation and success with a theorizing task?

Since there is, to my knowledge, no research focused on the human theorizer as a processor, one needs to rely on examining one's own practice and what others have said about theirs.

Let me begin with the reality that our intuitive theorizer confronts. This is an argument about the nature of the reality we encounter,[10] and about how reality serves as a resource for the intuitive system as it accomplishes its task. Theorizing is oriented to something outside oneself (one hopes); it is a relational rather than a monadic process. The intuitive processing system needs experience to develop any intuitions. It needs to lay itself open to the reality it will end up theorizing and be able to engage with it in ways I have glossed as "observation." Observation can mean "being there" in the environment we try to theorize, or conducting the less naturalistic observation that one does under controlled conditions, or being immersed in a domain of reality that comes with doing on-site interviews. Observation need not be continuous; it may mean making visits to the observed area over a period of months or years, as when one watches a high-energy physics experiment and its outcomes grow over time—a process that can take twenty years. My own experience suggests that these visits should be either frequent or aided periodically by online contact, to keep the inner processor engaged despite offsite interruptions. Let us leave the notion of "observation" as vague as it is at the moment and paraphrase it by saying that it amounts to the "exposure" of the intuitive human processor to whatever it is that happens in a field of study. This exposure, one assumes, could result in different types of knowledge—practical skills, descriptive information of the kind that results from a tourist's gaze, or the more analytic and conceptual knowledge we call theoretical. The question is: what helps the processor to come up with the last kind, which may be the least frequent and hardest to obtain? One answer surely is that scientists as trained observers are usually firmly anchored in a discipline. They will start their observations not only with particular interests in mind, resulting in focused observations, but also with a whole repertoire of background concepts, explanations, and theoretical hypotheses at their disposal. We know from experience that our inner processor brings this equipment to bear on what "it" or we observe. For example, when I worked at a particular university it often occurred to me that I was in a "Kabylean society," a notion that came to me from Bourdieu and meant that I was in a place where everything was always renegotiated and the results were unpredictable. Intuitionist theorizing surely includes such processes of pattern matching in the widest sense, with the patterns taken from the scientific literature we have absorbed, and being more analytic, empirically established, and perhaps explanatory than the ones we use in everyday life. However, if our processing systems were only doing pattern matching, this would yield few new theories since all the patterns would already be available to us. Perhaps we can think of the exposure we started out with as somewhat analogous to photography, where the term captures the amount of light energy that is allowed to fall on a film and is recorded as information in the form of significant areas of shadow and detail. We can think of the incoming light as "structured" in terms of the information that comes from the object or thing that is being photographed. Our exposed intuitive inner processor could similarly be thought of as receiving, via percepts and communication, pre-structured information from the reality that is being observed. I want to propose that this pre-structuring, assuming it occurs, is incipiently theoretical in the sense of being ordered, layered, laminated, sequentially arranged, directed, and so on. When reality is social, these orderly features may well be obliquely or directly referred to in language. They may be formulated, storied, and analyzed; signaled by labels and symbols or dictated by rules of law. Order may be inscribed in behavior, moods, and physical states, in conversations of gestures (think of dance, for instance), in the architecture of a workspace. Orders may also leave traces in writings, discourse, and visuals. Social reality is often subject to explicitly formulated norms and constraints—actual practice may not conform to the norms, as our notions of resistance (Willis 1977) and decoupling (Meyer et al. 1997) indicate, but breaches confirm the existence of norms. Social reality may also be intentionally set up in strings of elements that are causally related. The opposite of the sort of orderliness I have in mind is chaos. Much of our social reality appears not to be chaotic, but it is historically and in other ways contingent, and the number of dimensions and the possibilities of manipulation there are may well be enormous to the degree that we experience this reality as idiosyncratic. We may not be able to find "laws" that govern this reality or be able to create reasonably complete theoretical pictures of it and get it right. But my point here is only that ordering features exist and they are often visible and in fact signaled, and when they are obscure, they tend to shine through or leak out of what obscures them. Participants could not operate and accomplish what they do if things were not running for them in ways that are intuitively graspable and predictable; and when things seem not clear, as they do at times in financial markets, participants complain and resort to common, predictable back-up strategies like putting their money into Swiss banks, holding cash, or investing in gold. Marx's famous phrase "all that is solid melts into air" ([1844] 1967: 4), and Lash and Urry's (1987) assessment of the end of organized capitalism, suggested the end of certain aspects of our world as we knew it. What these authors confronted were major historical transformations in areas that had appeared stable. They did not suggest that the world would now become a series of undirected and unpredicted surprises that we would have to navigate afresh every morning.

One major resource for an intuitive processor, then, are the traces of the theoretical construction of the reality to which the processor is exposed. I use the term "traces" here in a Derridaean sense (see, e.g., Derrida 1988). Some of the theoretical construction of reality may be explicit, but theorizing that reality social scientifically is of course not just a matter of collecting a group's ethno-theories about how its reality works, and neither is it simply collecting explicit norms and rules of behavior. Contradictions between any explicit normative or symbolic order and what happens in practice will need to be theorized, and the rules themselves will need to be decoded and interpreted. There will also be gaps and contradictions in normative orders. Even written law and other written codes include traces of the deferred nature of the order they imply. Theorizing may involve taking the deferrals seriously and discerning in them the seeds of new orders, or of struggles that remain unresolved. I am not advocating a particular type of theory; extreme types, for instance, when they are firmly rooted in empirical traces, may well be the most interesting and innovative theories. My point is simply that our inner processor has much to lean on in these traces—but it also has much theory-discovering left to do.

It may be helpful at this point to introduce a distinction between a "discovered" theory that is theoretically adequate, and one that is more or less strongly grounded in previous knowledge but is not discovered, and rather is the theory through which we approach empirical research. An example of the latter might be network theory, through which we may want to collect and analyze new empirical data, saying we are using a network approach. Even when we have a theory in place that we take as our guidance, there tends to be theoretical work to do—for instance, the work of extending the theory to a new area. Luhmann's systems theory offers an example. In an early paper, Luhmann (1982) wrote about how systems theory pertains to a global level, to what he called the world society, but his work on the issue remained rudimentary and badly needed further development by other authors (e.g., Stichweh 2000). Intuitionist theorizing would surely help with this, particularly if extending the theory involves empirical work. But a stronger case for intuitionist theorizing can be made when we have to "discover" theoretical knowledge—when we are after what I called "theoretically adequate" theories. What counts as "adequate" can be linked back to the understanding we have of the reality investigated. When one thinks, as I do, that the reality investigated is theoretically constructed; and one is interested, as I am, in learning what this possibly quite imaginative construction and its transformative implications may be: then approach-based theorizing is not the methodology of choice, precisely because it already assumes a particular construction (say networks), sees the field in these terms, and focuses research on nodes and relations. If, on the other hand, one thinks that networks may be relevant in some cases but that other structural and cultural forms also matter, and may even dominate how a domain is structured, then identifying these forms becomes the main task at hand. Theoretically adequate theorizing aims to capture how a particular province of reality is theoretically constructed (including deferrals, negations, and their implications). Approach-based work has many advantages, precisely because it offers a language and concepts through which reality can be addressed, as well as findings from previous research that can serve as an example and benchmark for further research. It gives us a tool for seeing the things for which the shutters are already open, and that are within the optical power of the lens we already have. In contrast, theoretical knowledge that aims to adequately capture the theoretical construction of a particular domain may need to discover an appropriate language, and much else besides that is needed to understand and explain that domain. It will also draw on existing concepts and theories when they seem applicable.

The last point is important. As suggested earlier in this section, intuitionist theorizing is not theorizing without tools, with a mind emptied of previous knowledge. In this chapter I mostly leave out the question of what role the community of inquiry plays in relation to intuitionist theorizing—both as a target audience for theoretical knowledge and as a source of concepts and examples a theorizer has available. But I do want to emphasize that the intuitionist theorizer is part of this community, whose concepts and exemplifications are in the toolbox he or she has at his or her disposal. For example, the concept of a face-to-face situation proved to be a crucial tool for me, when studying trading floors where the primary orientation of participants was not toward others present, but toward a non-present, aggregate, and projected entity: namely the market onscreen. Intuitionist processing surely benefited from all I knew and could reread about the social situation, but it needed to "discover" that this specific social situation, and others like it, had in fact become a mediated, face-to-screen, "synthetic situation." Synthetic situations are structurally quite different from—and they now often occur prior to—the face-to-face situation. While sharing that preference for the underlying, the conceptual, and the analytic (of any kind) that distinguishes theorizing from good storytelling and other types of writing, what's specific here about the intuitionist theorizers' relation to the community may simply be that he or she is a chooser more than a follower. The intuitionist picks things out of the theoretical toolbox selectively and flexibly, controlled by patterns and priorities implicit in the area studied, while the follower selects an approach and trains the imagination and language on it prior to conducting any empirical work. The point here is simply that an intuitionist theorizer is not, and doesn't try to be, a blank cognitive slate when he or she conducts an inquiry—and that is different from any version of induction or phenomenology that recommends blankness. But our theorizer is also not simply accepting and applying a particular theoretical framework—doing this would lead to approach-based theorizing, in which the link to the community of inquiry consists in becoming a follower of a subgroup. As intuitionist theorizers seeking theoretical adequacy, we would not approach art, for example, with Bourdieu's book *Distinction* in hand, and start by matching the art world we observe with his fourfold matrix of a field. The criterion of adequacy assumes that an intuitionist processor can perceive the theoretical features dissolved in an area and bring them out, and these features may or may not correspond to patterns in the literature. The advantage of this can be the discovery of architectures and relationships that enrich our theoretical vocabulary. This, of course, is a full workload for our intuitionist processor—and also for the explicit reasoning circuits when things are consciously addressed.

Theorizing Technology: An Example

What theoretically adequate theorizing based on intuitional processing might mean in practice can best be illustrated by an example. In my study of institutional currency markets, the settings observed were the trading floors of big banks in global cities. The currency market is, with the exception of currency futures, an entirely electronic "over-the-counter" market, meaning that currencies are not traded in exchanges but directly between traders via conversational dealing windows and electronic broker systems that present dealing prices onscreen. When I first arrived on the trading floor of one of these banks, the most striking feature was the high-tech electronic environment. About 200 traders were intensely watching hundreds of colorful screens that seemed to surround them. I learned that the deals were done on an intranet, an electronic infrastructure that connected a network of banking institutions, through which market makers and proprietary traders mostly traded with each other. The environment was not quite what I had implicitly expected from reading teaching-related literature on electronic information and communication structures, which had offered images of webs and underwater pipes and satellite connections. There were too many screens, four to six for every trader, and an atmosphere of intensity and concentration that did not quite match my notion of technology. But I did not make this into an explicit question—I didn't drag the puzzling observation fully into consciousness and start processing it there, using the explicit reasoning system. It remained a preconscious awareness for several years as the study progressed through rounds of interviews having to do with markets, asset management, and trading in several global cities. It seemed as if I had from day one explicitly "understood" what the literature suggested the technology was—an infrastructural necessity that connected participants, transmitted information and communication between them, and could be matched to network society notions (I had also read Castells, 1996). I think I also felt impelled to neglect the technology because the traders I interviewed were not inclined to talk about it. The screens and computers were in the care of information technology experts sitting in separate but co-located units close to the trading floor. Traders treated their technology as transparent in a Heideggerian sense (1962: 98–107), were basically satisfied with it, and relied on the assistance of the experts who appeared within minutes when one of the systems failed to work. But my implicit intuitive processing system didn't see things as transparent, and was not so satisfied with what I seemingly knew. I gather this from certain recurrent impressions and feelings that popped into my head whenever I was on trading floors and stuck with me. The screens seemed like eyes or windows on the world. The many lines of colored text, and the images and graphs that scrolled down the screens often in rapid sequence, suggested that whole areas of life had been sucked into them from all major time zones—politics, social life, and nature included. They were the medium through which traders acted, talked, and saw the world. Seeing like a trader meant staring at screens, from which vast amounts of information and challenges to act stared back at the trader. Traders seemingly lived not with but in their screens. The screens were not like phones boosted by video capabilities. Going from phone trading to screen trading required a gestalt switch, as if going from a distribution to a concentration. Traders had previously used phone connections to deal and find out prices. But what I saw were not connections that linked human participants in widely dispersed locations together, allowing them to create a market. Instead I saw a market concentrated and speeding along on screens composed of layer upon layer of information. From the present perspective, this screen setting presaged the onset of the even more extended electronic environment that is now upon us, in which algorithms rather than humans increasingly execute deals. At the time of these observations (1999–2002) I published two papers with Urs Bruegger that hint at the unease I developed as a result of my recurrent impressions. One paper proposed to capture the sociological side of information technologies through the way they are used. That is, we were looking at how the technologies were social actions at a distance (Knorr Cetina and Bruegger 2002a: 909). The second paper latched on to the puzzling trading floor observations directly, using the phrase "inhabiting technology" to highlight the dominance of screens, and traders' immersion in them (Knorr Cetina and Bruegger 2002b). These publications started to take seriously what I had intuitively picked up, namely that the visualization of markets and their contexts on the screen made a difference for how we had to understand them. A short while thereafter I came up with the notion that the technologies involved were not just infrastructures carrying messages back and forth, but functioned like periscopes: they were reflexive systems of observation that "captured" the market and beamed it to an audience. The notion of a scope came to me seemingly out of nowhere. I do not recall taking it from the literature, and I do not know why periscope rather than telescope or some other optical instrument remained the analogy that stuck. I published a paper called "From Pipes to Scopes" in 2003 that introduced the notion and spelled out its major implication: that there was a significant difference between network coordination and scopic coordination, and that information and communication technologies that involved infrastructural (cable) networks did not automatically imply (social) relational networks— it depended on how the technology was used—i.e., on whether there were screens and what the screens enabled (Knorr Cetina 2003). Market participants did not have to go through network connections to find the market and engage in trading. It was beamed to all of them by a scopic system they shared (everyone in the interbank market had the same Reuters screens), simultaneously and in synchronicity, and that created a co-temporal community held together by its common focus of attention, rather than by any network connections. I later extended this work with research on other areas in which such scopic systems were used, and by the notion of the "synthetic situation" that attempts to capture how the face-to-face situation, a basic concept in sociology, has been transformed by the inclusion of screen technologies (Knorr Cetina 2009, 2012).

Let us assume that the concept of "scopes" and its implications—i.e., the new form of coordination it suggests and the historical replacement of a network market by a media-centered market—can count as theorizing a technology; and that the result is theoretically adequate—that it brought out the architecture of an area that was surprising and stands in contrast to that of other areas. Why do I think that much of what led to this result was intuitive theorizing rather than explicit theory building? First, I had no principal interest in technology, never saw myself as a sociologist of technology (I still don't), had no technology-related goals in my grant proposal, and had no incentive to publish on it. In fact, I would go as far as to say the issue of technology was "forced on" me against my explicit preferences and will. What forced me, I suspect, was an intuitive processor who responded to what it was exposed to, saw treating the topic as unavoidable, and proceeded to work on it. The challenge to network theory that emerged as a consequence of theorizing electronic technologies as scopes was another case in point. I did not go to the field with network theories in mind and in fact had no specific interest in challenging or confirming them in financial markets. They came up as relevant when the notion of a scope was in place, and they became part of articulating the consequences of that notion. But in order to "see" these consequences some preprocessing had to have happened in which the intuitive system was involved. Third, the continually reaffirmed observations of a screen environment that somehow converged with a market resulted for quite a while in no more than a feeling or sense that the technology presented a puzzle, rather than in anything I explicitly addressed. As indicated, the many interviews I conducted didn't help since the traders more or less refused to say anything of interest on the issue. Fourth, my intuitive system, I would say, labored on: it did not drop the subject of technology but continued to absorb and process observations. It surfaced the issue when it could—that is, when there were opportunities, such as the invitation to a conference called "Inhabiting Technology," whose title struck me as a good match for what I had observed, and the invitation to publish a paper for a special issue on economic sociology with prominent contributors (2003), for which I had no other topic. On this last occasion many of the previously implicitly absorbed observations came readily to mind and seemed bound "together" without me having to painfully piece them together or research them afresh. Fifth, my intuitionist theorizer (or some part thereof) processed things somewhat against the grain of what I was writing about explicitly at the time—the action system of trading, the global nature of the market, traders' relationships with the market. It was dissatisfied, I think, with the write-up of my conference talk on "inhabiting technology," which remained descriptive in nature. When I was finished with these writings it made a move: it drew the reluctant ethnographer and her explicit reasoning system to the culture of technology by causing the concept of scopes to pop into my head.

There were of course many points in that story when the explicit system helped—for example, I started to research network theories at one point. Once I had the concept of scopes I researched it in the natural science and optical literature, and as soon as I had the idea that the current market differed from a network market, my collaborator and I planned and conducted oral history interviews with older traders to confirm the notion. I did not, however, use our explicitly formulated methodical strategies of theory building to come up with the concepts and relationships I finally postulated. At a minimum, the notion of intuitionist theorizing points to just that—that we can do theorizing without method, so to speak, and feel we are successful with it.

Attention and Phenomenological Deficiencies of Theorizers

We may do theorizing without method, but not without taking into account some requirements our intuitive system seemingly has, and the impositions it makes. Let me pick out just two such requirements that are also implicitly indicated in the story above. The first pertains to attention, the second to feelings and the role of the emotional brain that mentioned earlier; the two are connected. To begin with the first, let me say that attention as a cognitive process is complicated, or as some analysts put it, "It seems that the more information we gather about how the mind and the body work, the farther we get from concrete, consolidated definitions of the attention construct and its component parts" (Weber et al. 2009: 405). Sociologists did not have much to say about attention in the last decades, and when the term comes up, it tends to be applied to macro-level trends, as in economics (e.g., Davenport and Beck 2001; Franck 2007). Cognitive science has studied attention processes based on psychological experiments, and this work has resulted in interesting theories and findings, but these do not converge in a consensus view. Also the relationship between these results and neurophysiological studies is sometimes unclear, as the two fields appear to operate in parallel rather than to share their results. I want to address attention nonetheless, drawing on my own experience and some research results. Let's begin by reconsidering the vocabulary of exposure I used earlier when I suggested that our intuitional system will need to become exposed to the area to be theorized. What I meant was sensory exposure, for example through direct observation of the target area, and that the perceptions of external events and other sensory stimuli activate our unconscious or preconscious information processing capacities. My own experience suggests the need for sensory exposure. At one point I collaborated with a student on a laboratory study,[11] with the student going to the lab and then reporting back what he saw, and also showing me his notes and transcripts. I could not, however, make much sense of these reports—I could not productively engage with the material, which came from a science about which I had only textbook knowledge and a laboratory context I did not know. After becoming exasperated by my inability to "understand" and analyze the data, I decided to join the student on his next fieldtrip "to see for myself" what was going on. It was just a four-day stay (the first of several), but it made all the difference; it transformed an inability into a productive capability that was even somewhat generative—it extended to activities I had not watched. Thus sensory exposure may be necessary, but the notion is limited because it does not capture the fuller sense in which intuitionist theorizing requires a sustained focus of attention that can also be in place when one is not in the physical presence of the target area. I switch then from the vocabulary of exposure to the vocabulary of attention, and posit that intuitionist theorizing requires that one maintain an intense focus of attention on a target area or problem.

Attention is a scarce resource. Hence a theorizer needs to learn how to best divide up his or her capacity for attention and how to allocate it to various tasks. This is not just a conscious activity of telling oneself "attend to this" and "attend to that." Attention would seem to also operate unconsciously, but to maintain this sort of latent focus of attention one has to know how to inhibit distractions. Distractions, one assumes, often come from the explicit system associated with the prefrontal cortex—from our explicit thinking about and planning our next moves, from communications that want attention (e-mail, phone calls), and simply from the regular business of our work. High-energy and high-intensity universities, for instance, do not allow much room for focused attention beyond their regular business. And yet if attention also operates unconsciously, presumably one can attend to the official business consciously while continuing to be attentive on the unconscious level to a research target. When we listen to an unrelated conference presentation, for instance, we can often get an idea or concept or argument out of the experience that helps with our own research. This suggests that on a latent level we are oriented toward our research goal when listening, and are implicitly processing what we hear in relation to it, while the explicit focus of attention is oriented toward the speaker's words and arguments. Although we listen to a speaker, understand what he or she says, and can report it afterward, we are not exclusively "with them" but also "with us," latently extracting from the talk what we can use for our own purposes. We are not consciously on the prowl for a concept or theory, and yet the unconscious mind is constantly searching under the hood of our official focus of attention for what is useful and stimulating in what crosses our path.

The interesting question is how one sustains that latent focus of attention—how the intuitive system makes it through the many distracting tasks that occupy our conscious awareness and time. Some results in the literature actually suggest that one can let the mind wander from a task, and that these periods of latency and "incubation," or time away from a task, may be a boon for problem solving. Baird et al. (2012: 1117) report a meta-analysis of incubation effects that show, for example, that creative problem solving will be enhanced after a break, and that the benefits of incubation intervals are greater when individuals are occupied with an undemanding task during their time away. More generally speaking, distractions, such as a wandering mind, can enhance creativity significantly, whereas focused deliberation on problems can undermine it. One way to interpret this is to say that mind wandering enhances creativity "by increasing the likelihood of non-conscious, associative processing"—or as

Kaufman and Singer (2012: 4) put it, "when we allow our mind to wander we may be increasing the chance that (the intuitive system) will make creative associations for us." This raises the thrilling possibility that being busy with undemanding tasks, while distracting, might not hurt our latent focus of attention and processing. It also suggests that demanding tasks will hurt. The question then is what counts as a demanding task and what doesn't? I see "demanding" not so much as a property of the task than as a property of the processing system that is related to what taxes the system under what circumstances.[12] In my own experience, going to a movie when I am mentally absorbed with a problem indeed does not hurt and may rather offer the break I need. But interestingly, lunch conversations and administrative meetings do hurt. The common denominator in those two cases may be the social interaction they involve, which can require more energy than watching or listening.[13] Another common denominator could be temporal; if, say, such meetings occur during periods normally devoted to focused attention and high performance and the meetings interrupt the flow, the experience is negative. But if they occur at other times the experience could be positive and even relaxing. There are other indications that support the idea that sustaining a (latent) focus of attention involves a strict temporal regime. Self-observation suggests that I attempt to maintain such a focus up to the last minute before an interrupting engagement and then take a "leap" into the engagement (rather than mentally or otherwise preparing for it), as if the two spheres were different finite provinces of meaning in the sense of Schutz (1945). Leaps back into the province of research are more difficult, if they can be accomplished at all. It can be part of the temporal regime to engage the "sub-universe" of sleeping for the purpose of maintaining a latent focus of attention on the target. This can be accomplished, I assume, by reading target material just before falling asleep—chances that the intuitive processing system remains "on target" during sleep could well be higher than if distracting material is consumed.

Of course, Schutz's "world of working" includes both research/theorizing and business meetings. But from the perspective of an implicit processor these two domains might well involve different stances toward reality instantiated in distinctive information processing circuits and attention networks. Schutz seemed to have anticipated this when he said the different realities involved distinctive "cognitive styles," with distinctive temporal, corporal, social, and logical dimensions. However, while I have experienced the discreteness of the provinces and the "leap" it takes to switch between them, on another level the provinces are not quite as finite. For example, if one were a scientist working on research before a business meeting, it would be possible to retain (or fail to slip out of) the scientific attitude of an observer during the meeting. This implies that as the latent attention remained focused on its previous target and stance, explicit processing and attention would suffer. One would therefore not contribute to the meeting as expected.

The account I am giving thus far sheds light on our attempts to manage attention through a temporal regime, as well as some of the phenomenological experiences this involves—the experience of multiple realities, more or less successful transitions between them, and the different demands these realities appear to make on our cognitive processes. Let me add a few more observations and issues to this. Schutz talked about the phenomenon whereby the transition into a particular province of meaning, say the fictitious world of a stage play or a joke, can mean that "the world of our daily life takes on the character of foolishness." It may be worth mentioning that one can experience this "foolishness" in the world of working, the one I am transitioning into and having to participate in "prefrontally," while the intuitive reasoning system is still busy with its latent focus on the "other" world to be theorized. Finding things foolish is not an optimal stance to have as a practitioner in one's working life. Intuitionist reasoning may bring with it social costs and deficiencies in one's functioning, resulting from the difficulties of maintaining more than one focus of attention, the dilemmas of transition management, and the possible tendency of experiencing social communication as an undermining rather than a supportive distraction.

Ideas about how to divide the attention pie assume that it is a finite cognitive resource. But instead of thinking of attention only as finite, we can also think of it as a resource that can be mobilized and that resides not only in the human brain and its cognitive processes, but also in interactions, in technology, and in institutions. Neurophysiology, for instance, distinguishes between three aspects of attention that are linked to separable regions of the brain: alerting, orienting, and executive control (Posner et al. 1987). Alerting (or alertness) in this context is the ability to sustain vigilance—and to maintain response presence. Whereas orienting is defined as the ability to select from the incoming sensory information the parts to attend to (Raz and Buhle 2006: 371, 374; cited in Weber et al. 2009: 406). Orienting can also occur before the sensory information is in place; for example, imaging and cellular recording studies are said to widely agree that "orienting to sensory information activates a network of neural areas even before a target is presented." (Fan et al. 2005: 471). This may serve as a source of enhancement of neural signals related to processing a target. However, orienting and alerting are not only neuro-physiological aspects of attention, but also behavioral concepts. Traders and the firms in which they work offer plenty of examples of orienting and alerting behavior—and of the technological and organizational means that are used to facilitate this behavior. When traders arrive on the trading floor they take off their jackets, and strap themselves to their seats, metaphorically speaking; from then on their gaze is glued to the screens. They orient themselves to the market and remain oriented to it throughout the day, taking lunch at their desks and rarely stepping away. Lunch at the desk may be provided by firms, which seemingly do what they can to allow traders to keep their attention focused on the market. Trading floors and seating arrangements are designed to enhance an intense focus; for example, they make it possible for traders to hear what goes on at other desks in related markets, while keeping their gaze fixed on their screens. The technology helps hugely: it more or less surrounds the traders, and it alerts and attracts the focus of attention through both the screen content and the medium itself—its colors, frames, signals, and placements. Traders also cry out when they see a strong market event (say a price decrease) onscreen, and when asked why they do this, they have said they are alerting themselves (and others) to activities to increase their responsiveness (Laube 2008). Abolafia (1996) and others have observed that traders' "vigilance" is not only an automatic response to a changing market but also a tool they use strategically. Traders experience an increased surge of "adrenalin" (their term) even before arriving on the floor of an exchange, as they orient themselves to their task before beginning to work. Traders also incorporate market rhythms into their behavior and bodily rhythms, suggesting that the body, too, is used as an attentional resource. Traders pay attention to the body language of others on the floor, and when they work in an open outcry exchange (some still exist), they use their body language to try and get the attention of others (Levin 2005: 218–19).

I use these examples to show that there are settings in which attentional needs, and the economy of attention and its demands, are well within the purview of institutions and their subprocesses—for example, by technology producers and providers, supervisors, and even those who design the setting. But there are also settings in which this is not the case—where institutional time regimes and procedures are not responsive to attentional needs. Intuitionist theorizing should be easier in the first kind of setting.

Does Theorizing Involve Emotions?

Persons who maintain an intense and narrow focus of attention on a target may find themselves in a state of flow: engaged in a seemingly effortless, automatic task performance and feeling as if they are operating without conscious thinking. Csikszentmihalyi (1988; 1990) described the flow experience as an optimal experience: an altered state of consciousness characterized by pleasurable feelings and emotional rewards that accrue from being thoroughly absorbed in a challenging task. If intuitionist theorizing, like the flow experience, requires an intense focus of attention, does it also involve emotional rewards? Recall that in the literature emotional processing is connected with the intuitive rather than the explicit system. This suggests that emotions or feelings (I use the terms interchangeably here) are likely to come into play, and may even be required to maintain and perhaps optimize implicit processing. Let us first consider what flow theory has to say, and then address theorizing.

There are several aspects of flow theory that are consistent with an intuitive information processing system engaged in subconscious task execution, and with what I have said about intuitionist theorizing, although they may also point to the flow experience as a special experience. For example, flow theory postulates that action and awareness are merged during the experience of flow, meaning "a person's attention is completely absorbed by the activity. There is no excess psychic energy left over to process any information but what the activity offers. All the attention is concentrated on the relevant stimuli" (Csikszentmihalyi 1990: 53–54). The description entails that the explicit system will be inhibited during flow (Dietrich 2004: 757). Intense concentration is associated here with decreased prefrontal functions, implying the disappearance of consciousness, a sense of timelessness, the loss of worries of failure, and an attentional effort that excludes other, intruding information. This suggests that intuitionist theorizing can result in the optimal performances associated with flow when one can volitionally narrow the attention to the task and avoid any additional business that demands attention. One may speculate that the long-term latent attention required for intuitionist theorizing leads to enriched and more frequent experiences of flow. Another consistency arises from a second postulate of flow theory. According to Csikszentmihalyi (1990: 55), the reason it is possible to achieve such complete involvement in a flow experience is that goals are usually clear and feedback immediate. When the goals are not so clear, as for all activities that are creative or open-ended in nature, the person "needs to learn to set goals and to recognize and gauge feedback in such activities." How would we do this in the case of theorizing? Most of Csikszentmihalyi's examples involve sensory-motor tasks such as playing tennis or climbing a rock, in which immediate feedback (scoring points, "not falling") appears to be built into the task. Is intuitionist theorizing a feedback-rich activity? In the technology-related example I presented, feedback may have come from the repetition and reinforcement of certain experiences; these repetitions could have resulted in an accentuation of the uneasiness I had with my explicit knowledge. If this is correct, repetition that provides an incentive for continued implicit processing and "sinks" information into the relevant long-term memory would be an advantage for, and a requirement of, implicit processing. I do have the sense that repeated sensory exposure to a target reality was indeed necessary in my field studies, not only to get interviews and observations done, but also to "ready" latent attention circuits so that they would be unconsciously on the prowl for useful input, and to launch the processor on its implicit reasoning and analysis path.[14]

With these consistencies and overlaps between flow theory and intuitionist theorizing in mind, let me now return to the question of emotions. One aspect of flow Csikszentmihalyi emphasizes is that it is enjoyable—and described as such in similar terms by musicians, basketballers, and others "regardless of culture, stage of modernization, social class, age, or gender" (Csikszentmihalyi 1990: 49). What makes the experience enjoyable in Csikszentmihalyi's account includes what I said before; we must be able to concentrate on what we are doing, the task provides feedback so that we know we are getting somewhere, and there is the inhibition of prefrontal functions that could cause worries about failure. In fact, the whole point of the theory is the connection between an activity that requires full concentration, and pleasurable feelings and emotional rewards. If intuitionist theorizing is similar to flow in relation to the implicitness of task execution and the intense focus of attention that is required, is it also similar in the sense of involving pleasurable feelings and emotions?

We can "update" Csikszentmihalyi's writings for our purpose in light of the neurophysiology of emotions I discussed earlier. Damasio (2009: 211) suggested that the brain is designed to attach a "value tag" or somatic marker to the incoming information, and that the marker signals the conjunction of certain categories of situations or outcome with certain categories of emotional response. All this may happen unconsciously. Damasio had an eye on decision making when he summarized his theory for economists and said that the marker "weighs in" on the decision process. I propose that the marker weighs in on maintaining the latent focus of attention and keeping the intuitionist processing system "on target" by "value-tagging" the research area to be theorized positively—if necessary against the other preoccupations the reasoning brain suggests. Recall that the marker is an emotional value that we have learned in the past to associate with certain phenomena, including, according to Damasio, "the premises of a problem, the options of actions, the factual outcome" of situations. I suggest that the emotional value relevant here is the feeling of excitement, stimulation, and challenge that some research contexts arouse. I experienced this excitement when I took my first step into a scientific laboratory, in my second laboratory study, and when I first stepped onto a trading floor. When I first entered the lab I did it hesitantly, feeling foolish—my reluctance fueled by the belief that what scientists did after all was thinking, and thinking could not be directly observed in practice (I had read too much philosophy of science). Yet once in the lab I was hooked almost immediately. What unfolded before my eyes was an action system: a collective, instrument-rich, buzzing work setting that could of course be observed! When I asked scientists the usual initial questions about what they were doing and why, they answered freely; it was also clear that their way of reasoning was not different from the sort of reasoning we all do—it posed no logic of inference problems, and one could fully understand it, though of course I did not possess all of their scientific knowledge or understand all of the technical language they used. What stimulated the excitement and got me hooked, I think, is that I saw (literally) almost immediately that my premise had been wrong. The options of action (doing an ethnography of science) were there, and the outcome would be positive for me and others. One could almost say I fell in love with doing the study. Ethnographies of science had to my knowledge not been done before, and the contradiction I saw between my expectations ("thinking") and what unfolded (an action system) were surely promising of new insights and warranted carrying out the study. Not all of the responses I am reconstructing here were fully explicit in the situation, but my emotional excitement was.

It is possible that this first excitement became a memory trace reactivated in my later studies, even though the stimuli that prompted it were quite different. In my study of CERN (the European Organization for Nuclear Research),[15] I was attracted, I think, by its "big science" character: the huge international research teams, constellations of equipment (accelerators and detectors), and the lab itself—a small city rather than an academic department. The contrast between what I saw and the bench-work science I had studied previously was amazing; I later decided to turn this into a topic of the project, which would compare small science with big science. In my study of trading, the attractor was the high-energy, high-intensity setting of an interbank trading floor and the postmodern impression it made (in comparison with a university). It's also possible that earlier memory traces rooted in biography played a role in the first and later cases. I had been drawn to images and tales of science before, had discussed science for years in the debates surrounding positivism in Germany, and found all of that pleasurable.[16] Among the territories of social reality that are within one's reach and offer themselves for liking or disliking, I liked those that were forward looking, esoteric, and strange (I am an anthropologist by training) more than those that celebrated the past (museums) or that were routine settings of social life. The point of these anecdotal illustrations is simply to claim that intuitionist theorizing involves feelings that arise from research areas that emotionally excite (or turn off) the theorizer. Since we can know the emotional quality of an object before we have consciously assessed it, we may have a bias toward wanting to "understand" a particular research field, without having good reasons or use for the choice. I have done studies whose emotional imprint must have been negative: Lisrel models of scientists in organizations based on questionnaire studies, for instance, that yielded results that were much like derivatives in financial markets. One wasn't sure what one had in hand at the end, the correlations were often hard to explain, and they were miserably low, with 9% of the variance explained. Such outcomes are normal in sociology, but no natural scientist would take such correlations seriously. While these projects were methodologically challenging, they did not give me confidence in the outcome or feelings of success, and they did not have lasting emotional appeal. I have avoided doing such studies ever since—not because I devalue them "objectively," but because their emotional value tag for me is "unpleasant" and "unsatisfying."

Emotion, to be sure, not only plays a fundamental role in background processes—like motivation for exploring a particular domain or for avoiding it—but also in moment-to-moment processing and decision making as well (Immordino-Yang and Fischer 2009: 313). It's a "rudder that steers learners' thinking," these authors state, helping the student to "call up information and memories that are relevant to the topic or problem at hand." As analysts, we evaluate implicitly but also emotionally that which brings us closer to the solution of a theorizing problem, by drawing selectively on our own previous experience and that of the field. Damasio (1994) suggests that, unlike the computational mode of the cognitive system, emotions are a form of "bio-computation, i.e. dirty, me-relevant computation" (Churchland, 2002: 228). The intuitionist processor, one assumes, is embedded in a biography shaped by plenty of me-relevant computations. These fulfill orienting functions not only by inciting attention and motivation, but also by evaluating simulated and actual outcomes—giving us a sense of moving in the right direction, and of which lines of analysis are worth pursuing.[17]

Concluding Remarks and Open Questions

In our cultures, human beings have long been seen as "thinkers." But what if we see them instead as "processors" of information? Shifting away from the thinker and toward the processor may seem like a small step, but it has the substantial consequence of taking us from explicit reasoning to implicit reasoning—to a level of information processing that appears to be efficient, high capacity (in terms of the number of variables and dimensions it can deal with simultaneously), pre-conscious (we can still consciously do something else), and not controlled by "thinking." For a scientific observer of reality to not be controlled by the "thinking" brain may seem odd, but this lack of control may actually be an advantage. First, from all we know now, implicit processing is the automatic default process; it happens anyway, even when we are not trying to bring it into play, and we are using our time efficiently when we work with it. Second, not being controlled by thinking may enhance creativity, allowing us to see the world in new ways. For example, we might

be better able to identify new patterns of empirical reality that the thinking brain neglects when it directs attention toward what is reasonable and
plausible. There is evidence for this; for example, a recent study finds that
an experiential thinking style (corresponding to implicit processing) is
positively correlated with creativity and an imagination scale, but not a
rational thinking style (Norris and Epstein 2011: 1043). What is reasonable and plausible for a researcher should be heavily influenced by disciplinary knowledge—by what is known and believed in the scientific fields
in which we work. Such guidance is important—everyone needs it, and I
always felt I profited from understanding the concepts and theories of a
discipline, which are much like the tools in a toolbox from which one can
choose. But new tools and approaches enrich disciplines, and an automatic
learning system may be good at analyzing any stimulation from the environment in ways that are potentially enriching. This point is supported by
anecdotal evidence from scientists (including Einstein) who report how
intuition has helped them. Note that "intuitive" here and in the literature
should not be understood to mean fuzzy, impulsive, or noncomputational;
neither is it an antonym for rationality. Conversely, conscious reasoning
is not the epitome of rationality, as suggested by the many researchers
who describe how it is often used for the confabulation of explanations
of behavior that are controlled by the unconscious system (see above; and
Evans 2008: 258). Note also that there are multiple connections at various
levels between the conscious and unconscious systems. In the literature,
the differences between the two systems seems to be better understood
than the connections between them; but understanding the connections
is surely a pressing issue, not only for the neurosciences but also for the
concept of theorizing.

I have long thought of myself as a processor when I am in the field,
drawing an analogy with a computer whose miraculous inner workings I
don't understand. Just as one can readily use a real computer for what it
is designed to do (e.g., calculation) without actually understanding how
it operates, I can use myself effectively to do what a processor is designed
to do: assimilate and come to terms with information. This was before I
knew anything about dual process theories, the emotional brain, or attention networks. Neurophysiological and cognitive sciences of the brain
take some of the wonder out of the process, while supporting the analogy of the theorizer as a processor. To go forward with the concept of

intuitionist theorizing proposed in this chapter, and with the goal to learn more about theorizing in the context of discovery, this literature does not contradict anything we may want to add at the level of behavior, institutions, technology, or culture. Resources for maintaining an intense focus of attention, for example, are mobilized on all those levels when activities are associated with maximal implicitness of task execution in practice, as suggested by the example of trading. Such a proposal to use multi-level analysis could resolve any conflict we might perceive between the more intra-individual and nano-level analyses the cognitive sciences offer and the interactional and collective levels the social sciences prefer.

3 Analogy, Cases, and Comparative Social Organization

Diane Vaughan

A GRADUATE STUDENT ONCE SAID TO ME, "WE LEARN THEORIES, but we don't learn how people theorize." Theorizing is the process of building an explanation: theory is the product. We read the polished final products, but the process of theorizing remains private, the undiscussed backstage of our craft. Perhaps this is so because we are not aware of our own process, or because theorizing is tacit knowledge, hard to articulate. How do we have theoretical insights? What are the sources of ideas and the cognitive mechanisms behind our interpretive work?

In the 1980s, as I started my career, I became aware that my own process of theorizing was analogical: Against tradition, I was creating explanations by drawing in theories and concepts developed to explain similar events or activities in social settings different from mine, both in substance and in level of analysis, because they nonetheless fit my data. Wondering if this were a common way of theorizing, I began exploring the possibility. Research in cognitive science showed that analogy was the primary way that children and adults explained the world to themselves. Analogical reasoning is the cognitive process of structural alignment and mapping between separate, distinctive domains and their parts (Gentner 1983). It is a complex process that we experience in a flash of recognition.

That flash of recognition of similarities across different domains matched my experience. Logically, if analogy was a common way of explaining the world to oneself, it followed that other scholars would use analogical reasoning in developing theoretical explanations. I began to search for uses of analogy in sociology. While other disciplines had acknowledged its role in the production of knowledge, sociology had all but ignored it. A few organization theorists had written about the role of correspondences in theorizing; however, they concentrated on metaphor, not analogy (Manning 1979; Morgan 1980). The exception was Stinchcombe (1978), who advocated a method of case comparison for historical sociologists that called for systematically searching for both analogies and differences across *similar* cases (i.e., social revolutions in nation-states). Writing before Gentner, Stinchcombe described historical case comparison as a search for structural equivalence relations. When a great number of structurally equivalent pairs were found, it constituted a deep analogy. The relative silence about analogy in sociology was in contrast to evidence of its use in some classic works. Although analogy was unnamed and no method discussed, the authors were generating theory by comparing similar activities across different social settings: cross-case rather than same-case comparison.

Goffman was a master at it. In *Asylums* (1961), his concept of the total institution was inductively developed from his fieldwork in a mental hospital, then further elaborated by cross-case comparison: of prisons, army training camps, naval vessels, boarding schools, and monasteries. The resulting theory was that the most important factor in forming the member was the institution, not individual characteristics, so the reaction and adjustment of the individuals to one total institution was analogous to those confined in the others. In *Power and Exchange in Social Life* (1964), Blau began with an analysis of love in a dyad using interactional data to identify basic principles of power and exchange. Then in succeeding chapters he elaborated his theory by considering first groups, then complex organizations, then inter-organizational relations.

These examples explicitly demonstrated analogical theorizing based on cross-case comparison, where the cases were different, stand-alone forms of social organization with different members. In *Street Corner Society* (1943), however, Whyte had innovated. His famous insight was that the informal rankings of cornerboys from the Norton Settlement House were analogous to their formal ranking on the bowling team, based on scores. His theoretical explanation was that the opportunity to change street rank through athletic skill was precluded by group dynamics, which limited social mobility, creating structural equivalence between member ranking in the informal organization of the corner and the formal organization of the team. Writing long before Stinchcombe, using ethnographic rather than historical data, Whyte had identified a deep analogy and the dynamic that created it.

I thought that if we could harness our use of analogy, making the heretofore invisible and automatic visible and explicit by developing it into a systematic method, it would have the potential for innovative theory generation. Moreover—and in response to the graduate student's complaint—it could be taught. I began experimenting with such a method, using cross-case rather than same-case comparison. Since I began this project in the 1980s, sociologists have become more aware of the importance of the theorizing process (Weick 1995; Becker 1998; Burawoy 1998; Hedström and Swedberg 1998; Swedberg 2012b). Moreover, analogy as a mechanism for theory building has received some support. Tsoukas (1993) recognized the potential of analogy, proposing Gentner's structure-mapping theory (1989) for building organization theory. More recently, Abbott identified analogy as a key heuristic for the social sciences, giving examples of concepts and theories that have been imported across disciplinary boundaries, traveling from one research topic to another, resulting in innovative theorizing (2004: 110–20).

Because it is seldom discussed, we know very little about how people theorize. Analogical theorizing is one way, among several others (see, e.g., Van Maanen 1995; Becker 1998; Abbott 2004; Swedberg 2012; Timmermans and Tavory 2012). Undoubtedly, others are undiscovered because people are not sensitized to their own theorizing process. My purpose in this chapter is to create an awareness of the uses of analogy in social research and to introduce the method of analogical theorizing. Analogy is relevant to this project in two ways: as a case comparison method and as a way of thinking analytically. I begin by briefly describing the method. Then, to demonstrate, I retrace how I used the method to develop a general theory from a three-case comparison, explaining how and why things go wrong, such that organizational actions and outcomes deviate from social expectations: *Controlling Unlawful Organizational Behavior* (1983), *Uncoupling* (1986), and *The Challenger Launch Decision* (1996). Despite variation in organization size, complexity, and function, each case demonstrated similar causal patterns, which combined with the differences to drive theorizing forward.

Throughout, I focus on the cognitive backstage of theory development: my iterative process and the choices I made, showing both the missteps that led to revision and the positive advances that produced new concepts and theoretical innovation. The comparison shows analogy operating at every stage of the research process: case selection, developing concepts and theoretical explanations; the material practice of comparison; and generalizing beyond the case to other examples. Although my examples are substantively specific, the method itself is theoretically neutral, so can be used for other substantive topics and by scholars with theoretical orientations and research methods that differ from mine. In the conclusion, I address the general uses and relevance of analogical theorizing for sociology and its potential for developing generic explanations, theoretical innovation, and theoretical integration.

Analogy and the Heuristics of Case Analysis

Analogical theorizing depends upon cross-case rather than same-case comparison to explain some similar event, outcome, or activity.[1] Supporting the legitimacy of this approach is the formal sociology of Georg Simmel (1950), who argued that the central task of sociology is to separate the social form of some phenomenon from its content in order to identify generic patterns across cases. So, for example, if comparing domestic violence, gang violence, and war between nation-states, we would be able to identify the general properties of violence found across social settings. The approach embraces differentially organized social forms, from the simpler and less structured, as in the earliest organizational studies of the Chicago School (Abbott 2009), to modern formal and complex organizations. Their comparability originates in a fundamental principle of group life. Regardless of differences in size, complexity, and function, all organizational forms have characteristics in common. They share basic aspects of structure: hierarchy, division of labor, goals, normative standards, patterns of coming and going. Further, they share common processes: socialization, conflict, competition, cooperation, power, culture. This means we can compare them, generating theory based on analogies and differences that we find (Vaughan 1992).

The focal point of explanation—our case—will be an event, activity, or outcome situated in an organizational form or forms: either a group, formal organization, complex organization, or some combination— substantively, a family, gang, neighborhood, community, profession, university, nation-state. The cases can be ethnographies, interview- or document-based, or historical studies, all producing lots of detailed information as a rich base for theorizing. The first use of analogical comparison comes in at the point of case

selection. We always begin research with a starting theory, concept, or definition in mind that shapes our selection of a case. So from the beginning, we are
making a comparison between our case and what we expect to find, based on
a theory, concept, or characteristics of other cases. More than one case can
be analyzed in the same study, or cases can be analyzed sequentially. Alternatively, a focal case can be compared with a case or cases done at a different
time and place by other researchers, these differences qualifying it as a cross-
case rather than same-case comparison (see, e.g., Burawoy 1979).

Case selection is a key heuristic in the discovery process. A case is selected
because of the event or activity to be explained. However, intentionally shifting the unit of analysis from one organizational form to another is essential.
Doing so can contribute to theory building in several ways: (1) when studying similar events in different organizational settings, we get different kinds
of data that reveal previously unrecognized aspects of the problem; (2) often
shifting the unit of analysis shifts the level of analysis as well, allowing new
insights into the micro-elements of a macro-level explanation, or vice-versa;
(3) it can be advantageous for elaborating theories and concepts focusing on
large, complex systems that are difficult to study; and (4) it promotes integration of the research and theory of different scholars studying events, activities, and outcomes in variously organized social forms and at different levels
of analysis, thus building a stronger conceptual base and moving us toward
general theory that narrows the scope conditions in which a particular theory
will apply.

Our first goal is to determine empirically what a given case is an example
of. The starting theory or concept is used as a heuristic to loosely organize the
data. A complex starting theory may be reduced to a set of its key concepts,
organized as a skeletal analytic framework to aid discovery. The case selected
is itself a hypothesis. A circumstance or event appears to be an example of
x based on certain characteristics of x that we know and recognize (or suspect) are there, either on the basis of research of our own, others' research,
or personal experience. The idea is to proceed in a systematic way that forces
us to discover and confront what we do not expect to find. To further this
goal, the analysis is framed as situated action (Vaughan 1996, 1998). Following
sociological theory indicating that social interaction occurs in layered social
structures and processes, we situate individual interaction within the organizational form in which it occurs and also within the organizational environment: relevant political, economic, cultural, institutional, and historical

conditions. Drawing boundaries is a creative aspect of the theorizing process that can limit or enhance the similarities and differences we find. By framing our analysis as situated action, we are forced to consider the relation between environment, organization, and individual choice, meaning, and action. Most often, empirical work focuses on one, or possibly two of these levels of analysis, not all three. With a situated action approach, we are forced to look in new directions, beyond our personal theoretical orientation toward micro-, meso-, or macro-, even though in a given case we may find we do not have data for all three.

We treat each case independently of others. Although the analogies—with the starting theory, with other cases—confirm what we suspect, the differences are crucial because they lead to theoretical innovation. The differences sensitize us to our mistakes. They can disqualify the case as an example of *x*, for it may turn out that we do not have an example of what we thought (see, e.g., Vaughan 1996, 2004). Whatever the result, identifying the defining patterns of each case is a necessary first step. The process of comparison is important to developing an explanation. Intuitively developed and practiced before I knew of the writings of C. S. Peirce, analogical theorizing conforms to Peirce's process of abduction (cf. Vaughan 1992). In a 1903 lecture and subsequent writings on how to theorize, Peirce saw theorizing as three interrelated yet independent and distinct operations: abduction, deduction, and induction (Swedberg 2013). He described abduction as a series of mental processes: a continuing iteration and adjustment between alternative hypotheses, theory, and data to either refine, correct, or expand a theory in new directions, narrow its scope, or define it as inappropriate. Abduction depends upon weighing anomalous findings against existing theories to construct new theories (Tavory and Timmermans 2009; Timmermans and Tavory 2012).

These several processes of comparison are essential to discovering both patterns across cases and the novel and unexpected. The discovery process is aided by the systematic use of research strategies that help us guard against our biases and force-fitting our data into a preconceived theory (Vaughan 1992: 195–99). Analytic induction calls for expanding and correcting the explanation to take into account discrepant information that contradicts what we expect to find (Lindesmith 1947; Katz 2001). Blumer (1960) argued for "sensitizing concepts" that point us in a general direction, telling us where to look rather than dictating what we will find. In contrast to Glaser and Strauss's (1967) take on grounded theory—that we proceed inductively, always beginning from an objective, neutral theoretical position—in order to let the theory "emerge" from the data, analogical theorizing assumes that we always have a set of theories and concepts in mind, so must make them explicit in order to reject, reconceptualize, or extend theory (Vaughan 1992). Concurring with Peirce, Timmermans and Tavory (2012) prioritize abduction over grounded theory, concluding that theory generation is not solely inductive, and must be an iterative, recursive process that takes alternative hypotheses—those theories and concepts we have "in mind"—into account.

Once the defining patterns for a case have been identified, the patterns can be treated as a heuristic device to see if the relevant features are found in other cases or theories that appear to be analogical. This works both backward and forward: once resolved, a case is weighed against the starting theory, concept, or case and also becomes a hypothesis for the next case. Critical to this method is the backward comparison: setting aside the substantive findings of the present case to clearly distinguish similarities and differences that specify the theoretical consequences of the comparison. When we do not take this final step, we discourage others from building on what we've done. The goal is to develop a body of cumulative knowledge across cases, based on the identification of generic patterns, incrementally narrowing the scope of phenomena to which they apply.

Theorizing Organizational Deviance: How and Why Things Go Wrong

To demonstrate analogical theorizing as both a cognitive process and a cross-case comparative method, I retrace my incremental development of a theory of organizational deviance from a three-case comparison. Although strikingly different substantively, all three were examples of how things went wrong in organizations that varied in size, complexity, and function: corporate misconduct in one, deteriorating intimate relationships in another, and NASA's Space Shuttle *Challenger* tragedy. Throughout, I attempt to make clear my theorizing process: the theoretical tools I brought to the project and how analogical reasoning and comparison led to new insights and concepts. Three caveats: First, I present an overview, based on the main ideas of my previous research as I moved from writing project to writing project. Each book appeared separately, in isolation from the others; here their stories are joined to show the connections between them. The resulting shortcoming is that each project cannot be presented here in the detail of the original, so the complete logic of the process and the theory that are crucial to explanation are not visible. Second, the need to condense and put the narrative in a logical order distorts the process of theorizing, which is more a meandering process with intermittent order than the linear one presented here. Third, none of what appears here would have been possible without the work of literally hundreds of scholars. For in-depth explanations of each case, the theory, and how the work of others went into its development, interested readers should see the originals.

Controlling Unlawful Organizational Behavior (1983)

As a graduate student, I specialized in the sociology of organizations and in deviance and social control. For my dissertation, I wanted to merge the two in a study of organizational misconduct. This was an innovative idea at the time. Organizational pathologies were not the domain of organization specialists. Instead, the topic was restricted to specialists in deviance and social control whose focus was white-collar criminals—high-status individual offenders, acting in their official roles, violating laws and rules to achieve corporate goals (Sutherland 1949). Fortuitously, a case hit the local papers that was exactly what I had in mind: one organization had violated the law, victimizing another organization. Revco Discount Drug Store, a Medicaid provider, had used a computer-generated double-billing scheme to defraud the Ohio Department of Public Welfare of more than a half-million dollars in Medicaid funds. I analyzed the case, the social control network that developed to investigate it, and the outcomes in organizational terms. My empirical analysis was followed by three chapters that I organized into the three topics that dominated the literature: the competitive environment, from the corporate crime literature; organization characteristics, from the organizations literature; and regulation, which mainly came from the sociology of law, but with some crucial bits of organizational sociology mixed in. The three chapters were thorough, and they were original because they merged the organizations and deviance literatures. However, they stood alone as disconnected pieces of the puzzle. They described but did not explain.

It was while revising my dissertation as a book that I discovered that my own process of theorizing was analogical. While working on the chapter on "organization characteristics," I discovered myself writing a sentence about organization characteristics as "legitimate means" to accomplish deviance. From the toolkit of concepts I carried around with me all the time, without thinking I had extracted one concept —legitimate means—from Merton's Social Structure and Anomie theory (1968[1938]) because it resonated with my data. Merton had conceptualized legitimate means as opportunity structures at the societal level. Thinking of organizations as the units of analysis, I saw that organization characteristics could be conceptualized as opportunity structures to attain organization goals unlawfully. His concept of opportunity structures came to me because of analogies—structural equivalences—between his problem, individual deviance, and mine, organizational deviance.

Realizing this connection, I saw how the parts related to each other and to the whole: I reorganized my three descriptive chapters into three interrelated parts of a causal explanation. For this abbreviated space, I reduce the theory (i.e., the three chapters) to its core concepts and subconcepts. The major elements of this theory, how they connect with each other, and the major subconcepts that constitute each are:

1. The competitive environment (competition, scarce resources, and norms), which puts structural pressures on organizations to violate laws and rules in order to attain goals (Vaughan 1983: Chap. 4, 54–66);

2. Organization characteristics (structure, processes, transactions, and technology), which provide opportunities to violate (1983: Chap. 5, 67–87);

3. The regulatory environment (autonomy and interdependence), defined as the relationship between regulatory organizations and the organizations they regulate, which tends to compromise the capacity to control and deter violations, thereby encouraging the decisions of individual organization members to violate in the organization's behalf (1983: Chap. 6, 88–104).

Although each of these three components is related to violative behavior, I saw that they were interrelated, such that misconduct resulted from the three in combination. All three factors were necessary to a causal explanation because they *combined* to affect individual meaning making, choice, and action. The subconcepts were interrelated as well, together explaining the dynamics within each of the three core factors. Thus, I concluded, misconduct was the product of an organizational system.

Reflecting on what I had done to arrive at this new place, I realized I had switched units of analysis, using Merton's societal-level theory, which was designed to explain rates of individual deviance, and instead applying it to organizations. Thinking in terms of organizations had exposed some weaknesses in Merton's conceptualization and at the same time had suggested how it might be altered to explain organizational misconduct. In fact, his theory seemed better at explaining the behavior of organizations than individuals. Below I describe some of the cognitive process of theorizing that led to (1) linking the three major concepts into a causal system, (2) developing the subconcepts within each core element and their relation to one another, and (3) a critique and revision of Merton's theory.

The Competitive Environment. Scripted into Merton's explanation but never made explicit were the ideas of competition and resource scarcity. His societal-level theory explained the crimes of the working class by arguing that not all can achieve the culturally approved goal of economic success because the legitimate means (opportunity structures) to that success were limited (education, jobs, etc.). Thus, Merton's unrecognized dynamic was that individuals had to compete for scarce resources. When stymied by blocked access to legitimate means, many resorted to illegitimate means to attain them. However, I saw that *both* means and ends could be in short supply. Thus, I reconceptualized both as scarce resources. Further, I realized that he neglected to note that even those individuals who have the opportunities to get into the competition still must compete for scarce resources: acceptance at graduate school, promotion, meeting the profit goals for the quarter, achieving tenure, winning the NCAA basketball tournament. Obviously, deviance was not solely a working-class phenomenon. Middle- and upper-class people could also be compelled toward deviance (Vaughan 1983: 54–66, 70–73, 85–87). The cross-case comparison had generated a critique of the social-class basis of his theory.

This realization led to the next theoretical advance. Analogically, it followed that what was true for individuals was also true for organizations. Organizations compete for scarce resources, which I defined broadly to include not only financial resources, but also qualified employees, sales territory, market share, members, customers, parishioners. Those organizations at the top of the organizational stratification system compete to retain their status among equals or move up, those in the great middle compete to maintain or increase theirs, and those at the bottom strive to stay in the competition or to keep from failing altogether. This continuous dynamic of competition and scarce resources, together with the unclear norms regulating business behavior, in combination exerted structural pressures on *all* organizations, regardless of place in the stratification system, to engage in misconduct. Marginal and failing organizations were wrongly viewed as the perpetrators of misconduct. Lacking resources, they were just more likely to be caught and punished.

Organization Characteristics. Adding the organizations literature led to a major break from the macro-level Mertonian-inspired part of the explanation, bringing meso- and micro-level factors into the explanation. Fleshing out the idea of opportunity structures, I saw that organization structure—the hierarchy, division of labor, geographic dispersion, specialized units—provided opportunities: (1) it created many locations where misconduct could occur; and (2) the specialization and separate locations of those divisions and subunits created an invisibility, blocking oversight and providing opportunities for individuals to violate laws and rules in the organization's behalf. I described the effect as "structural secrecy" to show how structure promoted misconduct through concealment.

But the meso-level explanation was not yet complete. The Revco case had indicated that the fraud generated by the double-billing scheme had gone on for a long time without detection. Why was it not detected? Revco carried out the fraud by submitting falsified claims entered on tape in a computerized invoice submission system. The welfare department reviewed these tapes using a computerized program that spot-checked for irregularities. Because of the clever way the falsified information was organized on the invoices, the computer spot check missed the continuing fraud. Again, my theorizing was triggered by analogical comparison. These data resonated with a theory designed to suit a different but structurally equivalent problem: economist A. Michael Spence's (1974) theory of market signaling.

Spence wanted to explain how firms make decisions when hiring from among a large pool of applicants. Given the high costs of getting to know each candidate well, firms elect a short-cut method of evaluation, treating information as indexes (characteristics of a candidate that cannot be changed, like race or sex) and signals, which vary (where a candidate earned a degree, letters of recommendation, previous employment). Because signals vary, firms rely on them as an efficient means to discriminate between candidates' qualifications. It struck me, first, that because signals vary, they could be manipulated; thus fraud was possible. Second, the high cost of thoroughly screening information means that any fraud is likely to go unnoticed. These insights led to my treating information as signals, and explained why early warning signs of the fraud were missed. Thus the concepts of "transaction systems," "technology," and "missed signals" completed the meso-level explanations.

Regulatory Environment. The theoretical problem remaining to be resolved was individual action: why do some organization members working in organizations that are subject to competitive pressures, and who have access to internal opportunities, act unlawfully to achieve an organization's goals while others do not? Since rewards and punishments influence choices people make, the ability of other organizations to impose costs affects the probability that opportunities for misconduct will be used. Thus the regulatory environment became the final conceptual building block of the explanatory scheme. Owing to the effects of autonomy and interdependence between regulatory and regulated organizations (Pfeffer and Salancik 1978), social control was systematically compromised, thus encouraging individual decisions to violate in an organization's behalf (1983: 88–104).

At the time of publication, I believed that my effort to theorize organizational misconduct was limited by the lack of micro-level data—in my case and in the white-collar crime literature generally. The model most frequently supported in that literature was the "amoral calculator" model, a rational choice theory. Whereas many cases, including Revco, appeared to fit, the data on organizational factors were always inadequate and other organization decision-making models, such as bounded rationality, had never been weighed. A serendipitous classroom experiment suggested how to move forward. In a lecture in my large undergraduate course on criminology, I used the theory to explain corporate crime, using the Revco case as an example. To simplify the theory, I reduced it to its major concepts and subconcepts, putting them on the chalkboard as an analytical framework to hang the major ideas on. It looked like this:

Competitive Environment	*Organization Characteristics*	*Regulatory Environment*
Competition	Structure	Autonomy
Scarce Resources	Processes	Interdependence
Norms	Transactions	
	Technology	

In the past, I had followed my corporate crime lecture with lectures on police misconduct and domestic violence, treating them as separate patterns of crime, with nothing in common. But that semester, as I began the police misconduct lecture, I saw that the theory qua framework fit the police data, adding meso- and micro-level insights to it. Encouraged and curious, in the following class I used the framework again to explain domestic violence. It worked: my students saw that all three cases could be explained as organizational phenomena. And I saw the heuristic possibilities of a simplified analytic framework and cross-case comparison for fleshing out a theory at different levels of analysis. The success of this experiment led me to think about writing a book on organization misconduct using these three as cases; plus I wanted to add a fourth case of misconduct in which the offender was not a corporate profit-seeker but a large nonprofit. This was not easy to find in 1983.

While I was searching for one, I worked on a project on deteriorating intimate relationships. I did not see this situation as organizational misconduct, but I did see it as an example of organization failure. Intimate relationships are, after all, the smallest organizations we create. Even though the participants may not have defined it as a failure, and even though the participants may have reconstituted the relationship as a friendship, as an organizational form (a group) the intimate relationship no longer existed. I did not guide the research with the analytical framework above because I was not expecting the analogies that I found. Surprisingly, the process of relationship decline took my 1983 theory in important new directions.

Uncoupling: Turning Points in Intimate Relationships (1986)

In "The Social Construction of Marriage," P. Berger and Kellner (1964) described how two people with separate identities come together and, in interaction, redefine themselves as a couple. This redefinition is a gradual process. Habits and routines that used to affirm the singular identities of each are reconstituted to affirm the partnership. The two people create new sets of social relations: in addition to the friends of each, they develop "our friends." They move in together. These actions publicly define them as a couple. Breaking up, I believed, was the analogue of this theory, but in reverse: a gradual process of "uncoupling" in which the two people again redefine themselves, in their own eyes and in the eyes of others, as single and separate identities again.

My chronological accounts from married and cohabiting couples, both gay and straight, confirmed that uncoupling is a gradual transition with identifiable stages. Both people in the couple make the same transition, but it starts and ends at different times for each. The main pattern is that one person, whom I call the initiator, begins leaving the relationship socially and psychologically before the other. By the time the partner being left behind realizes the relationship is in serious trouble, the initiator is socially and psychologically distant, making saving the relationship difficult. The puzzle to be answered was, how was it possible, in the smallest organization we create, for two people to get so far apart without one person noticing and acting to reverse the decline? I immediately saw analogies between uncoupling, Spence's market signaling theory, and the Revco case: a long incubation period, information that deviated from expectations introduced gradually, and early warning signs that were missed or ignored. However, the uncoupling case provided social-psychological data missing from both Spence's signaling theory and the Revco case.

Situated Action. Following Spence, I again treated information as signals. The key to the patterns in uncoupling lay in "the display of discontent": how the initiator communicated unhappiness and how the partner interpreted that information. The initiator's signals varied in strength, affecting their meaning. Some were weak signals. As the initiator's discontent grows, the signals become more frequent and stronger. But even the signals that initiators believe are strong and direct may not get the partner's attention. Why? Despite changes in the relationship, the partner does not define the relationship as a serious problem because the salience of these signals is reduced by (1) the pattern of information and (2) the social context. Each warning sign is interjected one at a time into an ongoing stream of information that the partner reads as indicators that all is well. The pattern of information renders the initiator's signals as weak, mixed, or routine.

Further, at the organization level, the partner's world view comprises taken-for-granted assumptions about what is possible in the relationship, based on the organization culture and the routines and rituals of everyday experience in the past. Those elements symbolize stability, tending to obscure change. At the macro level, the partner's interpretive work was shaped by institutionalized cultural beliefs in the larger society about the value of relationships, their socially expected duration, the priority of the group over the individual, and gender and commitment. Partners expressed cultural expectations about the quality of relationships: "All relationships have trouble. Ours wouldn't be normal if we didn't." "After a while, all couples lose their interest in sex." Within the context of layered cultural beliefs, the problems in their own relationship are normal, natural troubles, not signals of danger. As a result of this disconnect between the two people, the initiator has been in transition for some time. Only when the initiator is socially and psychologically ready to go does that person send a clear strong signal that the partner cannot miss or deny. At the point of physical separation, the initiator is prepared; the partner is not. The partner then begins going through the stages of the transition that the initiator went through long before.

Generalizing from the case in the last chapter of the 1986 book, I used examples to indicate that the process of uncoupling was analogical to other kinds of leave-taking, suggesting a basis for a sociology of transitions. The social-psychological data elaborated the original theory of misconduct in several ways. As the Revco case allowed me to elaborate on/break with Merton's theory by bringing in meso-and micro-level factors, so uncoupling elaborated the concepts of signals and signaling, adding the social construction of meaning, nested within organizational and macro-cultural factors. The case raised the possibility of a mistake contributing to organization failure, and showed how mistakes could be systematically produced in a very small organization. I did not know it at the time, but these conceptual developments would be crucial in explaining the data from my next case—the case of misconduct by a large nonprofit organization.

The Challenger Launch Decision: Risky Technology, Culture, and Deviance at NASA (1996)

The Space Shuttle *Challenger* exploded seconds after launch on January 28, 1986, killing the crew and Christa McAuliffe, the "Teacher in Space." Immediately a Presidential Commission was formed to investigate the accident. The cause was quickly identified as a technical failure. However, further inquiry revealed the NASA organization had failed as well. NASA managers were warned by engineers that the weather conditions that prevailed prior to launch were risky. The engineers recommended against launch, owing to possible dangerous effects on the shuttle's solid rocket boosters—the technical component responsible for the *Challenger*'s demise; but despite the warning, managers proceeded with the launch, apparently in order to keep to the launch schedule, violating rules in the process.

The case had all the markings of organizational misconduct: competition for scarce resources, cost/safety trade-offs and production pressures, and violations of rules in pursuit of organization goals: managers had failed to pass relevant information up the hierarchy as required. Moreover, the *Challenger* case was different in size, complexity, and function from the Revco and intimate relationship cases, a requirement for cross-case analysis. Drawing from my classroom experiment, I used the three core elements and subconcepts of the analytic framework heuristically to organize the data. Initially, my reliance on press reports and volume 1 (a summary of the five-volume Presidential Commission Report) confirmed my misconduct hypothesis. But when I was deep into the enormous body of archival data that the commission had amassed,[2] I discovered information that contradicted many of the aspects of the case that had, for me and the public, indicated misconduct (Vaughn 1996: Chap. 2).

I was wrong. Crucially, for the case to be misconduct, there had to be rule violations by individuals acting in their organizational roles in behalf of NASA goals. However, I discovered that the actions of NASA managers that the commission identified as rule violations actually conformed to NASA rules. With a short time to master NASA language, the commission had misunderstood. For the case to be misconduct, there had to be rule violations, and I hadn't found any. If not misconduct, what explained it? The commission's inquiry had revealed that NASA had been flying with known flaws on the solid rocket boosters since the first shuttle flight in 1981. I started over. The research became a historical ethnography: a reconstruction of the past to see how people at another time and place had made sense of things. For each launch decision, I analyzed engineering pre-launch risk assessments, memos, testimony, and interview transcripts to understand why, after a technical anomaly was discovered on the solid rocket boosters, they continued to fly. These historical records allowed me to compare testimony after the tragedy with what engineers and managers believed when they were making decisions.

I spent years reading engineering documents, without a clear picture of what I was finding or where it was leading theoretically. The discovery I initially experienced as a setback—a negative surprise—set me on a new path, filled with additional surprises (Vaughan 2004). These surprises I interpreted as mistakes on my part: mistaken assumptions, hypotheses, and theories. First among them, I found that in every launch decision NASA personnel had conformed to NASA rules. Affirming theorizing as a meandering rather than a linear process, after six years of research I concluded that this was not a case of amoral calculating managers and misconduct, but I did not yet know what it *was* an example of. The conceptualizing was incomplete, and a full explanation was a few years away.

In the end, the starting theory's three core concepts, their subconcepts, and the links between them nonetheless explained the case. The analytic framework and the original theory still applied, but had to be reconstituted to fit the developing explanation and new concepts. In the book, the competitive environment as structural impetus (competition, scarce resources, norms) became "The Culture of Production" (Chap. 6). Organization characteristics that provide opportunities (structure, processes, transactions, technology) are reconstituted as "The Production of Culture" (Chaps. 3–5) and "Structural Secrecy" (Chap. 7). The regulatory environment (autonomy and interdependence) and its connection to decision making also appear in "Structural Secrecy" (Chap. 7). Then in combination, they explain the *Challenger* launch decision in "The Eve of the Launch Revisited" (Chaps. 8–9).

The Production of Culture: The Normalization of Deviance. By production of culture, I mean how, in interaction, managers and engineers produced a cultural belief in risk acceptability of the solid rocket boosters in the years preceding the launch of the *Challenger*. By "normalization of deviance," I mean the remarkable fact that—growing concerns and objections of individual engineers in the year before *Challenger* notwithstanding—in all official risk assessments and launch recommendations, engineers analyzed evidence that the design was not performing as predicted and reinterpreted it as acceptable and non-deviant. I discovered a five-step decision sequence in which technical deviations first were identified as signals of potential danger, then, after engineering analysis, were redefined as an "acceptable risk," a formal category at NASA. This decision sequence—anomaly, risk acceptance, fly—was repeated, the repetition indicating the institutionalization of a cultural belief in acceptable risk. More amazing, NASA gradually expanded the bounds of acceptable risk. The first decision to accept risk established a precedent to fly with recurring anomalies. The production of culture and the normalization of deviance explained how they gradually accepted more and more technical anomalies. Again, my question was why.

The Culture of Production. Competition, scarce resources, and norms played out in new ways, perpetuating the normalization of deviance and decisions to launch. Powerful elites in the White House, Congress, and NASA set the agency goals high and constrained resources, changing NASA's R&D culture to one that operated more like a business. To meet performance expectations, NASA leaders accelerated the launch schedule and shaved costs, as if they were in the kind of bureaucratic production system that engineers normally inhabit. The norms of professional engineering contributed to the normalization of deviance. Engineers are trained to work in technical production systems that are organized by the principles of capitalism and bureaucratic hierarchy. During professional training and then on the job, they develop a world view that includes attention to costs and efficiency, production goals, conformity to rules, and acceptance of hierarchical authority. Compromise between cost and safety were routine. Documents showed that at the time decisions were made, engineers agreed that proceeding with launches was an acceptable risk. Explaining in testimony why they continued launching, they said it was not the best design, but it was working: ". . . you've got to have a strong reason to go in and redesign something, because it costs dollars and schedule. You have to be able to show you've got a technical issue that is unsafe to fly. And that really just was not on the table that I recall by any of the parties . . ."[3]

Structural Secrecy. Each question answered raised yet another. The production of culture explained how managers and engineers normalized the technical deviations, gradually expanding the bounds of acceptable risk; the culture of production explained why. But the problem had gone on for years. Why had no one recognized the anomalies as warning signs and intervened to halt NASA's incremental descent into poor judgment? Unexpected, and indeed startling, were the analogies with Spence's theory, Revco, and uncoupling: again, the data showed a long incubation period with early warning signs that were either misinterpreted or ignored. The NASA data allowed an explanation of missed signals that showed the connection between macro, meso, and micro levels of analysis.

Like uncoupling, at the micro level patterns of information obscured problem seriousness, affecting the definition of the situation. Early warning signs were affected by their position in a stream of information: some signals were weak, and others were mixed. Each time an anomaly occurred, it was examined and fixed, and the safety of the component was confirmed by the next successful mission: thus a signal that something was wrong was followed by a signal that all was well. When anomalies became more frequent and serious, the change was gradual. The technical deviations became a routine signal, not a signal of danger. Further, organization structure created missing signals. As information was passed up the hierarchy, it was condensed, eliminating ambiguities in the engineering analysis. Finally, the structure of safety regulation contributed. Autonomy handicapped the external safety regulators, leading to dependence on NASA for information. Unless NASA engineers defined something as a serious problem, they did not bring it to regulators' attention. Interdependence affected NASA's internal safety system. Because of budget shortages, NASA leadership cut the resources and authority of those internal safety organizations. In the absence of regulatory intervention, the cultural belief in acceptable risk of the solid rocket boosters persisted throughout the NASA organization.

The normalization of deviance in the years preceding *Challenger* was explained by the production of culture, the culture of production, and structural secrecy, in combination. I returned to the *Challenger* launch decision, now positioning it as one decision in a stream of decisions. Engineers were arguing against the launch, based on a new condition: the predicted cold temperature. They felt the condition made launching an unacceptable risk. As I put together the testimony and interview transcripts of all participating parties into a chronology, I realized this was the first time I had considered all of the accounts together. In striking analogy, I saw that the explanation of the history of decisions—the production of culture, the culture of production, and structural secrecy that had reinforced the normalization of deviance in the past—explained what happened on the eve of the launch. I concluded that the decision to launch was a mistake, the result of conformity to norms, rules, and patterns of the past, not deviance (for details, see Vaughan 1996, Chaps. 8 and 9). Analytic induction had driven the analysis to this unexpected conclusion.

This case confirmed that the method of analogical theorizing can lead to discovery of generic patterns and innovative theorizing. For the first time, I had data showing the direct link between macro, meso, and micro connections and outcomes: how elite leaders and powerful organizations in the political environment acted, changing the space agency structure and culture, affecting engineering decisions. The key new concepts were "the normalization of deviance," the "production of culture," "the culture of production." and "structural secrecy." The role of cultural beliefs emanating from the environment and organization, important in the uncoupling process, was repeated here as a major causal factor. Analogical to the new institutionalism (DiMaggio and Powell 1991), the case revealed cultural understandings as a mediator between institutions, organizations, and individual choice. Analogical to Bourdieu (1990), the case showed how the occupational habitus of engineers penetrated the organization, the pre-existing dispositions reproducing structure, culture, and ways of being.

The theory and several concepts generalized beyond the case. Structural secrecy, patterns of information, and missed signals were key in all three cases and were analogous to many examples of organizational failure, from national security before the September 11 attacks to child welfare offices and foster child abuse cases. Signals and interpretive work were neither solely social-psychological nor solely structural, but a product of the two. Although NASA's decision to launch the *Challenger* was an example of mistake, not misconduct, the normalization of deviance offered an alternative to amoral calculation as an explanation of how people who are upstanding citizens can engage in illegalities and deviant acts in behalf of their organizations. In addition, the concept may apply to other situations—neither mistake nor misconduct—in which behavior that outsiders view as deviant and unacceptable is viewed by insiders as normative and conforming in their organization and industry: for example, the practices of the banking industry in the 2008 U.S. credit crisis (MacKenzie 2011).

Theorizing didn't stop with the publication of the book. The cross-case comparison expanded my understanding beyond the explanation of each case individually. Although I started with an interest in organizational misconduct, at the end my interest was in the general subject of how things go wrong in organizations. Pursuing this broader agenda in a review of the literature on mistake, misconduct, and disaster in "The Dark Side of Organizations" I identified analogies and differences between the three types (Vaughan 1999). In all three, the outcomes resulted from the intersection of environment, organizations, and individual choice, meaning, and action. Thus the outcomes they produced could be treated as the result of organizational system failures. From the comparison, inductively I arrived at a set of definitions to be used heuristically—as Ideal Types—in future research. Though different, each of the three types (also my three cases) fit the larger category of organizational deviance, which I defined as "an event, activity, or circumstance occurring in and/or produced by a group, a formal or complex organization that deviates from formal design goals and/or normative standards and expectations, either in the fact of its occurrence or in its consequences, and produces a suboptimal outcome" (Vaughan 1999: 273). Mistake, misconduct, and disaster all fit this general definition, but to account for variation, each had a more precise definition of its own. Finally, I concluded that although the theory (as it stood after the *Challenger* analysis) developed from three cases of organizational deviance, it also seems applicable to deviant organizations, in which deviance is the formal goal of the organization (Rafter 2011): for example, state geno-cide, organized crime, terrorist organizations, and instances of corruption that are organized and thus expected and non-deviant at the societal, country, community, or industry level.

The Relevance of Analogical Theorizing for Sociology

In this chapter, I introduced analogical theorizing, a Simmelian-based method in which analogy operates both as a cognitive process and as a material prac-tice of cross-case comparison.[4] In my demonstration across three substantive cases I have shown that analogy comes into play at every stage of the research process: case selection, developing concepts and theoretical explanations, and the material practice of comparison. I suggest that these uses of analogy are common to the theorizing process, regardless of a researcher's preference for quantitative or qualitative methods, or whether the research design is inten-tionally cross-case comparative, or, I strongly suspect, whether or not the scholar doing the work is a sociologist.

Moreover, analogical theorizing is integrated in the research processes of citation, importation, and generalization. In the simple act of citation, often we are making a cross-case comparison, identifying either a similarity or a difference between our own case and the one we cite. We also are theorizing analogically when we import another work into our own in a more significant way, bringing in a theory or concept from research done in a different time or social setting to frame our case, to explain all or part of it, or to contest the other research. Importation occurs countless times in any published work. Here, because of space limitations, I demonstrated this in a limited way: I imported Merton into the explanation of the first book, Berger and Kellner framed the second, and Spence was generic to the explanation in all three. Finally, analogies are integral to generalizing beyond a case to other examples having similar generic patterns, as I indicated in the Challenger case concepts of structural secrecy, the normalization of deviance, and signals and inter-pretive work (for others, see Vaughan 1996: 400-415).Since I began the proj-ect, additional empirical cross-case comparisons have been done by scholars of different theoretical orientations, in different subdisciplines of sociology, using different modes of analysis. These examples show that cross-case com-parison can be the core of a single study, and need not be as time consuming as my three-book sequence. In historical sociology, for example, Tilly (1985) famously wrote a theoretical essay analyzing war making and state making as organized crime. Goldstone and Useem (1999) identified five principles of state-centered revolutions, then examined thirteen case studies of prison riots to identify analogies and differences. Using nonparametric statistics, they found that state-centered principles could be usefully extended to explain prison riots. In contrast to these two macro-level applications, Katz (1988), a symbolic interactionist and ethnographer, compared six types of crime, inductively raising a theory of situational transcendence that worked across types. The offender's emotional response to particular situations allowed him or her to transcend it, so that at the moment the crime was committed the criminal offense became a morally justified act in the offender's eyes. The variety of methods and the rich and novel insights in these examples suggest the promise of analogical theorizing for theory generation in sociology. Notably, none of the authors discussed the role analogy played in their theorizing or the method behind their work.

Swedberg (2012) has stressed the importance of teaching how to theorize. My purpose in this chapter has been to transform the invisible and unacknowledged process of theorizing into a visible, intentional, systematic process of cross-case comparison that can be taught. Moreover, I have shown how situated action, using concepts and theories as Blumerian sensitizers, and analytic induction, lead to theoretical innovation. In the introduction, I indicated that shifting the unit of analysis from one organizational form to another can contribute to theory building in several ways: (1) when studying similar events in different organizational settings, we gain access to different kinds of data that reveal previously unrecognized explanatory factors; (2) often shifting the unit of analysis shifts the level of analysis as well, allowing new insights into the micro elements of a macro-level explanation, or vice-versa; (3) shifting the unit of analysis can be advantageous for elaborating theories and concepts focusing on large complex systems that are difficult to study; and (4) it promotes integration of the research and theory of different scholars, studying organizational actions in various social settings and at different levels of analysis, moving us toward general theory. My three-case comparison demonstrates points 1 and 2 above, so I will not repeat those here, instead focusing on its advantages in relation to points 3 and 4.

Some aspects of large complex systems may be difficult to study, either because of access problems or restricted data availability, or because their size, complexity, and the kind of data that are available do not readily lend themselves to fully answering the research question. Looking for answers in an analogous circumstance at a different level of analysis can be productive. Recall that Blau (1964) started with the intimate dyad, where details of inter-action were available, then applied those same principles to groups, complex organizations, and some inter-organizational forms, elaborating his theory along the way. The development of concepts, too, can benefit from cross-case comparison at different levels of analysis. Consider "loose coupling," which has a long history (Gouldner 1968; Weick 1976). Weick used the concept to explain educational organizations as loosely coupled systems, commenting that because of measurement difficulties with education systems, the con-cept lacked precision, but still could be used heuristically, as indeed it has been. Then Perrow (1984) introduced the concept of tightly coupled systems. Tight coupling also has enjoyed widespread use, but similarly left some degree of ambiguity. Greater ambiguity is desirable because it opens new research questions. Qualitative research on social movements, networks, or cohabiting couples, for example, could explore the extent to which parts of an organiza-tional unit are interdependent, bringing greater clarity about what it means to be tightly or loosely coupled, the range of variation, circumstances when both can coexist in one organization, or how an organization can move from one to the other.

The fourth point, how analogical theorizing can build toward general the-ory by promoting theoretical integration, speaks directly to the issue of disci-plinary specialization. We tend to develop a professional niche for ourselves, whereby we selectively study a particular organizational form that has a par-ticular function: nation-states, corporations, families, hospitals, courtrooms, social movements. While our depth of knowledge and expertise enhance our ability to develop theory within our own area, the overall result is that the production of knowledge occurs in fragmented rather than integrated ways. While in-depth study of one type helps us to more clearly specify the patterns and variations within type, disciplinary boundaries prevent finding support for and challenges to our own theories that could come from reading across types. Also, specialization blocks exposure to theories and concepts devel-oped to explain similar events or outcomes in other organizational forms. Finally, specialization leads to methodological preferences that consistently locate our work at the same level of analysis. We tend to define problems at either the macro or micro level, but typically not both. We see and investigate a problem in a way that limits our interest in data at other levels of analysis and precludes our integration of other theories or concepts that might bridge the gap between macro-specialists and micro-analysts.

Analogical theorizing can promote theory building by theoretical integration across disciplinary specialization and the macro-micro divide. Framing a case as situated action is one way to bridge this gap. Creative selection of cases for comparison is another. Everett Hughes, influenced by Simmel, was fond of asking his students, "What do a prostitute and a doctor have in common?" Interested in professions, Hughes answered that both are entrusted with client secrets that, if revealed, had legal implications for the client (Becker, personal communication, November 1991). Traditionally, we think of comparative work as same-case comparison. Breaking away from structured professional predispositions and using our natural inclination for analogical reasoning in the research process can stimulate both theoretical innovation and theoretical integration across subdisciplines within sociology, and between sociology and other disciplines as well (on signaling theory, e.g., see Vaughan 2009: 704–06). Analogical theorizing has demonstrated the capacity to develop a cumulative conceptual base and to move us toward general theory that integrates macro, meso, and micro levels of analysis. I am not suggesting that there is some perfect explanation or analytic endpoint that can be found for a case or across cases. However, a stronger conceptual base, discovery of generic explanations, and intra- and inter-disciplinary exchange of theory and concepts not only leads to better theory, but also benefits sociology as a discipline.

4 The Unsettlement of Communities of Inquiry

Isaac Ariail Reed and Mayer N. Zald

THE PRAGMATIST ACCOUNT OF THE RELATIONSHIP BETWEEN knower and known, and of the development of ideas, informs many of the accounts of theorizing in this book. A particularly strong pragmatist theme is the interruption of habit. For Richard Swedberg, James March, Karen Knorr Cetina, Karl Weick, and others, theorization occurs when routine streams of thought and intellectual work habits are interrupted or upset by "reality," thus creating problems for conceptualization spurring ideational innovation (Peirce 1903; Peirce 1992b; Peirce 1992c; James 1950; James 1907; Dewey [1922] 1930). Applied to social scientific research, this emphasis on interruption suggests both a focus on how the bureaucratic humdrum of academic life can be subverted, and on designing various creative ways for theoretical speculation to develop out of the interaction between a scientist and her data.

In this chapter, we continue this theme of interruption, but we place theorizing explicitly in its social context and translate it as the idea of the unsettlement of a community of inquiry. We define a "community of inquiry" here as a scholarly community of variable size whose self-definition and occupation with certain problems make the networks of communication between the community's members especially dense.[1] We then consider how individual social scientists interact with such communities of inquiry, and how bridges that develop between a community of inquiry and aspects of that community's social environment can create unsettlement in the community's communications, which in turn can spur the kinds of creative theorizing central to the project of this book. We thus analogize the unsettlement of a scholarly community to the political, cultural, and social unsettlements and restructurings that have long occupied scholars of collective behavior and social change. Much as "unsettled times" (Swidler 2001: 99–103) in societies are times of high rhetoric, ideology, and emotion, so too does the unsettling of a community of inquiry prompt the kinds of abstract thought, conceptual reformulation, and emotional excitement that are the hallmarks of theorizing in social science.

Our development of these themes builds toward the following argument:

> Theorizing, which via conceptual breakthrough advances social science, is (often, though not always) a product of collective conceptual unsettlement that leads to renewed attempts at abstraction, redefinition of the core terms of an area of inquiry, and the creation of new problems and new perspectives. This happens via a process wherein communities of inquiry constituted by dense communication about research become unsettled via connections to various aspects of their environment. This unsettlement creates a time of "high rhetoric," emotional energy, and conceptual reconfiguration, within which theoretical breakthroughs may be achieved. This process may lead to a reconfiguration of the community of scholars such that new boundaries are established, creating a new substantive field or area of inquiry.

Constructed as a hypothesis, we would propose that the relationship between unsettlement and theorization follows an inverted-U function, with unsettlement of a community or network of researchers increasing the level of theorization to a certain point, after which unsettlement begins to cause the community itself to disperse, and that dispersion reduces theoretically innovative communication between researchers. Our work in this chapter, however, is dedicated to conceptual specification via the consideration of illustrative examples rather than hypothesis testing. After discussing the role of individuals in unsettling communities of inquiry, we propose a typology of sources of unsettlement for these communities. These sources occupy a gray area between "internal" and "external" sources of intellectual change. The sources of unsettlement are: two different kinds of anomalies in the object of study, radical technological changes that affect the economy of theorizing, inter-community idea migration, and something we call "bridging the zeitgeist."

This typology is given a specific twist, however. We emphasize the way in which these sources are different in the social sciences than they are in the natural sciences. We do this by arguing that sociology is both a science and one of the humanities. This brings us into dialogue with the literature on "what's wrong with sociology" (Cole 2001) and with the longstanding question of how to characterize the knowledge project of the social sciences and social theory (Bhaskar 1979; Bernstein 1978; Habermas 1971; Reed 2011), something we discuss before setting out the typology. Near the end of the chapter, our arguments about sociology as a human science and about bridges between a community of inquiry and its environment point us toward a third argument about the relationship between "sociological theory" and "social theory." This, in turn, leads to some practical suggestions regarding theorizing in the social sciences, with which we conclude.

Theorizing in Social Context

It is important to resist a view of theorizing as a relatively asocial process, done by a lone theorist in relation to her privately gathered evidence, in contrast to finished theory as that which is brought forth into public view when verification or falsification is required. This image of science is mistaken because it reduces creativity to an individual psychological process, on the one hand, and because it limits the social aspect of science to the singular process of intersubjective verification or falsification, on the other. Instead, we maintain that individual psychological processes of discovery or serendipity intersect in complex ways with communities of scientific inquiry. Thus, while we accept the classical point from the philosophy of science that the specific, idiosyncratic way in which a scientist comes to an idea (e.g., in a dream) should be separated, analytically at least, from an account of how that idea comes to be taken as true, we do not accept some of the conflations that have been attached to this point. Considered more broadly, both discovery and justification are deeply social, even if one can make a normative philosophical distinction between the two processes and how they should be idealized (Aufrecht 2010). Thus we attempt here to address how theorization is itself a social process, and to develop some hypotheses about theoretical growth and change.

We define theorizing as the process, within a community of inquiry, of developing abstract and generalizable languages for understanding and explaining social behavior. To specify how this definition relates to theory growth and change as it is typically understood in sociology, we can begin by noting the definitions of theory and the typology of theory growth developed by David Wagner and Joseph Berger (1985; see also Wagner and Berger 1986; Berger, Willer, and

Zelditch 2005). First, they divide theory into (a) meta-theoretical "orienting strategies"; (b) "unit theories" that model or propose to explain a variety of sociological phenomena, and, finally, (c) "theoretical research programs"—"set[s] of interrelated theories, together with research relevant to evaluating them" (Wagner and Berger 1985: 705). Then, given these divisions, they typologize theoretical change in the following way: elaboration (refinement for precision and explanatory power), proliferation (expansion of a theoretical application to another domain), and theory competition (for theory competition, see also Lakatos 1970: 115). These basic processes lead to some secondary processes as well: variation (specification of different ways a theory can be applied or used in building explanations), and integration (synthesis of different, and even competing theories).

This typology provides, in our view, a reasonable "internal" description of the process of theorizing, one that draws on Imre Lakatos's concept of a research program, and that recognizes a link between "metatheory" and "unit theory." And we believe many sociologists would be comfortable with the idea that theory develops through elaboration, proliferation, competition, variation, and integration. However, Wagner and Berger's approach tends to underestimate (or perhaps deliberately exclude) the social context of theorizing, preferring instead to provide an extremely autonomous view of theory growth as the royal road to scientific rationality. Berger and Wagner do not connect theory development to broader changes in society, to shifts in the interests of intellectuals in general, or even to inputs from disciplines and subdisciplines at the boundaries of the community of inquiry that is doing the theorizing.[2]

What, then, spurs theory growth, via elaboration, proliferation, competition, variation and/or integration? For the Wagner and Berger approach, the answer is quite clear: inconsistencies in explanations offered, and the inability of theories to explain certain social phenomena whose importance cannot be avoided from the perspective of a given research program. In other words, what spurs theorization is precisely what Thomas Kuhn called the accumulation of anomalies. But if we think about scholarly communities as *communities*, we will quickly come to see that anomaly accumulation is only one of many possible prompts to theorizing that can affect a community of inquiry.

In contrast to the Berger/Wagner approach, which defines theory development well but does not account for its social location, the sociology of knowledge provides several useful models for conceptualizing the impact of the social world on knowledge creation. Without undertaking a full review of the developments in this field, we can nonetheless look here for inspiration.

Pierre Bourdieu (1988) discussed the fiscal and demographic pressures on the French academy and how these were translated into struggles over symbolic capital. In the 1980s, Richard Whitley (2000) reconceptualized the sciences as work organizations, primarily competing over and redistributing the resource of "reputation." And, in a perspective inspirational for the analogical theoretical strategies pursued here, Scott Frickel and Neil Gross reconceptualized intellectual change on the model of social movements, developing a theory of scientific/intellectual movements (SIMs). Taking up the Kuhnian project of accounting for scientific discontinuities, they describe for the conditions under which challenges to the scientific status quo are likely to emerge and to succeed (Frickel and Gross 2005: 204–05). They enumerate some of the social sources of intellectual change, such as generational shifts, lack of fit between the world views of certain high-status actors and those of the field at large, the different social backgrounds of those who enter the academy, and so on.

These perspectives from the sociology of knowledge gain insight from viewing scholarship as an institutionalized form of work, and more broadly, a social struggle. We agree that the social sciences and the humanities, like the natural sciences, participate in a modern university system and marshal various symbolic, organizational, and material resources in efforts to secure position within that system for lead investigators, their students, and their colleagues. It is furthermore clear that these scholarly endeavors operate in an environment that is somewhat autonomous from other areas of risk and reward in modern society, and is thus structured as its own field of struggle, as Bourdieu would emphasize.

However, in this chapter we address the gray area in between the internal development of anomalies identified by Wagner and Berger and the pressures, positionalities, and competition for resources (material and symbolic) that are the classic foci of the sociology of knowledge. When we look at this aspect of the knowledge process, new questions emerge about potential differences between natural and social science, questions whose answers might inflect our understanding of theorizing in sociology. In a way, the literature already recognizes this, albeit not as conceptually central. In Frickel and Gross's account, and especially in Whitley's characterization, some rather clear differences emerge between the intellectual dynamics of different disciplines. For Whitley, sociology, in particular, seems to have low interdependence between its workers, leading him to term it a "fragmented adhocracy." Why is this? And why is it, furthermore, that certain aspects of the Frickel and Gross model— such as the different world views or social backgrounds of new generations of practitioners—seem to matter so much more in the social sciences and the humanities than they do in the natural sciences?

Sociology as a Human Science

For a long time, sociologists have debated the answers to these questions in terms derived from, or misappropriated from, Thomas Kuhn—arguing that the social sciences are not yet "mature" sciences, or, in contrast, that the social sciences are "multi-paradigmatic" sciences or constituted by multiple, competing "research programs" (Ritzer 1975a, 1975b; Berger and Zelditch 2002). In strict Kuhnian terms, a multi-paradigmatic science is impossible. Paradigm dominance—and thus the possibility of normal science—is constitutive of mature science *qua science*. In this way, discussions about Kuhnian paradigms in sociology, though iconic for "post-positivism" and quite common in humanistic parts of the discipline, are incomplete in the vocabulary they provide for understanding the production of social knowledge. In contrast, we seek here a shift in this language, and thus we discuss the social sciences from a different point of view.

In our view, many discussions about the social and/or intellectual structure of the social sciences tend, perhaps because of the continuing prestige and influence of the natural sciences, to underthematize a key issue, which is also essential for understanding the process of theorizing in the social sciences. They underestimate the degree to which the social sciences retain various bridges to the culture and politics of the surrounding society, and the movements, events, and emergent forces within that society, in a way that the natural sciences do not, or do to a lesser degree. In particular, communities of inquiry in the social sciences are subject to "external" influence not only in the forms familiar from the analysis of the political economy of big science, but also in more subtle, and more deeply discursive ways whereby the very problems, objects of investigation, and theoretical terminology of the social sciences can be transformed by shifts in the political orientations, cultural interests, and social backgrounds of those who involve themselves in social science research.

In a 1991 article, Zald argued that sociology as a discipline was a "quasi-science" and one of the "quasi-humanities," and we develop that view here.[3] He suggested that in its effort to achieve scientific status, sociology had neglected its opportunities to become a better humanistic discipline. Sociology could do this, Zald suggested, while maintaining a clear emphasis on "explicit comparison and concern for generalization" and a dedication to "evidential criteria for choosing among interpretations" (Zald 1991: 179). As part of the historical and empirical argument for considering sociology this way, Zald noted how, in sociology, "the press for reformulation may occur because of moral and political currents in the larger society; because events in the larger society and the moral and political evaluation of them lead one to reflect on the adequacy of current formulations" (Zald 1991: 178), as well as because "anomalies" build up. In our view, this has important consequences for how we view theorization in sociology, in particular, and in the human sciences more generally.[4]

In Zald's original formulation, the core concerns or problem-orientations of sociology follow a pattern that in some ways approximates the humanities more than the natural sciences. For, in sociology, the core concerns are, like in the humanities, "civilizationally rooted." Zald's example of this is the rise and fall in sociology of the study of formal organizations, which shows elements of both Kuhnian "normal science" (wherein "research findings accumulate and the research terrain is exhausted" (177)), and of how civilizational concern impacts the relevance and research energy devoted to a subfield (the paradigm faded in part because practitioners "lost their connection to the larger issues which had generated the original question"—namely, moral concerns about the overgrowth of the administrative state and increasing power of managers vis-à-vis stock-holders).

To this we would add the point that there is a way in which the *objects* of research change in social science in a way that would appear quite odd to natural scientists (or for that matter, to a philosopher of natural science).Stephen Cole (2001) makes two arguments relevant here. First, standard textbooks in the natural sciences and the social sciences are quite different. In the natural sciences most of the texts describe key developments that are the accumulated consensus of generations of research; the frontiers are barely mentioned. In the social sciences, and possibly especially sociology, all or most of the text is devoted to current or recent topics of research; it is mostly at the frontier. Second, Cole argues that the objects of study in sociology are in a constant process of change. For example, if one is interested in the status of women in the professions, that status will have changed over some describable time period. Thus the ontology of social life is itself a historical object of analysis (Reed 2011, Hacking 2004).

Furthermore, the interests of faculty and students change as societal processes lead to rising and declining issues of public concern. One of us recently had the experience of asking an entering cohort of graduate students what their interests were. Hardly any of their specific interests would have been in the curriculum fifty years ago. Students were interested in public policy and the environment, public policy and poverty, the rise of female-headed households, and so on. Fifty years ago, most or many sociologists thought that social science was too underdeveloped to make much of a contribution to policy debates, and the field of women's studies had not been created. The changing objects of study in social science are subject to a shifting attention space within communities of inquiry, and within the disciplinary fields that emerge from or act as frames for the claims emerging from specific communities of inquiry. Here again the reigning model of the social structure of natural science is not the most appropriate. Rather, we would do better to recognize that communities of inquiry have limitations to their attention spaces that emerge from their own network structures (R. Collins 1998: 81–85), and that these attention spaces are influenced by the communication of social problems *from* various public spheres into the sphere of university research (Hilgartner and Bosk 1988).

When Cole delineated these aspects of sociology, he intended them to be part of a critique of "what's wrong with sociology." However, what Cole saw as a problem, others saw as an advantage. Responding to his original 1994 paper in *Sociological Forum*, ten feminist scholars published a commentary "What's Wrong Is Right: A Response to the State of the Discipline" (Fitzgerald et al. 1995) In their view, the developments of feminist theory, queer theory and other topics sprung loose by the social changes and movements of the 1960s and 1970s showcase the ability of sociology to open up and respond to the previously buried and invisible parts of social life, marginalized by orthodoxy, patriarchy, and homophobia. They contribute to scholarship and the development of theory and knowledge. Sociology need not mimic the natural sciences to be of intellectual value.

Furthermore, it is possible that *progress* in sociology, and in the social sciences more generally, can occur in ways foreign to (our image of) the natural sciences. In particular, as Zald (1994) argues, progress and accumulation are separable concepts. There are a variety of ways that a community of inquiry can advance (and can judge itself to have made progress, a judgment that may differ from the judgments of those in other communities of inquiry), not all of which are tied to the accumulation of replicable empirical observations. Indeed, Zald argues that in several key fields of sociology where progress has been great, the accumulation of facts has, paradoxically, not been particularly significant. He metaphorically links this to the Schumpeterian idea of "creative destruction" (Zald 1995: 458), and thus suggests that in many instances conceptual progress or advancement—and in particular a move closer to truth about the (changing) object of study—may be accompanied by a loss of knowledge. In this chapter, we specify that this notion of progress is autonomous from fact accumulation by suggesting that there are many different possible prompts to theorizing in the social sciences, and such theorizing can lead to progress, *even though—indeed because—it upsets the working conceptual order of a community of inquiry.*

If we consider sociology in this way—as a science and one of the humanities, and as capable of progress in quite different ways—it becomes clear that the prompts for *intellectual* transformation that Kuhn identifies as "anomalies" are, in the human sciences, *much more varied, and much less strictly internal to the "puzzles" set by a paradigm* than they are in the core physical sciences that were the true objects of debate for the classical philosophy of science, its modern adherents, and the Popper-Kuhn-Lakatos debates.

Our proposal, then, is that the ways in which a community of inquiry in the social sciences is influenced by its social environment will be significantly more varied qualitatively, and significantly greater quantitatively, than is common in the core natural or physical sciences. Some of the ways this is so have been well covered in social theory. For example, Anthony Giddens discusses the "double hermeneutic" that obtains between the social scientists' conceptual architecture and the concepts and working theories of those she studies (Giddens 1987). This is evident in Weick's work on firefighters, wherein Weick takes both his own and the firefighter's theories of organizations and reliability seriously and constructs a hermeneutic dialogue between them. This is one route whereby "outside concerns" might enter social science—and it is one much meditated upon by ethnographers. However, there might be other routes as well. What is needed is a model of the development of theory in communities of inquiry that accepts both *variation in the degree* to which "civilizational concerns" or "social meanings" affect the ongoing framing and conduct of research, and the *different pathways* whereby the influence of such concerns and meaning occurs. In what follows, we set out the preliminaries of a research program on this issue.

Change in Communities of Inquiry: Individuals and Bridges

Consider as the basic unit of analysis the community of inquiry, loosely corresponding to subfields of a discipline in the contemporary academy, and, in sociology, to the kinds of research programs that make up Berger and Zelditch's volume *New Directions in Contemporary Sociological Theory* (2002). These communities of inquiry are characterized by links between mentors and students, co-attendance at small, focused conferences, sustained e-mail communication, frequent co-authorship, and dense co-citation networks. They also share certain abstract theoretical terms that constrain research designs, create the interpretive schemas by which new problems are understood, and ultimately make up the language game of useful, central concepts that are essential to the sociological explanations built within the program. These abstract theoretical terms have varying cognitive ties to those of other research programs.

If this is the basic unit of analysis, then the question is: What causes theoretical growth, breakthrough, and ultimately the conceptual transformation of the abstract communication terms that help tie together a community of inquiry? Such an analysis, we believe, would have to be carried out at two levels simultaneously—one that examines the intersection of individual biographies with the dynamics of communities of inquiry, and one that examines how a community of inquiry develops relations with various aspects of its social environment. We examine each of these in turn.

Individuals

We see two essential ways in which individuals, or very small groups of individuals working together closely, contribute directly to the dynamics of a community of inquiry. *First*, it is clear that individuals, with their own idiosyncratic biographies, intellectual interests, and educations, can serve as a source of variation in the inputs that are brought into a community of inquiry working on a defined set of problems.

New students replace old ones, retirements shift the emphasis in problem choice, and the creativity, status-strategies, and charisma of individuals can matter a great deal, particularly if the community of inquiry is small, or if individual members of the community of inquiry are especially well positioned in relation to the institutional structures of the academy. Furthermore, individuals' own idiosyncratic interests could lead to shifts in scholarly attention because individuals' day-to-day lives may be less "walled off" from their scientific endeavors than we think. Sociologists of social movements may be *in* social movements; ethnographies can be particularly thorough if they draw on longstanding practical knowledge of a given milieu; and so on. In this way, discourse in the social sciences is subjected to a wider and more intense *bricolage* process than is likely to be found in the natural sciences.

One version of this "variation based in individuals" is directly connected to the theme of this volume, and is in fact evident in its very construction. For, while it is the case that the community of experts in a given subfield of social science may be largely concerned with transmitting to a future generation a narrow, technically demanding set of methodological practices, the historic connections of the social sciences to social theory and to general intellectual threads in the larger society imply that the palette of discourse for a given individual social scientist can reach far outside what is normative (or even known) within a specific community of inquiry. In James G. March's case this is evident in his ability to reach into the classic political theory of Rousseau when discussing problems in the modern theory of representation and its tendency to measure the common good by aggregating the public opinions of individuals (March and Olsen 1984), and in his use of the contemporary social theory of Susan Sontag to address theorization. Similarly, Karl Weick draws on the writings of the painter and installation artist Robert Irwin (1977) to elaborate his own process of theorizing. Perhaps this phenomenon could be used to measure individual variation: the breaching of boundaries around a subdiscipline or a topic might be indicated by the extent to which scholars who are part of a community of inquiry reference intellectual sources that extend beyond the citations that signal membership in the community, and particularly references that do not signal disciplinary membership either (see Shwed and Bearman 2010 for an example of measuring heterodoxy in citation).

But, *second,* it is also clear that the impact of individuals or small groups on a community of inquiry derives from the human capacity to synthesize disparate ideas and be creative. The capacity for intelligent individuals to reconstruct a community's discourse, problems, and solutions to problems cannot be underestimated. A great deal of interpretive social theory focuses on producing careful internal accounts of this aspect of individual dynamism— reconstructing the influences on, and synthesis of, classics of social theory so as to spur a shift of attention in the field, for example. Thus, for example, Marx's synthesis of political economy, socialism, and dialectics is shown to have been more Aristotelean than previously thought (Engelskirchen 2007), and Talcott Parsons is shown to have been engaged in a project of understanding the United States in contrast to the rise of authoritarianism in Europe in the 1930s (Gerhardt 2011). Individuals, then, may directly affect the direction of communities of inquiry via their idiosyncratic biographies or their synthetic abilities. But they may also serve as *conduits* that increase or strengthen links between the community of inquiry and its environment. This brings us to the second source of unsettlement: the links between the community of inquiry and its larger environment.

Links to the Social Environment

The environment of a community of inquiry includes other communities of inquiry, the academic field at large, and the society at large. Links to this environment, or "inputs" to a community of inquiry from this environment, come in many forms, and they include both the pieces of social reality that are the focal point of study and other kinds of inputs from "society." Because of this, it is essential to any model of the dynamics of a community of inquiry that we come to some basic theoretical understanding and categorization of these inputs and links. We offer the following typology, which we explicate below: anomalies that emerge within a paradigm or research program working on a certain defined set of social phenomena (of which there are two kinds); radical technological change; inter-community idea migration; and bridging the zeitgeist.

Strict Kuhnian anomalies. In the Kuhnian model, unsolved puzzles for a community of inquiry become overwhelming, leading to a sense that accepted theories, assumptions, and methods are inadequate, and thus to a search for possible reconceptualizations. This seems to be clearly what Berger and Wagner have in mind when they discuss research programs and theory development. For example, they discuss how the conflict-spiral theory in social psychology responded to anomalies that could not be ignored. Initially, the theory posited, and supported with a great deal of research, that the following mechanism obtained between interdependent actors: use of threats so as to project strength by A leads to a loss of face for B, so B responds with a threat of B's own, leading to a "spiral of conflict" (Deutsch and Krause 1960) However, the theory could not account for situations in which threats between interdependent actors lead to the mutual *coordination* (such as when a threat of punitive action leads to concessions and the avoidance of conflict). Thus Shomer, Davis, and Kelley (1966) posited a difference between threat and actual use of punishment devices, and thus restated the basic theory while expanding its empirical purview. Sometimes, à la Lakatos, this kind of development in relationship to anomalies happens via *competition between* rather than *refinement of* various theories (example from Wagner and Berger 1985: 710–12).

Object-change anomalies. However, in social science, historical shifts in the nature of social relations can also produce anomalies, which then prompt theoretical revision. This appears to be the sort of anomaly that Michael Burawoy has in mind when he discusses Marxism as a research program. The nature of capitalism, and in particular its mechanisms of exploitation and consent generation, changes, and these changes are, furthermore, spatially and temporally uneven. As a result, Marxist researchers are always revising their theory of capitalism—and this is a mark of the way in which Marxism is a progressive research program rather than a degenerative one, as Lakatos himself believed (Burawoy 1990).

Another example of this type of object-change anomaly is the way in which research on social movements had to shift its overall theoretical architecture in response to the emergence of objects that were clearly social movements, and clearly very important ones, but which seemed to stretch the explanatory capacities of previous theories. In the 1940s and 1950s social movement research was dominated by a set of ideas centered on the core insight that social movement participation was a result of a flight from the anomie and isolation of individuals in modern society. Although Erich Fromm (1941) and Eric Hoffer (1951) had very different backgrounds and life experiences, their (now classic) books *Escape from Freedom* and *The True Believer* reflected a similar understanding of the development of fascist and communist politics in the first part of the twentieth century. Neither book drew on extensive interviews or other empirical data, but both presented a diagnosis of their times. William Kornhauser's *The Politics of Mass Society* (1959) converted this diagnosis into a theory of the organization of political participation that was much more subtle and persuasive. But it, too, centered on one kind of political participation—namely, the entry into politics by low-status individuals without elite and institutional guidance. However, the 1960s and 1970s saw the emergence of a different set of movements with participants from different social backgrounds, *and* the emergence of scholars who identified with the goals of the movements. This change in the object of study (and in the hermeneutic relationship between author and object of study) contributed to the rejection of the mass society theories. (See Buechler 2004, 2011, for a review and discussion of these issues.)

Radical technological changes. The imposition of massive technological change on a field can elevate the usual mundane cost-benefit calculations about scientific problem solving and methodological innovation to a qualitative change in outlook, leading to extensive theoretical justification of a new approach. The clearest example in sociology would be the way in which the lower time and money costs of analyzing large sets of network or discursive data has allowed for a quantitative solution to empirical issues that would have not been possible prior to the new software analysis programs. So, Fiss and Hirsch (2005) demonstrate how quantitative discourse analysis contributes to the careful analysis of the transformation of the language in which globalization is discussed. Or, Shwed and Bearman (2010) employ network analysis to examine the development of scientific consensus through the growth of common references in substantive fields. In cultural sociology, an important debate is emerging on the use of "big data" in the subfield that has long embraced interpretive and ethnographic approaches (Bail, 2014). In the work of these scholars, the conceptual research design itself, and the theoretical justifications that accompany it, would have been senseless before high-speed computation became readily available.

It is important to understand what is really going on here. For a community of inquiry, technological innovation is unsettling *not* because it is a threat to theorization or will somehow change the goal of sociological explanation, but rather because it changes the contours and confines of theorization, suggesting new routes for thought. In other words, technological change shifts the "economy" of abduction, identified by Peirce and articulated by Swedberg: "Once you have gotten some new ideas through abduction, you have to make a judgment of economy since work on any one hypothesis entails a serious investment" (Swedberg 2012: 10). Technological changes affect the feasibility of testing certain hypotheses, and thus shift the economic structure (of effort, money, time, etc.) that influences (and rewards) theorizing itself.

Inter-community idea migration. As many different commentators have noted, the metatheoretical issues that underwrite the social sciences do not seem to disappear (Alexander 1981; Wagner and Berger 1985; Seidman and Wagner 1992). Rather, they seem to be inherent to the problem of studying human subjects scientifically. The self-referential aspects of consciousness, the question of the basic motivations of thinking human beings, the difference between moral and self-interested action, the emergence of collective action problems, and the tragedy of the commons—these are just some examples of problems in the social sciences that refuse to either disappear or obtain strictly empirical resolution. Rather, they exist at a presuppositional level. This intellectual situation has the effect of making the cross-migration of ideational accounts and root theoretical metaphors highly likely (e.g., Kahn and Zald 1990).

So, for example, sociologists' interest in collective goods was raised following the development of the concepts of "the tragedy of the commons" originally developed by Garrett Hardin (1968), a zoologist and microbiologist who focused on human ecology, and "the logic of collective action" developed by the economist Mancur Olson (1965). Another example in sociology is the contentious way "the rational actor" has migrated between different communities of inquiry in economics and sociology, and the different interpretations and criticisms of the concept that have been developed and put to use for the solution of research problems in different subfields (see Hechter and Kanazawa 1997; Goldthorpe 2007; Adams 2010 for commentary). We characterize this intercommunity idea migration as intellectual links enabled by various individual, social, and institutional means.

Bridging the Zeitgeist Political events, cultural movements, "civilizational" concerns, and so on routinely enter social science via a variety of pathways and mechanisms, both individual and institutional. These "human concerns," which circulate in and out of the social sciences routinely, can, under certain circumstances, exert tremendous influence on a given subfield or community of inquiry.

There are many examples. Social movements such as the feminist, gay rights, and environmental movements have contributed to the development of research, courses, and training programs. Widely noticed human made disasters contributed to the development of research on them (Perrow 1984; Vaughan 1997), and also indirectly to the study of high-reliability organizations. Jeffrey Alexander's (1995) study of late twentieth century social theory suggests a similar bridge between the world views that informed progressive politics, the intellectual currents of social theory, and specific sociological research programs such as modernization theory and world-systems theory.

Finally, consider again the study of social movements and revolutions. Forty years ago, students of movements and revolutions paid little attention to how society repressed them. When scholars did pay attention to repression, they assumed that most subjects tried to avoid the costs of pain, deprivation, and even loss of life, and thus that repression worked. But research in Latin America showed the risks that mothers would take in challenging regimes that had kidnapped or slain their sons and husbands (Loveman 1998), and in particular, work after 2001 on terrorism has begun to adjust theoretical accounts to recognize the limits of generalized conceptions of costs and repression, and to develop more nuanced approaches to these issues (see also McAdam 1986 for an early example).

Theorizing the Unsettlement of Communities of Inquiry

Changing objects of inquiry, intercommunity idea migration, and bridging the zeitgeist can all be hypothesized to be more frequent occurrences in the social sciences than in the natural sciences, though confirmation of this requires further study, and—of course—the sociology of science has studied in detail the impact of social forces on science, such as the role of activists in AIDS research (Epstein 1996). Here, though, we want to point out that, if the sources of intellectual unsettlement are understood in this expanded way, the Kuhnian and Lakatosian ways of thinking about scientific change must also be revised.

First, the dichotomy between revolutionary science and normal science should be revised into a *continuum of conceptual unsettlement*. Instead of imagining periods of normal science followed by periods of crisis, consider instead that communities of inquiry can approximate, to differing degrees and because of different conjunctions of causes, the "normal" and "revolutionary" ends of this continuum.

Second, we hypothesize a link between unsettlement and theorizing in social science, based on an analogy to the unsettlement of societies or polities. Kuhn's original argument in *Structure of Scientific Revolutions* was also based on an analogy to a specific kind of social unsettlement, namely revolution. Kuhn argued that, much as certain members of a political community might be fed up with a set of institutional structures and therefore advocate for a radically new set, so too might scientists act this way about a paradigm, and in particular its core theoretical components. This allowed him to suggest that, much as revolutions are times in which "political recourse fails" because the basic political rules of the game are in dispute, so too paradigm disputes are times during which *logical* recourse fails, leaving scientists to convince each other via exemplary practice. This is perhaps the most fundamental way in which Kuhn was "post-positivist."

We here pursue a similar analogical strategy, but with a different outcome. Research in cultural sociology has suggested that "unsettled times" are those in which high rhetoric, ideology, and fundamental values are contested.[5] By theoretical analogy, we argue that *when influences unsettle a community of inquiry, theorization increases, because theorizing is for scientific communities the equivalent of what "high rhetoric," disputation over values, and ideology are for polities.* Thus, as with ideology during unsettled times, so with theory when communities of inquiry become unsettled: its creation increases and

intensifies, emotional attachments to (or against) certain theoretical arguments take on outsized importance, and new or long-neglected perspectives
are quickly developed. Conceptual generalization is pursued, much energy
is devoted to getting new research projects that use these concepts off the
ground, and the possible applications of the new set of concepts becomes
viewed as almost infinite. This moment of energy and unsettlement is what
Clifford Geertz, drawing on the work of Suzanne Langer, describes as the way
in which a new idea is taken up as "the conceptual center-point around which
a comprehensive system of analysis can be built" (Geertz 1973).

For Kuhn, normal science was a space where, within a given paradigm,
scientists could solve puzzles, and adequately verify or falsify each other's
solutions to these puzzles. Revolutionary science was, in his initial formulation, more rhetorical and by implication less rational—thus leading his interpreters to develop his ideas into a critique of the rationality of science, which
he subsequently disavowed (Fuller 2001). Our argument is different: although
communities of inquiry may need to be relatively "settled" to accumulate
empirical knowledge in a straightforward way, *progress* is not the same as
accumulation (Zald 1995), and thus unsettlement of communities of inquiry
can lead to progress via theoretical breakthrough, and thus to (a version of)
scientific rationality. Furthermore, the sources of unsettlement are multiple,
and their relationship to the "internal" problems of a community of inquiry
can be subtle. Indeed, it will be our argument that there is an important way
in which the social sciences retain, via a generalized theoretical discourse, a
well of potential unsettlement that can be returned to time and again, in the
progressive pursuit of better social science.

The Sociological Theory/Social Theory Bridge

We see the argument of this chapter as a first step in a research program on
the organization and intellectual structure of sociology as a human science.
Here, however, we would like to articulate one clear implication of this model,
as it has been discussed so far, for theorizing in the social sciences: a different
understanding of the relationship between social and sociological theory.

In his chapter, Steven Turner—after noting how much theoretical exposi-
tion of the classics "confuses, not to say enrages, conventional social scientists"—distinguishes between "mundane theorizing," "system building," and
"high theory." In the latter, the theorist takes on the most essential arguments

across generations and civilizational moments, constituting precisely the sort of conversation that would be incomprehensible from the perspective of a well-organized research program, and thus conducting high-concept *brico-lage*. All of these forms of theorizing, Turner argues, but especially the last one, are likely bad for one's career. The implication of this (besides depression for theorists) is that "social theory" tends to take place outside or on the periphery of the institutional structures of modern social science. Only outside the bureaucratic-professional machine, in other words, can the true *bricolage* of theorizing at the highest level happen. Simultaneously, Turner also admits that "ideological passions are not only the subject, but at the very heart of social theory."

In nonetheless advocating for this sort of theorizing as essential, Steven Turner inverts the argument of his longtime opponent and sometime co-author Jonathan Turner, who draws a bright line between *social theory* as a kind of social philosophy, and *sociological theory* as the general concepts that make up sociology as an explanatory science, and who resolutely affirms the latter (J. Turner 1981, 1985). Those familiar with argumentation in theory journals in (American) sociology since the mid-1980s will immediately recognize this debate (for iconic examples, see Turner 1985; Lenski 1988; R. Collins 1989; Gieryn 1982; Seidman 1983; Allan and Turner 2000; Lemert 2000). We should also note that Steven Turner's ideas about the dominance of sociological theory over social theory apply to the United States more than to Europe—an issue that could be the subject of a separate essay that uses the typology of sources of unsettlement here as a starting point. But how should we think about this longstanding divide between sociological and social theory as it relates to the dynamics of communities of inquiry in the social sciences? Consider the following possibility.

Rather than treating social theory and sociological theory as antagonists, view social and sociological theory, *together*, as forming a bridge or link between cultural and political "issues," societal concerns and movements, and generational shifts, on the one hand, and the progressive and accumulative development of research programs in the social sciences, on the other. Social and sociological theory, in other words, together form a two-way street between "civilizational concerns" and specialized empirical research in social science. They do this by creating a discursive, and to some degree institutional, space where social concerns can be articulated in abstract language, and wherein empirical social science can be made to "speak to" the concerns of the day.

First, social theory, as manifestly interdisciplinary, becomes a facilitator, precisely by its broad nature and multiple meanings, of inter-community idea migration. Social theory is an extra-disciplinary device whereby concepts from other disciplines can be translated into useful theoretical constructions for sociological research and vice versa. Second, social theory, with its more literary, appreciative, and normative dimensions, encodes social and political concerns and develops concepts to respond to them in an environment less burdened by the strict analytical and denotative/definitional constraints of explanatory sociological theories and models. In doing so, *it may be more or less ideological,* because being shorn of ideology so as to directly drive objective empirical research is not, in fact, the primary conceptual goal or utility of social theory. Rather, precisely insofar as it is *not* sociological theory, social theory *thematizes* at a generalized and abstract level of discourse matters of broadly social or "public" concern. These issues can then be *translated* from social into sociological theory. The reverse pathway is also possible—from empirical research, to newly revised sociological theories, to shifts in social theory with all their accompanying ideological implications.

Here are just a few examples of this bridge:

— In many of their texts, Goffman and his followers among interactionist sociologists remain relatively coy about their attitudes toward the interactional mechanisms they identify, and certainly tend not to make political pronouncements on what they signify for Western Civilization. But philosopher Alasdair MacIntyre (1984: 115–17 and elsewhere) does exactly this, suggesting that Goffman's sociology, and especially the conception of the strategic actor dedicated mainly to self-enhancement rather than to accomplishing the social good, fits well with the social theory of Weber and Nietzsche in diagnosing the ills of modern society.

— The complex and contested relationship between strictly analytic or "scientific" Marxism (Little 1986) and its more normative or "critical" elaborations reveals an extended history of concept translation, normative interpretation of new conceptual developments in social science, and attempts to find scientific support for the possibility of certain normative or utopian goals.

— "Postcolonial" interpretations of texts, and reconstructions of historical narratives, started as an intellectual movement within the critical analysis of literature and history—two core disciplines of the humanities. It then became "postcolonial theory," a highly evaluative, philosophical enterprise that took on directly foundational assumptions about "modernity" that informed many different social science disciplines (for an overview, see Gandhi 1998). It then moved into comparative historical sociology, and from there into a "postcolonial sociology," which, in its role as a sociological theory, proposes a series of abstract propositions about the nature of empire and its relationship to capitalism (Go 2008), yet simultaneously resists jettisoning its normative project, retaining a link to social theory more broadly understood (Go 2013).

Conclusion: Implications for the Cultivation of Theorizing in the Social Sciences

Given our argument, how should we cultivate the capacity for theorizing in social science? If the link posited between unsettlement and theorizing holds, then links between groups of scholars that are particularly designed to increase conceptual unsettlement are called for. The institutional structure of social science already has some venues wherein abstract ideas can be developed in a social context without the strictures of the verification of hypotheses being strictly imposed. The "informal" side of academic life appears, to some degree, to fulfill this purpose: graduate workshops, writing groups, professional conference presentations, miniconferences, and colloquium series are all places of discussion and elaboration.

Perhaps, however, more specific and directed efforts are required. A journal could be developed that is devoted to papers that build, rather than test, theory, and thus applies different criteria in the evaluation of what makes a good paper. A series of publications in such a journal might focus on *potentially* scientifically useful links between social and sociological theory. Such a journal, in other words, could create a space designed to enhance the social theory–sociological theory circuit. This would have salutary effects, in our view, on empirical sociological research. For, even if the end product of sociology is viewed as knowledge *qua* empirical explanations that rely on analytic and middle-range sociological theory, the quality, scope, and power of these explanations will suffer in the long term if "social theory" cannot function as a constant source of unsettlement for communities of inquiry in sociology. Certainly, even without creating a journal, the relationship between sociological theory and social theory could be re-examined and developed, perhaps in a conference on the topic or in a series of critical exchanges at other conferences. The link between issues of public concern and theorizing is harder, of course, to control. But it may be also be that courses could be offered in "social theory and contemporary problems," "theorizing the financial crisis," and so on.

Ultimately, these suggestions rest on the core premise of our argument vis-á-vis social scientific knowledge and theorizing in the social sciences. That argument emphasizes (1) descriptively, the frequency and variety of intellectual links that connect a community of inquiry in social science to "the outside world," and the way these links tend to "unsettle" a community of researchers, and (2) normatively, the utility of these links for theorizing in social science, insofar as such unsettlements spur theorizing and potentially theoretical breakthroughs. In suggesting this normative judgment, we rely on the idea that progress in social science does not always come in the form of accumulation of findings, but also in such breakthroughs.

C. S. Peirce himself struggled with the way in which discoveries, intellectual breakthroughs, and new theoretical architectures were both individual and social projects. His fundamental category of the "community of inquiry" leaves open a great deal of space for argumentation about how precisely that community is, or should be, structured in the pursuit of truth—though his essay on belief makes clear that openness to falsification via evidence undergirds creative and competitive communication in a successful science. At the end of his life, Peirce began to reshape his understanding of the relationship of truth to action, including in it an individualist ethics. Perhaps, as his biographer Joseph Brent (1998: 340–44) argues, this reconceptualization was related to Peirce's own exclusion from the academic community of his time. Thus we are drawn to conclude that alienation used for creative purposes—a process that is emphasized, in different ways, by Richard Swedberg and Stephen Turner in this book—is an important part of theorizing. Simultaneously, however, we should recognize how deeply our theoretical communiqués, including those we engage in with ourselves, bear the imprint of habits derived from those in our scholarly realm who produce in us the fundamentally social experiences of solidarity and competition. These social relationships are subject to reconstruction, much as the individual mind is. Our argument here is that there are aspects of these relationships in social science that have been repeatedly disavowed. If, instead, they were accentuated by reflection, progress in social science—particularly progress characterized by theoretical innovation—could become more profound.

5 Three Frank Questions to Discipline Your Theorizing

Daniel B. Klein

explanandum: The thing to be explained.
—*Oxford English Dictionary, 2nd ed., 1989*

RICHARD SWEDBERG'S FLAGSHIP PAPER, "THEORIZING IN SOCIOLogy and the Social Sciences: Turning to the Context of Discovery," invites us to try to teach students to theorize, and it guides us on how to do so. Also, the paper enhances our appreciation of real theorizers. Michael Polanyi (1963: 96) suggested that "we need reverence to perceive greatness, even as we need a telescope to observe spiral nebulae." Swedberg's essay shows the considered reverence proper to the edifying of young scholars and the inspiring of their abductivity.

When Swedberg asked me to participate in the present project, he suggested that I further explore ideas that Pedro Romero and I raised in a paper titled "Model Building versus Theorizing: The Paucity of Theory in the *Journal of Economic Theory*."[1] The paper criticizes certain cultural norms in professional economics, norms that allow so-called theorists to pass off mere models as theory. The *Journal of Economic Theory* (*JET*) is one of the worst offenders, and one of the most prestigious. Romero and I maintain that a model qualifies as theory only if the article offering the model answers three questions:

1. Theory of what?
2. Why should we care?
3. What merit in your explanation?

We examined all of the regular articles in the 2004 issues of the journal and concluded that only 12 percent answered all three questions, and thus that only 12 percent of the articles in the *Journal of Economic Theory* qualify as theory.

The problem Romero and I addressed does not afflict other social science fields to the extent it does economics, and especially not the audience for this book. So the aspiration in the present essay is first to recap the Klein-Romero critique and then to use the three questions in the service of teaching and improving the kind of theorizing Swedberg has in mind. Whether the essay helps with what Swedberg is trying to get at—the context of discovery, the creative experience, abduction—is for the reader to decide. Facing the three questions is a kind of training, a training that builds discipline. Such training might have played a role in making the abductive theorist what he or she is. Swedberg says that "[r]ules are typically helpful for the beginner" (2012: 16). Perhaps the three questions help one to discipline his or her theorizing; they might help one to build out the theory.

The Critique of the *Journal of Economic Theory*: Motivation and Method

Axel Leijonhufvud (1997: 193) notes about the economic profession, "For many years now, 'model' and 'theory' have been widely used as interchangeable terms in the profession." Treating the two sets as identical would have two implications: "theory" ⇔ "model." We dispute both "implies" arrows. A formal model, either mathematical or diagrammatic, with quite explicit equilibrium conditions, is neither necessary nor sufficient for theory.

Model not necessary: An economist who develops math-free explanations will often not be credited as a theorist, no matter how original and persuasive the explanation and no matter how important the explanandum. In economics, "theorists" usually means model-builders *and only* model-builders. But to suggest that "theory" implies "model" is to suggest that Hume, Smith, Marx, Menger, Weber, Durkheim, Veblen, Keynes, Coase, and others did not do theory. As Diana Strassmann (1994: 154) puts it, some ideas do not have "even the remotest potential for mathematical expression."

Model not sufficient: Our concern is to challenge the semantics that hold that every model is (or entails) theory. We maintain that scientific culture understands *theory* to entail requirements of importance and usefulness.

Theory must serve real purposes of the science, thus arguably meriting attention from the scientific community.

In her book *Lament for Economics* (1938), Barbara Wootton wrote a kind of proto-heterodox critique. She provided an example proving that model does not imply theory:

> The nursery poet, for example, who wrote:
>
> > If all the world were apple-pie
> > And all the sea were ink,
> > And all the trees were bread and cheese
> > What should we do for drink?
>
> certainly poses a problem to which it is not easy to give a ready and satisfactory answer. Yet no University Chairs have been founded for the study of this particular group of problems, although these would unquestionably become of the gravest importance, should the conditions postulated in the first three lines of the poem be realized. And the simple reason is, first, that nobody has the slightest grounds for supposing that the world is likely to turn into apple-pie, the sea into ink, or trees into bread and cheese; and, second, that there is also no reason to suppose that this strange poetic fancy is linked with the prosaic world of common experience in any way which would make the study of the one likely to throw light upon the workings of the other. (Wootton 1938: 31–32).

If an economist were to construct a model addressing what we would drink under those conditions, would we regard it as theory? Surely not. Not every model entails a theory.

The outpouring of criticism of formalistic economics is well known. The most basic criticism of model-building remains Wootton's: What *in the world* are you talking about? Why should we care? Leijonhufvud (1997: 196) characterized the problem this way: "Formalism in economics makes it possible to know precisely what someone is *saying*. But it often leaves us in doubt about what exactly he or she is *talking about*."

We specify three necessary conditions for a model to be a theory:

I   *Theory of what?* The proponent of the model indicates some set of real-world phenomena X, and offers the model as at least a partial or potential description of the conditions and mechanisms giving rise to X. That is, the model helps explain X. It is a way to understand X.

II   *Why should we care?* The proponent believes and tries to persuade us that

X is of import and might be inadequately explained/understood, that it might merit some of the community's attention. Thus the proponent establishes X as an explanandum. Only if he genuinely believes in the need for better explanation and tells us why we should feel likewise might the explanation deserve to be called a scientific explanation.

III   *What merit in your explanation?* The proponent makes a case that his explanation merits attention and resources. Here, it is useful to distinguish two situations hinging on whether the explanandum is previously identified.

2. If the explanandum is previously identified, then *What merit?* reduces to, *How's yours better?*—that is, how is it better than alternative explanations, even just simple or naïve ones? Thus the proponent sets out alternative explanations and attempts to persuade us of comparative virtues of his explanation, virtues that warrant its holding a place instead of, alongside of, or in conjunction with other explanations.

3. It is sometimes the case that a theorist organizes and identifies matters into an explanandum more or less for the first time, or at least in a novel and original way. That is, he not only runs with the football, but also discovers or invents the football that he runs with. As Allan Gibbard and Hal Varian (1978: 669) note, "Perhaps it is initially unclear what is to be explained, and a model provides a means of formulation." Such formulation is found, for example, in much of the work of the economist Thomas Schelling who, by providing many empirically meaningful illustrations, freshly identified classes of things to be explained, such as commitments, promises, threats, focal points, and tipping points. In such cases of freshly discovering the "football," it is not fair to demand "How is yours better?," since alternative explanations may not be available. No one has ever run with that football before, so it is inappropriate to demand better running. The demand of merit, therefore, needs to allow theory to be original both in the explanation and in the explanandum. *What merit?* allows for such complex originality. But it still demands some proof of merit— "proof" in the common-language sense. That proof will inevitably entail argument that the freshly formulated explanandum-explanation complex is important and useful.

Regardless of whether the explanandum is familiar or newly discovered, the demand of *What merit?* is not a demand for demonstrated dominance. Auditors may assent to hear out a new theory, even if *in some respects* it is manifestly weak (Booth 1974). But it also must claim to be strong *in some respects*. And, if we are interested in economic science, some of those respects must go beyond mere equilibrium storytelling and modeling craftsmanship. Without claims to empirical import or relevance, the basic demand for merit is unmet. The explanandum-explanation complex must claim some merits in advancing our understanding of genuine real-world concerns. If the proponent's explanation is complicated, difficult, or bizarre, it must at least promise offsetting benefits (or advantages). Further, our demand is only for a *claim* of such benefits. The claim may be unpersuasive, but here we demand merely a *claim* (which, of course, need not be explicitly stated as such). Absent a claim of promised benefits, an explanation does not merit the title *theory.*

"[I]t is reasonable," said Wootton (1938: 30), "to ask the economic theorists at least to show that they have some apparently probable ground for thinking that their present abstractions will eventually ripen into something of concrete and practical utility." We say that the showing of "some apparently probable ground" is a requirement of theory. Our requirements also conform quite nicely with Thomas Mayer's vision of scientific standards:

> Imagine that academic economic research . . . was sold in the market place . . . Those who want to understand how the economy functions would force suppliers of models to compete in terms of how well the model explains the observed characteristics of the economy. Each modeller would then try to show *that his or her model is superior to its rivals.* (Mayer 1993: 130, emphasis added)

In our article, Romero and I consider George Akerlof's "The Market for 'Lemons': Quality Uncertainty and the Market Mechanism" (1970) and explain why we say it passes all three hurdles. We then turn to another example, from the 2004 *JET*, and explain why we say it fails them. We then relate our approach to discussions by four thinkers with strong mainstream reputations—Daniel Hausman (1992), Allan Gibbard and Hal Varian (1978), and Robert Sugden (2002)—and conclude that our distinction between models and theories, and our bases for distinguishing the two, are highly congruent with their thinking. We then go on to explain the scheme of our investigation in greater detail.

We read every regular article in the 2004 issues of the *Journal of Economic Theory* to test whether it met our three demands of theory: *Theory of what?*, *Why should we care?*, and *What merit?*[2] For each question, it is sufficient for our purposes that the article *purport* to answer it. We are testing for the existence of certain requisites of theory, not the soundness of the theory. An article might pass all three of our tests and yet be quite nonsensical and worthless for understanding the explanandum.

The challenge facing us was to make our testing transparent, accountable, and credible. To meet those challenges, we broke down the analysis into a series of subtests. The results of the subtests include our judgments and details about the papers, including pertinent quotations. All of the subtests, quotations, and judgments are presented in a spreadsheet that was appended to our article.[3] One can spot-check our analysis by scrutinizing an article and deciding whether we have applied the tests fairly.

The spreadsheet first provides a quotation indicating the purported subject matter. We strove to select the passage that best describes the purported subject matter. The next columns of the spreadsheet contain the first three subtests:

> Subtest 1: Does the article illustrate an explanandum in a factual way, including by historical cases or even just anecdotes?
>
> Subtest 2: Does the article illustrate an explanandum with any fictitious examples or thought experiments (other than the model itself)?
>
> Subtest 3: In telling the model, does the author use language suggesting an economic context or scenario?

The next column arrives at the first major question:

> Major question 1: Theory of what? Does the article delimit an explanandum with reasonable clarity?

The assessment of *Theory of what?* draws on the prior subtests. Sufficient for passing is that the article provides any kind of illustration of the explanandum, either factual or fictitious. But that condition is not necessary. The article might be scored "yes" on *Theory of what?* by virtue of the economic context and language of the model itself. But whether economic language in the model will save a model is a judgment call—a "yes" at Subtest 3 will not always make a "yes" to *Theory of what?* An example will illustrate.

The tenth paper in the list is titled "Local Coordination and Market Equilibria." The article states its accomplishment as follows: "We reformulate the stability analysis of competitive equilibria as a coordination problem in a market game whose non-cooperative equilibria coincide with competitive equilibria" (Chatterji and Ghosal 2004: 276). It provides neither factual nor fictitious characterization of an explanandum. As for Subtest 3, yes, the model uses economic terms, including *traders, sellers, buyers, commodity bundles,* and *endowments.* But the storytelling of the model does not map intelligibly to anything we might imagine in our natural knowledge of worldly phenomena to be explained. If the article is supposed to be an explanation, it never fills us in as to what the explanandum is supposed to be. Thus, it fails *Theory of what?*

Only papers that pass *Theory of what?* have the potential to pass the remaining major questions, *Why should we care?* and *What merit?* To approach those two questions, we pose another subtest:

> Subtest 4: Does the article refer to an alternative explanation, including even just a naïve one?

The subtests that come next help to break down the article's empirical referents. In articles, the segment that begins and ends with the formal presentation of the model almost never contains any empirical content. That structure is depicted in Figure 5.1.

Only one 2004 *JET* article introduces empirical content in the midst of the presentation of the model.[4] In the cases where the model presentation contains no empirical content, we may then distinguish two locations for empirical content: preceding the model and succeeding the model. In asking whether the article goes beyond illustration to greater utilization of empirical learning, we apply two separate subtests:

> Subtest 5: In the paragraphs preceding the model, does the article refer to any empirical learning that goes beyond mere factual illustration (anecdote or individual incidents)?

> Subtest 6: In the paragraphs succeeding the model, does the article refer to any discussion of empirical knowledge cited as evidence for one explanation or another?

Those subtests, along with the previous ones and our general reading of the article, lead to:

> Major question 2: Why should we care? Does the article say why any economist should expend energy on better explaining the explanandum?

FIGURE 5.1 Model-building articles almost always have three parts.

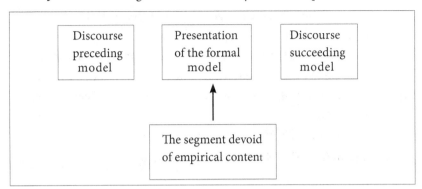

To pass *Why should we care?*, the article must either: (1) indicate *some inadequacy* in how alternative explanations (perhaps even just naïve ones) explain the explanandum, or (2) suggest that it is freshly identifying the explanandum and indicate how such identification might be useful. Either way, the indication of prior inadequacy helps to provide the research's scientific motivation. For this scoring, subtests 4 and 5 are particularly useful, but passing those tests is neither necessary nor sufficient for passing *Why should we care?*

The next column contains the last major question:

> Major question 3: What merit in your explanation? In the case of addressing a previously identified explanandum, we may ask more specifically: Does the article say how its explanation has advantages relative to or in conjunction with an alternative explanation? Otherwise, does the article say how its explanandum-explanation complex promises benefits?

To pass *What merit?* the article must either allude to an alternative explanation, even a simple or naïve one, and say why its model explains features that the alternatives do not explain (or not as nicely), or it must promise benefits of a freshly formulated explanandum-explanation complex. Passing *What merit?* does not hinge mechanically on Subtests 4, 5, and 6.

Here follows a recapitulation of the six subtests and three major questions, in abbreviated form:

> Subtest 1: Does the article illustrate the explanandum in any factual way?
>
> Subtest 2: Does the article illustrate the explanandum with any fictitious example?
>
> Subtest 3: Does the model use language of an economic context or scenario?

MAJOR QUESTION 1: Theory of what?

Subtest 4: Does the article refer to an alternative explanation?

Subtest 5: In the paragraphs preceding the model, does the article refer to any empirical learning that goes beyond mere factual illustration?

Subtest 6: In the paragraphs succeeding the model, does the article refer to any discussion of empirical knowledge cited as evidence for one explanation or another?

MAJOR QUESTION 2: Why should we care?

MAJOR QUESTION 3: What merit in your explanation?

Results of the Content Analysis of *JET* 2004

Our investigation includes all sixty-six of the regular articles published by *JET* in the 2004 issues (vols. 114–19). The results are summarized in Figure 5.2.

Our analysis finds that twenty-seven of the sixty-six articles do not satisfy *Theory of what?* They stumble at the first hurdle and do not qualify as theory on that basis alone. In our original article, Romero and I provided illustrative quotations, usually from the papers' abstracts, of twelve of the twenty-seven articles, to show some of the ways in which they failed to satisfy *Theory of what?*[5] If one were to ask an author of one of any of the twenty-seven articles, "What in the world are you talking about?," the only responsible answer would be: "Nothing."

Of the thirty-nine articles that passed the first hurdle, twenty-nine stumbled at *Why should we care?*, so 44 percent of the articles have the profile (Pass, Fail, Fail). Of the ten articles that passed the first two hurdles, two stumbled at *What merit in your explanation?*, so 3 percent of the total fall into the category (Pass, Pass, Fail). Only eight articles—or 12 percent of the sixty-six—passed *Theory of what?*, *Why should we care?*, and *What merit?* In our original article, we briefly examine samples at each of first two stages and then all eight articles at the last.

Another economist with an impeccable mainstream reputation, E. Roy Weintraub, wrote, "Economics at the end of the twentieth century is a discipline that concerns itself with models, not theories, so how did this happen and what does it mean?" (Weintraub 2002: 7). Romero and I conclude by offering some ideas to consider in addressing Weintraub's questions.

In 2008 another article about *JET* was published that complements ours. Research like that which appears in *JET* is often defended as laying the groundwork for subsequent work that hammers out applied theory fitting the

FIGURE 5.2 Summary results of the content analysis of JET 2004

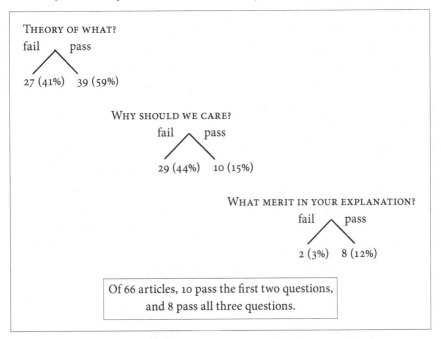

real world, and that tests such applied theory with empirical data. In this view, abstract work is like higher-order investment in knowledge, generating lower-order applied knowledge. Philip Coelho and James McClure (2008) examined the 1980 issues of *JET* for articles in which the word "lemma" appears at least five times. There were twelve such articles. They then looked at all the articles that cite those articles and investigated whether the twelve *JET* articles laid the groundwork for empirical application and testing. They concluded as follows:

> The 12 articles with five or more lemma generated 237 citations to them in the following (approximately) quarter century. Nine of the 237 citing articles contained empirical data, two had empirical data that had something to do with the propositions of the original article, and none had a definitive test leading to an acceptance or rejection of a proposition of the original article. In short, the 12 originating articles have to date defined no operational propositions. (Coelho and McClure 2008: 82–83)

Epilogue to Klein and Romero (2007): The editors of the *Journal of Economic Theory* were invited to reply to the article, but did not. The author of one of the *JET* 2004 articles, John Quiggin, wrote to us about our article and its treatment of his *JET* article (Quiggin 2004). The email exchange is reproduced in a subsequent issue of *Econ Journal Watch* as journal correspondence.[6] We had scored Quiggin's article as passing *Theory of what?* but failing *Why should we care?* and *What merit?* Quiggin protested the latter scores and reproduced text from his article to meet those questions; that part of the exchange is easily accessible at the link provided in note 6. I replied as follows:

> Pedro and I recognize that we might have mis-scored the paper. We looked again. It still seems to us that the paper does not say much to answer *Why should we care?* Can you elaborate on a real-world problem that your formulation helps to resolve? Do you maintain that your formulation is a better way to get at the results of traditional investment models? If so, better in what way? Is the betterness mainly a matter of economic insight, or mathematical sophistication? We still find that the motivation is obscure.
>
> We understand that asset price standard deviation may not really get at risk meaningful to investors. Is overcoming that failing the paper's motivation? Does your formulation get at how investors think of risk? If so, we still have trouble seeing that motivation. (Klein, as part of Quiggin 2007: 360)

John Quiggin concluded the exchange with the following reply:

> I suppose our disagreement comes down to tastes in how you write articles. I don't think it's necessary to convince an audience of economists that price determination in asset markets is an important problem, and having suggested a potential improvement interesting enough to satisfy the referees, I'll leave it to the profession to judge whether or not it's worthwhile. You obviously feel these points should be spelt out more in the article.
>
> As a result my interpretation of the message of your article is "*JET* articles aren't written the way we (Klein and Romero) would like". This is fair enough, but fails, for me, to answer your own question, "Why should we (the profession in general) care?" (Quiggin 2007: 360)

To my mind, Quiggin's reply is unsatisfying. The exchange provided him an easy and open opportunity to answer the further questions put to him in my reply, and thus the two questions on which we had failed his article. Instead he invoked the authority of the *Journal of Economic Theory*—the very thing that our article was testing.[7]

The Three Questions Turned toward
Swedberg's Theorizing Project

In interrogating the *JET* articles, the three questions—*Theory of what?*, *Why should we care?*, and *What merit in your explanation?*—were used to check whether the article provided *some* answer, *any* answer, to each of the questions. In turning now to Swedberg's theorizing project, the "we" of that circle is mostly free of any penchant for irrelevant and useless models. For Swedberg's theorizers—or, let us say, "our theorizers"—the questions may be useful in getting them to learn to give for each question not just some answer, but a *good* answer.

Now I speak to our theorizers as coach or counselor—one appointed by Swedberg. We turn the questions to our theorizers in a genial manner. There is no need to carefully separate the questions and hold anyone's feet to the fire. For our theorizers, the questions work as a set and may be managed as a set.

Running like a spine through the questions is the explanandum-explanation complex. In the complex, the explanandum and the explanation are counterparts. That means that whenever you speak of one, you should be able to speak of the other, as of parent and child.

Swedberg's article gives a prominent place to the naming of central concepts. He notes that neologisms often horrify (2012: 20), yet I propose a term for "the explanandum-explanation complex," viz., "explexus." The first four letters—"expl"—correspond to those of *explanation* (as well as the Latin *explanare*), and "plexus" connotes a complex of some mystery, like the complex of nerves that runs under each clavicle, the brachial plexus.

Our terminology differs from that used by Carl G. Hempel and Paul Oppenheim in their famous article "Studies in the Logic of Explanation." They write:

> We divide an explanation into two major constituents, the explanandum and the explanans. By the explanandum, we understand the sentence describing the phenomenon to be explained (not the phenomenon itself); by the explanans, the class of those sentences which are adduced to account for the phenomenon. (Hempel and Oppenheim 1948: 136–37)

For the thing to be explained, all of us use "explanandum." But for "those sentences which are adduced to account for the phenomenon," they use "explanans." But the ordinary word "explanation" suffices for what they call "explanans." They, however, use "explanation" for what I am calling "explexus." It seems to me that it is the larger complex consisting of the "two major constituents" that calls for an exotic term (my "explexus").

One might ask: Rather than introduce a neologism, why not just call the complex "theory"? Indeed, Swedberg writes of "developing a theory, including an explanation," and of "completing the tentative theory through an explanation." He says, "a fully built out theory includes an explanation" and "the theorizing process is not over till an explanation has been produced" (Swedberg 2012: 14, 16, 25).

But Swedberg also says, "Theorizing . . . means an attempt *to understand* and explain something . . . " (14, emphasis added). The word "theory" holds several facets aside from explanation, including understanding, prediction, and control. The facets are distinct but they relate to one another. When one sees, appreciates, or knows a good explexus, one better understands. In providing a good explexus, then, one advances understanding. Also, in providing an explexus one may aid prediction or control: If you believe a theory that smoke is caused by fire, then when you see fire, or someone fixing a fire, you might predict smoke. Also, you can, to some extent, control smoke by controlling fire. Explanation, understanding, prediction, and control are distinct but they tend to move together. Perhaps one could focus on understanding, and set up "the thing to be understood," and so on. But explanation seems most worthy. Explanation connotes statements and discourse, whereas understanding may be only tacit. As for prediction, it is often too ambitious, and control sounds menacing. If a theory can be said to have a spine, that spine is the explexus.

By the way, while Swedberg's essay provides wonderful and copious connections to thinkers who have treated of theorizing, there is no mention of David Hume, who said that "philosophical decisions are nothing but the reflections of common life, methodized and corrected" (1748: 170). Hume's ideas about causation and human understanding (in the first book of *A Treatise of Human Nature* and in *Enquiry Concerning Human Understanding*) are highly pragmatist. He says our minds form groupings of things based on resemblance and such, and learn to develop and focus on associations based on temporal priority and contiguity, *in whatever ways prove useful to us*. All this is the nature of causation. He places great emphasis on causation being an ordering in human minds, and, thus, in a sense, portrays all of us as theorizers. Hume associates causation with necessity, but it is clear that the decision as to *which* necessities we shall *focus on* is made pragmatically; it is not useful to say that *the absence of heavy rainfall*, a necessary condition for a fire, caused the smoke. Likewise, Hume suggests that we formulate the thing to be explained, the explanandum, creatively and pragmatically, as when he writes:

> These instances [of things that we collect mentally as a set based on their resemblance] are in themselves totally distinct from each other, and have no union but in the mind, which observes them, and collects their ideas. Necessity, then, is the effect of this observation, and is nothing but an internal impression of the mind, or a determination to carry our thoughts from one object to another. Without considering it [that is, necessity] in this view, we can never arrive at the most distant notion of it, or be able to attribute it either to external or internal objects, to spirit or body, to causes or effects. (Hume 1739: 165)

Causation, for Hume, was a matter of focal or useful associations. A "corrollary" (1739: 172) was skepticism: How can one invoke an associative regularity between one set of things (explanations) and another set of things (explananda) for an event as singular and unlike all others as that suggested by the statement "God created the universe"?

So, one counsel to our theorizers is to consider putting Hume on their reading lists.

Now I reposition them from third-person plural to second-person singular. That is, now I address *you*, young theorizer! Consider putting Hume on your reading list.

Think about the three questions—*Theory of what?*, *Why should we care?*, and *What merit in your explanation?*—in tandem, or as a set. When you find problems in answering one of the questions, a remedy may be found in adjusting your answer to one of the other questions. Likewise, shape your explanandum and your explanation in tandem. Your explanandum has to dovetail with your explanation. You might improve this dovetailing by adjusting the explanandum, not the explanation. Swedberg (2012: 32) cites Everett C. Hughes (1984: 503) on looking for "likeness inside the shell of variety." The likeness, or resemblance, is something that your theorizing may clarify and help to establish. If you think of yourself as a creator, even an artist, your creation, your work of art, is the entire explexus.

But it also pays to zoom in on one question at a time. In answering *Theory of what?*, you are disciplining yourself to make clear what it is that you attempt to explain—that is, to identify the explanandum. I trust you are not building equilibrium models like those in *JET*, but, still, for many a social science author, Leijonhufvud might nonetheless say that the work "leaves us in doubt about what exactly he or she is *talking about*."

And giving *some* answer to *Theory of what?* is not good enough. You have to give a *good* answer. Give clear illustrations, whether historical, factual, anecdotal, or merely fictitious, as when Schelling (1960: 54) provides the parable of a husband and wife becoming separated in a department store, or when Adam Smith (1790: 181ff) gives the parable of the now-rich poor man's son who looks back on his putatively successful life. If the illustration is clear, people can relate to it. As Deirdre McCloskey (2000: 78) says, people find it much easier to move from the concrete to the general than from the general to concretes.

By multiplying and varying your illustrations of the explanandum, you may also find its boundaries. It can be helpful to bring up a concrete example that resembles your explanandum in some respects, but differs in other respects that keep it from being an illustration of your explanandum. By clarifying what you do *not* pretend to explain, you clarify what you *do* pretend to explain. You delimit the explanandum.

By giving numerous clear illustrations—and factual is a plus, all else equal—you start to build out the basis for testing your theory. Unlike the blowhard, you give the reader something with which she may respond at the end: "But you said you were going to explain *this*, and I don't see (or don't buy) your explanation." Don't be afraid to find out that you, too, are a bit of a blowhard. What, after all, *is* your motivation to theorize? Better to find out now and begin correcting it.

Now, though an economist, I am quite permissive about the nature of explananda. What people say in such-and-such circumstances, what people think, what they feel are all viable explananda. Particular norms, practices, or moral or cultural patterns can be the explanandum.

Even what a particular person said or did on particular occasions might qualify. Why did Smith make an organon of moral sentiment being enshrouded in sympathy?[8] To explain that would take quite a theory.

If some particular speech acts of Adam Smith may be a good answer to *Theory of what?*, that is because he is Adam Smith. Not just anyone's speech acts will serve as well. If just anyone's served as a good answer, then all of the *JET* authors could have said that their explanandum is their saying what they say in the abstract of their article, even the articles that are purely model-building.

Here we see that theorizing is inevitably embedded in a discourse situation, entailing one or more circles of "we," and that our three questions depend on such embeddedness. Indeed, one of the questions is, "Why should we care?" One might reply: Who is "we"? That is how Quiggin replied in the exchange succeeding the critique of *JET*. He essentially said: My "we" is not your "we," and I abstain from entering further into your challenges of my article in *JET*.

Minding the three questions, then, impels you to mind your "we." Conflict is ineluctable among interpretations and judgments, and hence among circles of "we." They compete with each other. Along with fashioning the parts of your explexus, you are also choosing scholarly traditions and communities.

You can hope to innovate and alter those communities, but any such innovation proceeds as a development on them. Our third question— *What merit in your explanation?*—insists that new explanations of previously identified explananda show their merits in relation to old explanations. Innovations are new, but the standards by which they are judged are usually old and change only incrementally. Thomas Kuhn (1959) spoke of the relationship between scientific tradition and innovation as "the essential tension."

If a merit of your explanation is that it explains more reliably or more neatly than the rival explanation, mind the quantitative aspect. *More* reliably or *more* neatly can often be treated quantitatively. Quantification is not necessarily something apart from theorizing. It may inhere in theorizing. Make your quantifications as transparent, as accountable, as possible. Besides answering merit, quantification will help show why we should care and what you are theorizing about.

Rules May Be Loose, Vague, and Indeterminate

So to aid your appreciation of theoretical work and improve your own, think about explexus and the three questions. If we believe that explanation and understanding are related in a quite general way, we might try to discern the explanatory aspect of most any work in the social sciences, since, even if empirical, historical, or discursive, it presumably proposes to aid understanding of something in some way.

Consider the present work. It would not be called theoretical or explanatory. Perhaps it would be called an essay. Yet the explexus lens can be applied. The thing to be explained, the explanandum, is some features of our sensibilities of good theory, our judgments about whether a theory is worthwhile. We cannot hope to render such sensibilities "precise and accurate," as Smith would say; the aim is not to make them grammatical. Rather, they are "loose, vague, and indeterminate" (Smith 1790: 175–76; see also 327). But that is not to say that they are arbitrary. The Smith material drawn on here is a discussion of the rules of virtues. Even loose, vague, and indeterminate rules *are rules*. He likens them to "the rules which critics lay down for the attainment of what is sublime and elegant in composition." Although "there are no rules whose observance will infallibly lead us to the attainment of elegance or sublimity," "there are some which may help us, in some measure, to correct and ascertain the vague ideas which we might otherwise have entertained of those perfections." The three questions (*Theory of what?*, *Why should we care?*, and *What merit in your explanation?*) are helpful disciplines in theorizing and in the assessment of theory. I thusly explain—albeit only partly—our judgments about theorizing: Works that we praise have good answers to the three questions, and those we blame often do not. How well the author answers the three questions partly explains our judgments about his or her theory. That is the spine of my nascent theory.

It is not possible here to provide many illustrations of the explanandum, or many demonstrations of the explanation. That impossibility is part of why this chapter would be called an essay and not a theoretical work. This essay hopes only to offer a number of illustrations, to begin to develop a theory and begin to test it.

Illustrations and demonstrations might be divided into two categories on either side of the benchmark of "mediocrity," which Smith calls the point of "propriety": Above propriety are things that are praiseworthy and below, blameworthy (Smith 1790: 26, 27, 80). The article that Romero and I wrote blames a majority of the articles in the 2004 volume of *JET* for failing to satisfy some of the basic proprieties of theorizing. Here, however, I do not examine any work deemed blameworthy. To do so would be difficult, given our lack of common knowledge of any such work, and insufficient space to make criticism fair.

The Three Questions and Coleman and Hoffer (1987)

In their book *Public and Private High Schools: The Impact of Communities*, James S. Coleman and Thomas Hoffer (1987) integrate theory, evidence, and narrative. The integration is rich and persuasive. The messages are of great moment. Coleman and Hoffer work with different categories of school—public, Catholic, and other private categories—and investigate differences in how well the students do. The jacket of the book says: "the authors are able to point to the crucial role of school-community relationships in explaining these differences." The explananda are patterns of differences in how well the students do, including the *growth* of academic learning over a two-year period; the explanations are differences in the features of communities to which the families belong.

The explexus, in simplified form, is the following: Students in Catholic school do better than those in public school and in other categories of private school, and "the first prominent explanation for the difference is the functional community that exists around a religious body to which the families adhere and of which the school is an outgrowth" (214). The mechanisms of functional community are conveyed throughout the book, as when the authors write: "The feedback that a parent receives from friends and associates, either unsolicited or in response to questions, provides extensive additional resources that aid the parent in monitoring the school and the child . . . " And: "[T]he norms that parents, as part of their everyday activity, are able to establish act as important aids in socializing children" (7). Such resources are discussed also in terms of social capital, networks, and intergenerational closure—the parents have relationships with one another. Coleman and Hoffer emphasize the intergenerational dimension, noting that religious life is "one of the few remaining strong bases of functional community in modern society which includes both adults and children" (215).

The book's answers to *Theory of what?* and *Why should we care?* are clear. The interesting question is, *What merit in your explanation?*, which in this case becomes, *How's yours better?* How is the functional-community explanation better than the other explanations?

One explanation might be that Catholic schools spend more money per pupil, but the opposite is true (35). Other explanations are separated out by virtue of control variables, on family income and structure, parental education, race, and so on. Issues of missing variables and selection effects always haunt such a study, but for the results on the students' academic *growth*, these concerns are greatly reduced, since a student's twelfth-grade performance on the test is effectively controlled for by *that student's* tenth-grade performance. For the evidence about what happens to students in their years immediately after high school, and so on, the selection issues may be more serious—and presumably have been taken up in the great deal of subsequent literature on the book.

A big point of the book is to highlight the importance of functional community in relation to "value community"—that is, same values among the families. Value community is strong when private families converge on some independent private school to their liking. But "[i]n the private sector, many schools are based on value communities that have little grounding in functional communities" (12). Catholic schools have functional community, and that is Coleman and Hoffer's explanation for why they generally do better.

Coleman and Hoffer engage *How's yours better?* candidly and scrupulously. They write: "We attempted to find an alternative explanation for the exceedingly strong Catholic school effect on the dropout rate . . . One possible explanation concerned Catholic religion *per se*: It might simply be that Catholic students were less likely to drop out of school than others, whether in a Catholic school or not, because of greater social integration in the Catholic religious community itself" (214). They summarize their argument for the relative merit of the functional-community explanation: "But this did not account for the difference, for while Catholics were slightly less likely to drop out of public school than were non-Catholics, they were no less likely to drop out of Catholic schools. Nor was it true that the degree of integration with the religious community, as measured by frequency of church attendance, was responsible for the special protection against middle-class dropout provided by Catholic schools" (214). But they are careful to qualify the argument, being fair to the competing explanation: "However, . . . those who regularly attended church, whether Catholic or not, [were] considerably less likely to drop out than those who never attended church" (214).

One might challenge the book on *How's yours better?* by probing whether the evidence can be interpreted within the kind of explanation we would associate with Milton and Rose Friedman (1980: 140–78), that, especially for an excludable service like schooling, private enterprise usually outperforms government enterprise, because private owners have decisive authority over their resources, are residual claimants, and must satisfy their trading partners to win their support and participation. Such probing would need to look more carefully at the results for the non-Catholic private schools. Coleman and Hoffer acknowledge that small sample sizes become a problem if types of non-Catholic private schools are subdivided (e.g., 98n). Also, the reader finds that the non-Catholic schools are treated differently in different places in the book, sometimes with a "high performance private" category—for which a ceiling effect on the results of the student tests poses a serious data problem— and sometimes not. Also, families sometimes pony up for private schooling because their child is troubled (or *is* trouble)—a point the book might have given more attention (see 97–99, 112–113, 117, 234)—which raise concerns about selection effects (especially for the forms of evidence other than student academic growth). Coleman and Hoffer do not directly engage the Friedman explanation. The explanation of Coleman and Hoffer highlights "a set of resources which are not provided by schools themselves, but are provided by these social relations that exist among the parents of students in the school" (216). Is that explanation something apart from the Friedmans' explanation, or is it an application and development of the Friedmans' explanation?

In the book the authors richly develop the explexus. They are also praiseworthy for being willing to step above the explexus and ask: What important things does the explexus leave out of view? One dimension beyond their data is whether "a functional community can strengthen the advantages of the already-advantaged and block the opportunities of the disadvantaged" (232), and they refer to the "graphic portrayal" provided by August Hollingshead's *Elmtown's Youth* (1949). Thus they pause to recognize that certain families may wish to lighten the effect of the functional community in which they are embedded.

A Co-authored Work of Mine, on Urban Transit

There is a strong tradition of transportation researchers at the University of California, Irvine, and when in 1989, at age 27, I joined the faculty there, I fell in with them. During the ensuing years, Adrian T. Moore and Binyam Reja, then doctoral students, and I wrote a book called *Curb Rights: A Foundation for Free Enterprise in Urban Transit* (1997a). It is fair to say that the book offers a theory. The reception has been mixed: The book does not get cited much, and yet many reviews in leading journals were quite positive.[9] We also published an article that offers a condensation (Klein, Moore, and Reja 1997b).

I see value in thinking of transportation systems as consisting of three parts: vehicles, routes (or corridors), and terminal capacity. In maritime transportation we have boats, water routes, and ports. In air transportation we have airplanes, flight routes, and airports.

Looking back on my years in the transportation community at UC Irvine, the community was fairly conventional in the sense that its purposes were oriented toward status quo arrangements. Much of the research was funded by government agencies. Its theoretical bearings tended to be bound by a posture of looking to advise policymakers on how to tinker with the status quo. Such an outlook is characteristic of academic transportation research generally.

In the seminar discussions about urban transit, we would discuss such things as urban development patterns, commuting behavior, transit's competition from the private automobile, ridership rates, vehicle capacity utilization, economies of scale, network densities, and the optimization of routes and schedules. My background differed from that of others in that I had come up through libertarian intellectual communities. In actual practice, transportation is, of course, heavily governmentalized: Many of the key resources are government-owned, much of the expense is paid by the taxpayer, and there are many critical restrictions on voluntary private action. I questioned much of the status quo. Shouldn't transportation be more of a spontaneous order? The idea is that a tolerably good foundation of property rights and freedom of contract conduces to a system of activities that achieve coordination, including innovation, better than does a more governmentalized system. Confining our thinking to road-based transit (not rail), Moore, Reja, and I pondered how private ownership and entrepreneurship could function and studied different actual urban transit episodes. We came to focus on a part of the urban transit system that seemed to escape attention, namely, the capacity of terminals: bus stops, bus stations, curb zones, taxi stands, and staging and congregation areas. Terminal capacity had been rather invisible in urban transit research, but the more we pondered it the more we saw how critically important its role is. In pondering free-enterprise urban transit, it was not sufficient to consider private ownership of bus fleets or deregulation of fares, routes, and schedules. Terminal capacity—"curb rights"—was an essential piece of the puzzle.[10]

One of the key issues in route-based urban transit is interloping. Suppose you invest in setting up a scheduled service, but opportunistic jitneys—small, unscheduled vehicles, such as vans, that ply a route—swoop in to offer rides on attractive terms to the passengers waiting at the stop, passengers who might not congregate there if they could not fall back on your scheduled service. If interloping is rampant, then it might be impossible to maintain scheduled service. And if the scheduled service then folds, maybe the passengers will no longer congregate and even the jitneying will unravel. The anchor of scheduled services gives rise to interlopers, but the interlopers dissolve the anchor.

In other cases the market might be so thick that jitneying can thrive even in the complete absence of scheduled service. So how should jitneying be handled? Our thought, in brief, is that the matter at each "terminal" should be decided by the entrepreneur who owns the property or holds a long-term lease from the local government to the curb zone along the street. On a foundation of property rights, interloping becomes a matter of trespass.

You might think: But in the United States we don't have problems of interloping at bus stops. That is largely true: The bus stops are government property and people abide by laws against unauthorized use of them. But would it be possible to prevent interloping and yet enjoy the virtues of the invisible hand? Local governments could lease out curb zones to private parties, in a way to foster competition among them. Another key would be free entry—that is, freedom of entrepreneurs to develop terminal capacity on private property as they see fit; that would require the liberalization of restrictions that now prevent them from doing so.

There are variations in curb rights within the United States today. Moreover, different times and different places in different countries have exemplified variations in curb rights that make for different episodes or experiences in urban transit. (Here space does not permit enumeration of notable different experiences; see the book, pp. 33–79). The different historical and international experiences constitute an array of different types of experience. We schematize the array as a typology (pp. 91, 128). The typology is our explanandum. Our explanation of the different types of transit experience is the variation in curb rights (and other conditions, notably the thickness of the market). Our analysis also helps to explain how various problems in urban transit relate to weaknesses in the underlying structure of property rights in terminal capacity (pp. 107–15). Our chief explanatory factor—"curb rights"—lends itself to policy reform suggestions, which are provided at the end of the book. Even if the reform suggestions are not possible politically, the theory helps us understand road-based transit.

Abduction and the Three Questions

I continue the memoir of Adrian Moore, Binyam Reja, and me doing *Curb Rights*, but now turn to the three questions and Swedberg's topic of abduction. As for the first question, *Theory of what?*, we had somehow learned enough about different transit experiences to have a body of material to fashion into an explanandum. The impulse toward historical and comparative study was natural among us: Moore had a master's degree in history, Reja came from Ethiopia, and I was researching the history of private toll roads. We read enough of the literature on different transit experiences to feel that we knew of all the different kinds of transit experience that had been given scholarly treatment. Swedberg (2012: 8) quotes Pasteur's dictum, "chance only favors the prepared mind."

As for the question, *Why should we care?*, real human troubles involve urban transit, giving rise to problems and issues. There is strong interest in mitigating the problems and addressing the issues. Transit policy is obviously a matter that many people care about, and for good reason.

Before addressing the third question, *What merit in your explanation?*, something should be said about coming up with the explanation. Did it involve a creative flash, an abductive leap?

I think it is important to say that, from the very start of our collaboration, Moore, Reja, and I shared a broadly libertarian outlook. In a sense, we had a broad theory from the beginning, namely, something to the effect that social affairs work better when resources are privately owned and people are free to compete within the bounds of property, consent, and contract. But such a theory is unoriginal. If we were to make some such theory worthwhile, we would have to sharpen it and move it beyond free-market commonplaces. We impelled ourselves to do so by addressing the question, *What merit in your explanation?*, and, in particular, *How's yours better?* That is, how is our explanation better than the familiar—and briefer—rehearsals of free-market verities? By asking yourself the tough questions, again and again, you feel impelled to come up with something that is better.

Something that is quite crucial to whatever success one might ascribe to *Curb Rights* is an equilibrium model presented in diagrammatic form (pp. 86–89). The model plots activity at a curb zone and involves two functions, passenger congregating and jitneying, and the domain of one is the range of the other—that is, congregating is a function of the number of jitneys that come by per hour, and the number of jitneys that come by is a function of the number of people who congregate at that curb zone. A diagram of this kind can accommodate both stable and unstable equilibria and illustrate tipping-point dynamics.

Somehow I came up with the diagram. I had had training in game theory and had written game-theoretic papers with tipping points. Also, I was an avid reader of Thomas Schelling, and the diagram is very similar to ones in *Micromotives and Macrobehavior* (Schelling 1978a). If there was an abductive moment in our project, it was when the diagram was first drawn: Different variants of the model, or different equilibria (or disequilibrium dynamics) within the models, correspond to different types of transit episodes, which are distinguished principally by differences in curb rights. I think I first drew the diagram alone in my home. But I do not recall anything more than that.

Our model is what makes the connection between explanandum and explanation as elegant as it is. Such elegance is one answer to the question, *What merit in your explanation?* The model helps to show how just one or two differences in conditions give rise to different types of outcomes, with the outcomes bearing resemblance to different types of transit experience.

Another merit of our explanation is that it helps us understand how defects in transit systems relate to features of the rights regime. In particular, the theory helps us see that many transit services in the United States are inert and unresponsive because there are critical restrictions on private action, because so much of the system is owned by governments, and because there are pervasive subsidies from taxpayers (and those subsidies are rendered on the producer, rather than user, side of the market). In this respect, our theory helps to incorporate the topic of urban transit into a broader understanding of how social coordination is related to the rights regime.

Although I do not recall much about the abductive moments of my work with Moore and Reja, these recollections might be helpful in understanding the process of successful abduction (if we may suppose the work a success).

It is hard to say how you come up with a theoretical insight. But once you have an insight, you can explore it. The better prepared you are, the better you can assess its merit, promise, and potential. Ask yourself the three questions, *Theory of what?*, *Why should we care?*, and *What merit in your explanation?* Your job as a theorizer is to formulate a complete explexus, consisting of both an explanandum and an explanation. Ask the questions again and again. That will help to direct your reading and thinking. In your knot of scholarly companions and peers, make a custom of asking each other the three questions. Challenge each other: *Theory of what?*, *Why should we care?*, *What merit in your explanation?* It will make you and your colleagues ever better prepared. Ask yourself the three questions to test your theorizing as it develops. The test results will help you refine and direct your theorizing.

An important ingredient is hope. Challenge yourself and your peers in a way that offers hope. Ask the questions as an aid to finding the way forward, not as a way to stifle theorizing and silence yourself or your peers.

Then we hope that abductive breakthroughs will come.

6 Mundane Theorizing, *Bricolage*, and *Bildung*

Stephen Turner

HOW DO THEORISTS THINK? WHAT IS IT ABOUT THE WAY THEY think that makes theorists different from other kinds of social scientists? We can answer this, in part, by identifying the externals of the process—for example, by looking at what theorists read and engage with and by reconstructing intellectual trajectories. We can consider the testimony of theorists in their autobiographical reflections, which can point to their obsessions and influences. But these approaches leave out a great deal, and the stories that one tells, about others or about oneself, have the usual limitations of narrative—the necessity of selectivity and the subordination of the effort to the need to make narrative sense. What gets left out? Theoretical thinking has very different properties from the rest of social science. What are these properties? Thinking through a problem often involves more or less random access to one's own mind, in a mental state that allows it to be open to making new associations and pulling up memories of facts and traces of past inferential thinking that can be analogized. Chance, the chance of coming up with something, favors the prepared mind, but works against the overprepared mind, the mind that only runs on rigid paths. Clichéd thinking is the deadly enemy of innovation. These considerations point to what is so difficult to describe: how it is that theorists come up with their innovations.

The process of capturing expressible ideas and thoughts from the fleeting mass of associations that the mind makes is mysterious. Everything of importance operates on the tacit level. Insights may come, and indeed often do come, from thinking that goes on while one sleeps. It is a commonplace experience to face a series of unsolved problems, or simply to get stuck in writing, and to find in the morning, or even to awake to find, that there is a solution to them or a path around them. Michael Polanyi wrote about these processes as they figure in scientific discovery ([1946] 1964: 13–14), but the lessons apply to "theorizing" of all kinds. People often report coming to a new insight while lecturing on a topic. Edward Shils mentions this experience. Robert Merton used lecturing to classes as an aid in working out his ideas (Cole 2004: 831). I think this must be a common experience. There must be some deep cognitive science reason for this as well, perhaps in the fact that articulating an idea in a new setting, activating new connections, produces new insights. There is also a close connection between articulating thoughts and devising new ones, and the self-correction and evaluation of one's own articulations. The discipline of writing is itself a source of novelty. One often comes up with new insights in the course of smoothing out a final draft. This kind of "discovery" or self-discovery is not the same as theorizing, but it is particularly relevant. The insights central to theorists are often of the kinds that involve making connections that include more disparate elements than those in more structured kinds of problem solving. And this would fit with the idea that one can derive from biographies and autobiographies, that theorizing, at least on a high level, requires a large amount of background knowledge that is unsystematically collected.

Although the mental processes that produce insights are opaque, examining the externals of theorizing nevertheless provides a starting point for exploring the process of theorizing. We can use these externals to differentiate some of the kinds of theorizing that occur in social theory and such related fields as sociology and organization studies. In what follows, I distinguish three kinds of theoretical thinking: a very basic kind, in which the theorist makes sense of something novel by analogizing from something that is already understood; a second type, consisting of puttering or *bricolage*, in which the theorist seeks a kind of coherence between available theoretical ideas; and a third type, in which the theorizer takes on the available theoretical schemes provided, especially by the classic thinkers and their heirs, to provide a coherent alternative or challenge to them. Thinking at this level is truly an effort at ongoing intellectual self-construction, or *Bildung*. Thinking at this level, I conclude, involves a particular kind of passion, and includes some uncommon intellectual characteristics and compulsions. Identifying them may provide some basis for enabling readers to determine whether they have a vocation or calling for theorizing, and for understanding the strange passions of those who do.

Social Theory as Vocation

The last sentence in the previous paragraph is a conscious reference to Weber's "Callings" essays (Weber [1919] 1946; Weber [1919] 1994; Weber [1919] 2012), and it may serve us as a miniature model of the problem of understanding theorizing itself. Framing an essay like this, one with a vague prompt about theorizing, requires some sense of one's audience, including an idea about the kinds of references the audience is familiar with. The audience for this chapter can be expected to at least have some familiarity with the "Callings" essays. So the reader would immediately see the analogy between Weber's problem and the problem of the essay. Weber's point in the first, sociological part, of each of those essays was to take abstract ideas, "science" or actually the much broader "*Wissenschaft*" in one and "politics" in the other, and begin the study of these as callings with mundane considerations about the human activities that the ideas correspond to.

In the case of "Politics," the lesson Weber outlines is a rather brutal one: politics has been dominated by political parties, not only in recent modernity, but for millennia. To be "in politics" or to be a politician, much less a leader, one must make a career in a party or face the reality that it is only within party politics, and with the cooperation of party politics, that political achievement is possible. To think otherwise is to be a utopian, not to say deluded. The message about "Science" is not so brutal, but it is brutal enough. Science is an organized human activity; scholars at a university must jump through many hoops, few of which are rational. Expectations that merit will be rewarded are out of place: the only person suitable for university life is one who can stand having hacks and incompetents promoted ahead of them.

Who might be suited? Only a very odd person, a person with very special passions and mental qualities:

> . . . if someone is not able to, so to speak, put on blinkers and get completely caught up in the idea that the fate of his soul depends on whether he makes the correct conjectural reading of this, precisely this, passage in this manuscript—then he should stay well away from science. He will never within himself live through what may be called the "inner experience" of science. If one does not know this strange exhilaration, which all outsiders only smile at, this passion, this feeling that "millennia had to pass ere thou camest to life, and other millennia wait in silence" to see whether this conjecture is correct, then one does *not* possess the vocation for science, and one should do something different. For nothing is worth anything for a human being, as a human being, unless he is *able to* do it with *passion*. (Weber [1919] 2012: 339)

In theorizing "theorizing" I have just lifted this theme and substituted the term "theorizing" for *Wissenschaft* (Weber's more general term translated here as "science"). To the extent that this works, it is because there is an analogy to the problem I am addressing in this chapter. It works for the audience for this chapter, which can be assumed to have at least an acquaintance with Weber's titles, and perhaps a vague recollection of the texts themselves. It is a kind of shorthand for a large group of ideas that do not need to be expressed, but can simply be invoked by making this analogy—ideas about careers, academic integrity, an inner self or soul that chooses the fate that results in spending a life on this strange passion in the stranger world of academic life, with its relentless politics, cynically pseudo-meritocratic structure, and so forth. The reader who knows the essays and the commentaries on them, of course, gets more of this than the reader who does not.

But there is also a grave point raised by the analogy: that embarking on a life of theorizing is a serious matter; that one is destined for probable failure both in the local setting of an academic career and in the larger sense of achieving anything of permanent value. The rule of "science" is that everything that is achieved is surpassed, and that the fundamental business of science is precisely to surpass past science. The only meaning to be gained from science is this: if you are lucky enough, your work may temporarily improve on or surpass that of your predecessors. Your work will certainly be improved on by your successors, if only by being comprehensively debunked.

The passion is trickier still. Weber said that he stayed in academic life to see how much he could stand. And there is a kind of obstinance that science requires. But there are rewards as well. And the chemistry of these rewards and frustrations, the stuff that the passion responds to, is complex. This is not an activity that ordinary people take up as a "job." It requires talent of a particular kind, but the talent needs to be matched with a specific kind of passion.

Social theory, to an extent unlike most of academic life, has a special problem with passion. The subject matter of social theory, and of much sociology today, is ideologically loaded. The core concepts themselves have ideological content and are already the subject of passions: the passion for resisting injustice and oppression, for example. Chemists have passions, even passions for chemicals, but the passion for understanding chemicals is rarely confused with other passions. In social theory the opposite is true. Ideological passions are not only the subject, but at the very heart of social theory. The motives for engaging in social theory are often derivative of those passions. And theorizing itself is quickly labeled in terms of its supposed ideological affiliations and significance. This is not entirely inappropriate. Much of it, indeed, makes sense only within a rigid ideological framework. Theda Skocpol's famous thesis to the effect that the state in the late nineteenth century became an autonomous power (Skocpol 1979), for example, makes sense only against a background of Marxist theorizing in which the state is the executive committee of the bourgeoisie. The actual constitutional history of the United States during this period involved the federal government, flush with expanded legal powers as a result of the Civil War and subsequent constitutional amendments, and with a large domain of federal land in the West, applying governmental solutions already present in state governments. The federal geological survey—whose creation Henry Adams called the first modern legislation—was a case in point. It was modeled on state surveys that had gone on virtually from the time of the founding. Nothing about any of this had much to do with "class" in any sense. Most of the states were agrarian. The powers involved were new only to the federal government, not to "the state." Does this disconfirm Skocpol's general point? Whether this fits or does not fit her thesis is essentially a theological question, not a historical one. And one can find many instances of this kind of theological problem in the endless discussion of class fractions and class identity in Marxist writing (for example, Carchedi 1987; Wright 1997).

Is this "theorizing? One is tempted to say that this too is a theological question, but in another sense, it is one only in analogy to the idea of political theology, in which atheism is itself a theology. Every theory can be converted into ideology, or can be read as ideological, in the sense that it can be said to support or have affinities with some political stance. But in the "vocation" sense there is a difference. What differs is what is potentially up for grabs, or revisable. Michael Oakeshott speaks of "arrests" and "platforms," by which he means problematizations of some concept or situation and the stable and unproblematized discursive grounds on which it is possible to discuss what one has problematized (Oakeshott 1991). For the ideological thinker, some of these grounds can never be problematized.

Mundane Theorizing: Analogy as a Method

For Skocpol, and for many others, the distinction is of little moment, because the level of theorizing is low. She begins with a model or explanatory form. In this case, it is the model of the state controlled by a ruling class and operated in its interests. But there is an anomaly, in this case a state that behaves as though it is not controlled. And there is an explanation of the anomalous fact in the form of an added notion that preserves the substance of the original theory, in this case the basic picture of society and historical development as class struggle. The theory is an epicycle. The main idea is not challenged.

This is an instance of what we might call mundane theorizing. It starts with a theory and extends it to cover something other than what it was initially created to explain, in this case various forms of state action that do not fit the original model of the state as the executive committee of the bourgeoisie. Some bridging work is needed to make it fit the new context. Some of the bridging may be translation: finding what corresponds in the new setting. In this case, we find an anomaly to deal with, and we need to add something. This work of extending the application of a concept or model (such as the classical Marxist one) and finding out the extension doesn't work, then finding something that does work for the case at hand, is normal social science: low-level but essential. What we add, however, is going to be an extension of some other model. We add by extending analogies.

A simpler example, again from academic life, will help to clarify this. It is obvious that much of academic life involves what is traditionally called clientelism. In the primitive Polynesian form, there are "big men" who can do favors or give protection in exchange for loyalty and services of various kinds. Academic life works in an analogous way. Of course, this reality is concealed by the usual meritocratic verbiage of letters of recommendation, academic politesse, and the rest of it, and has to be. It wouldn't work if it weren't concealed. So it takes an act of unmasking or of classifying the meritocratic language as a form of misrecognition and bracketing or critically examining it in order to apply the concept to the familiar material of academic endorsement, editorial decision making, and the like.

A lot of what theorists do involves mundane theorizing of this analogical kind. "Mundane" is not a term of opprobrium; "analogizing" describes a basic tool. Moreover, it can be very difficult to do. A lot of economic theory, perhaps all of it, works in this way: there is some odd phenomenon that needs to be explained, and it is explained by inventing a concept that allows the extant theory, or some extant theory, to be applied. A notion like "public goods" is a typical bridging concept. It makes something not a traditional "good," such as a bottle of ketchup with a price tag, into a "good" to which one can then impute a price. In sociology, the Merton/ Lazarsfeld practices described in *The Language of Social Research* (Lazarsfeld and Rosenberg 1955) and *Continuities in the Language of Social Research* (Lazarsfeld and Rosenberg 1972), and by Hans Zetterberg in his book on theory construction, *On Theory and Verification in Sociology* (1963), and later relabeled as grounded theory, worked in this way. One had an explanation of something and applied it to something similar, or what one could construe as similar, and used more general language to cover the similar cases.

One can of course do this without a "theory," and in a sense there is something more basic and pure that begins simply with a puzzle or problem. In sociology, the core puzzle, as I have claimed elsewhere, is produced by the situation in which one's own expectations and acquired habits of understanding and social prediction, or "practices," what we would now call social cognition, fail us, forcing us to repair our understanding with an explanation (Turner 1980). Minimally, all this need be is a kind of translation, which allows us to predict and understand by substituting a word—for example, they say "soda" when we would say "pop" and others would say "coke," to choose the classic geographically determined American terms for soft drinks. But in more elaborate cases one needs more: what we count as corrupt, others count as obedience to familial obligations. And to make sense of this translation, to make it intelligible to us, we need to tell more about the larger set of rules and expectations of which these obligations and expectations are a part. I called this describing one game (in the Wittgensteinian sense of language games) as a variation of another, with the thought that one understood the first "game" in some primary sense and understood the other by analogy.

What this account does is to respect the tacit and unmentioned parts of the social situation: the things that are understood in the primary sense that do not get challenged or changed in the new setting. If they are not problematic—if, for example, our facial expressions mean the same thing in both settings—they are not problematized and made into a sociological puzzle to be solved by this kind of explanation. We assume that our expectations work until we learn otherwise. Nor can we do otherwise: the social as distinct from the non-social can only be revealed in this way. This places a major constraint on the ambitions of social theory: there is no fixed autonomous subject here, with a body of data about which to theorize, but rather a set of puzzles that are revealed to us by our own attempts to make sense of other people.

Whether "explanations" in sociology in the end can go beyond this, or whether this is merely a special case, are issues in the philosophy of social science. One could argue that we cannot go beyond this: the objects we create to problematize and theorize about are always constructed in a way that depends on aspects of our tacit knowledge that are inaccessible to us, and consequently can only become explicit when we are presented with an actual alternative. But we do not need to adjudicate such questions. The basic format of getting in trouble with our concepts and needing to think our way out of our troubles is characteristic of theorizing generally, as is the use of analogy. And if we look at higher levels of theorizing, we can see that analogizing and getting in trouble with our concepts still play an important role.

Sometimes we come to recognize that we have problems with the application of our concepts when things that appear to be similar do not behave in similar ways. In such instances, generalizing in the way recommended by grounded theory, for example, does not work. If one compares like with like, it does work. But whether something is "like" something else is a matter of discovery, or at least we can discover that what we take to be "alike" is not. This is why social theory often begins with taxonomy. Taxonomies create categories of like objects that are alike in a definable way. They enable us to group things in a way that allows us to avoid the confusions produced by general terms, including of course the terms that we use in explanations of different practices, like corruption. But they also help with attempts at generalization, because new taxonomies can help us reveal commonalities within the new taxonomic category. Taxonomy is the sister of analogizing: it is a map of where to apply analogies to similar cases.

The Next Level: Basic Coherence

There is another class of theorizing that works with mundane tools but produces what appear to be novel results. Some examples from organizational theory will work as examples: John Meyer and Brian Rowan's "Institutional Organizations: Formal Structure as Myth and Ceremony" (1977) and Ken Benson's "Organizations: A Dialectical View" (1977), both citation classics. One could also use the classic articles of neo-institutionalism as examples. These papers are synthetic works: they bring together several "theoretical" ideas from different sources and use them to create a unified account, which is then applied to a novel setting, in this case complex organizations. This differs from the clientelism example above, in that the problem is not merely one of translating or bridging, though it is that. It is one of combining the products of several bridging activities into some coherent picture.

Here we see the beginnings of what Lévi-Strauss called *bricolage*, or puttering. The key to puttering is its aimlessness—well represented by the carpenter Popo in V. S. Naipaul's novel *Miguel Street,* who never made a stick of furniture, and was always planing and chiselling and making what I think he called mortises. Whenever I asked him, "Mr Popo, what you making?" he would reply, "Ha, boy! That's the question. I making the thing without a name." ([1959] 2002: 10)

Perhaps the authors of these constructions made them with a general picture in mind, which they filled out. But the aims were open; the outcome was not determined in advance. The thing they made was to some extent dictated by the materials themselves and what they could make of these materials by the intellectual equivalent of planing and chiseling to make them fit together. The materials were the ideas and "theories," perspectives, and whatnot that they had lying around the workshop, or, as the case may be, the office or seminar discussion, or the results of undirected reading around. They may have been driven by some sort of dissatisfaction with the available pictures, and by predilections for particular kinds of sources. But the task is to make something, something coherent enough to present as a picture, and to make a better picture than the one you were dissatisfied with.

One could ask many questions about this kind of theorizing. What is its purpose? What is "success" here? Is this supposed to be a way station to "science" and if so how does it help get to the supposed destination? But it must be said that these questions are ordinarily not on the mind, consciously or at least centrally, of the theorist. The problem is rather to make sense of something that does not make sense, such as the relation between various perspectives and descriptions. Part of the attraction for the postwar period of systems thinking was the promise that it was a method that would integrate apparently conflicting perspectives. And of course one motive for putting things together differently is the rejection, for whatever reason, of other attempts to put things together.

There is a market for synthesis, but it is difficult to provide syntheses that interest others. We may have our private sense of how things hang together, and worrying about how our different ideas relate is a major motivation for theorizing. And this is perhaps a clue to the answer to the "vocation" question: theorizing requires a capacity for thinking analogically and a strong drive to seek coherence, as well as, at the level beyond the most mundane, a wide set of materials to work with. But at this next level the desire for coherence, as distinct from gaining the understanding provided by mundane theorizing, becomes central, indeed a nagging force that produces effects like the one that Weber describes when he talks about the strange "exhilaration" of scholarship ([1919] 2012: 339).

But here we run into a tangle of problems. It was said of Phillip Rieff that he thought "only seventeen people understood him" (and as Gerald Howard commented, "it seemed that he was trying to whittle the number down" [Howard 2007]). But among the usual motives of theorists is to communicate to others their sense of how things hang together, or to orient a field, or to undermine and reject a vision one opposes. This is difficult. It is difficult to articulate a theory or theoretical viewpoint, and difficult to convey it to people who understand much less about theory and have different referents and background knowledge.

Start with the gap in understanding. There is a difference, and there should be a difference, between the theorist and the larger audience of the theorist. The theorist presumably knows more and different things. But merely a grasp of trivia does not a theorist make. What the theorist does with these trivia is what is important, and valuable to an audience. One thinks in these cases of the classic sociologists, and indeed the classic thinkers at the time of the disciplinary foundings. They knew much more than their followers, and put it together in a distinctive way. The successors knew what they put in their picture, but not the rest of it: what they left out, and what was submerged.

But if the differences in perspective between theorist and consumer of theory are related to this, they have many other aspects. I recall a comment by Jessie Bernard to the effect that she didn't think of the work of people like Durkheim as classics because they were, as she put it, her contemporaries. Theorists tend to treat other theorists who are contemporaries, and some who are not, as rivals, with the same access to the world that they have, but with different comparative advantages—different knowledge and different competencies. For the most part, they know the same sources, or most of them. The function of a canon, for them, is that it ensures that they have some common areas of knowledge with other theorists and, to a much diminished extent, with their audiences.

How different is the level of knowledge? Usually it is very great, for reasons that will become apparent in the final section. But the main reason is this. Originality is hard to come by in social theory. Falling into old errors, in contrast, is difficult to avoid. The basic explanatory forms have all been tried, retried, concealed and retried, and retried again. The problems with the explanations are well known. One can, like Pierre Bourdieu, who was certainly a sophisticated thinker well versed in the classics, invent a new terminology, develop a vast following of people who apply this terminology, and construct an elaborate defense of it, and in the end be outed, as Jon Elster (2010) has done, as just another functionalist.

For the user, this is not a problem. The conventions of article writing in the social sciences demand a theoretical framework and content relevant to it. This convention has been challenged recently in the organizational studies literature, and rightly so. As an editor for years at *Social Studies of Science*, I can attest that the main part of my job is excising the theory sections of the papers I edit. Rarely do they add anything; typically they are muddled. Authors squeal with pain over this because the theory section was the hardest to write and the part of which they are most proud. It is true that the inclusion of "theory" is a useful form of discipline that helps ensure that the material in the paper is relevant to its point. But the content of the theory section normally adds little but confusion. It deserves to be submerged.

The usual issue between theorists and researchers is this: researchers want testable propositions and theorists don't give them any. This reflects a basic difference in aims: the theorist wants coherence; getting it may require making a claim that can be turned into an empirically testable proposition, but there is no need for this to be the case. There is, however, a point of common ground. Explanations in the social sciences often have problems, which we can think of as gaps and as mechanisms that fill those gaps. The usual examples of mechanisms involve correlations that are mysterious or inexplicable. But there are other instances.

A simple example involves a taxonomy, or near taxonomy: Weber's classification of forms of authority, and specifically the form "charisma" ([1922] 1978: 215–16, 241–45). Weber gives a quite elaborate description of the process by which the charismatic figure gains authority by meeting tests, and hints that there might be a biological element to the response to the charismatic figure. But the key relation is a mystery: why does the mere fact of extraordinariness—the quality of the charismatic leader—produce obedience as a response? What does the theorist do with this kind of problem? There is a toolkit, notably the toolkit of rational choice thinking. But this seems to be excluded by the kind of relation involved, which is irrational. There is psychology and cognitive science, too. Nothing exactly matches up to charisma in either domain, but there is a body of psychological management research that tries to measure charisma. As is usual in these cases, the measures reinvent the concept of charisma in a way that has little to do with Weber and does nothing to solve the gap problem.

My solution was this: to find an analogy that could be explicated in rational choice terms and that involved psychology. Certain kinds of decisions produce the feelings that are characteristic of charismatic followership, or similar to them. What did people feel when they committed to Adolf Hitler, or to Martin Luther King Jr.? Certainly they thought that something profound would happen through these people, and that these people had demonstrated through their deeds the extraordinary qualities that would allow extraordinary outcomes to occur. This amounted to inverting the apparent causal relation between emotion and decision: the emotion did not make the decision irrational; rather the emotion was the result of a decision-situation created by the leader that promised great rewards for the great risks of followership, risks mitigated by the presence of other followers whose joining would help ensure the success of the leader.

How would one arrive at this kind of explanation? Basic empathy helps. So does knowledge of the world—in this case the world of gambling. This is not explicit knowledge, but the kind of tacit connection one would call up in thinking through a problem. One knows that basic decisions can be gut wrenching and result in strong commitments to the choice that one makes: that fear and risk are a major component of such decisions, and that leaders are in a position to create and make real these kinds of choices. The situation is familiar—it is not so different from a choice about what gamble to make in a poker game. Putting this into a rational choice framework is merely a way of making this situation more intelligible. And it allows a place for the agency of the charismatic leader in producing the situation, advertently or inadvertently, which fits with Weber's own account.

This is a gain in coherence. A gap has been filled: there is no longer a mystery about why extraordinariness connects to obedience. But it also is a mechanism with empirical implications. The implications are not, alas, the kind of thing a sociologist would be able to test on survey data collected in the General Social Survey or a psychologist with an artificial situation and paper and pencil test. But one could imagine strapping a subject into an fMRI machine (for a specialized brain and body scan) to see whether the brain areas that activated in response to a choice like this given by a leader would include the emotional areas of the brain, the amygdala perhaps, as well as the decision-making areas, and in the appropriate sequence, thus providing some evidence that the causal processes conformed to the explanation. This would require a lot of bridging, too: getting an experimental design, designing the stimuli, excluding alternatives and confounders, and the like. The results would be ambiguous, simply because of the problem of generalizing from an artificial situation. But it would be "empirical" in a stronger sense than anything the General Social Survey or a normal social psychology experiment would allow, if only because it would measure something actually going on in someone's head, rather than inferring something about what is going on there.

There is no guarantee that the mechanisms proposed by the theorist would be testable in this way, and in any case these are all still indirect tests at best. But from the point of view of the theorist, this is not the achievement. The achievement, for the theorist, is this: things hang together that did not hang together before. Whether the account is true or not is a separate question, which may or may not be answerable, though it is answerable "in principle" in some sense. There is no appeal to occult entities or angels (though Weber himself comes dangerously close by failing to explain charisma in other terms and in this way implying that charisma is a real originary power of its own). In a problematic passage in which he speculates that the Mormon Joseph Smith may have been a charlatan rather than genuinely charismatic, he seems to have fallen off this ledge (Weber [1922] 1978: 242).

So how does one come up with this "theory"? First there is the puzzle of following such leaders as Hitler and King: why did people do it? Then there is the taxonomy, which puts them in the category of Napoleon and Jesus. Then there is the problem of the gaps, in this case the question of what makes this work: is it a real power, or something else? One could arrive at this question on one's own, but it helps to have been struggling with Leo Strauss's critique of Weber's passage on Joseph Smith, which appears in a text that sociologists, as distinct from social theorists, would never read: *Natural Right and History* (Strauss 1953: 55), the aim of which was to show that Weber's project of a value free social science is impossible to carry through. Thinking that Strauss is wrong and wishing to disprove his ideas provides a motivation for the theorist: the nagging sense that something deeply wrong about Weber is revealed by this apparent error. Recognizing the force of Strauss's critique does not depend on anything in sociology: Strauss was motivated by a retrograde philosophical argument over the status of natural law. This motivation has nothing to do with conventional sociology, but everything to do with the understanding of the historical Weber.

This kind of theorizing is pure *bricolage*. One could not deal with the problem of the gaps in Weber's account of charisma on the basis of what a graduate student studies in a "theory class." One needs to have read around and to have experienced the world, and to have experienced, in thought, something of the different intellectual traditions that inform experience. This is characteristic of theory at a high level. Again and again, one finds that the major theorists in social science have brought extensive knowledge of something other than the literature of their own nominal disciplines to bear on the problems they address. Claude Lévi-Strauss, for example, the child of an artist, had a strong interest in and knowledge of art, was trained in philosophy, and in his student years and early career was a socialist activist who used ideas borrowed from linguistics (Wilcken 2010). It would be absurd to think that one could say in advance what background would be useful to a theorist. Indeed, it is precisely the variety of available sources that enables the theorist to say something new—together with what Vilfredo Pareto called the instinct for combinations and the relentless nagging of unsolved problems.

Theorists and Their Quarrels

Critique and dispute are the mother's milk of theory. The passions of the theorist are closely connected to this fact. Without the motivation to prove other theorists wrong there would be little motivation to puzzle over a stray passage in Weber about Joseph Smith, or to refute Leo Strauss. In *The World According to Garp*, John Irving (1978: 88–89) tells the story of an American novelist who is living in Vienna trying to motivate his writing. The novelist defines an enemy for himself: the mild-mannered liberal nineteenth-century Austrian novelist Franz Grillparzer, whom he makes into his nemesis as a horrible hack. The thought is not alien to the making of social theory. One needs to be motivated to replace and surpass what is already there. Making a kind of Schmittian friend-foe distinction is a natural step in motivating critique.

But it is also a motivation for taking one's "enemies" seriously. And this is often an important step in a theorist's growth. Defining an enemy is a mark of respect. What is deadly is regarding a theorist as unworthy of the attention required for a serious critique. Theorists are particularly prone to failing to see the innovations in the thought of other theorists—they see them "as contemporaries" as well as people struggling with the same issues, with mostly the same tools. They are likely to see in someone like Bourdieu, as Elster does, the things that make him look like a derivative hack, and to fail to see what excites consumers. If one knows the elements of a construction like Bourdieu's already, one finds it difficult to see what is added by the terminological innovations, which seem to be gimmicks. As to the rest, it is not new, and has, in the words of the computer software business, known problems.

Bourdieu was a synthesizing and system-building thinker, who sought coherence on a much more ambitious level than Meyer and Rowan. And there is another distinction worth noting here. All systems, like the careers of all politicians, end in failure. But as a means of calling attention to one's views, as J. S. Mill noted long ago, creating a system is unparalleled. It forces one's readers either to cease critiquing or to master the details of the system. But this is not the only kind of coherence. It was said of Thorstein Veblen that he thought systematically but wrote unsystematically. There was an older style of German philosophical criticism that evaluated the entire careers of philosophers, and tried to discern an underlying "research intention" behind the many texts that they produced. This made system-builders out of everyone, retrospectively. And there is also a kind of career in which the quest for coherence forces the thinker into revision, and the kind in which dialogue, conversation, critique, and new developments force revision. In his autobiography Edward Shils (2006) records such a life, but in some sense all theory beyond the mundane and synthetic has this character, even if it appears in the form of a system.

This range of forms of "theory"—especially criticism that takes the form of explication—confuses, not to say enrages, conventional social scientists, who see most of it as pointless and repetitive. Editors and readers complain routinely about having to put up with "yet another paper about what Weber meant." But it would be an error to think that one could pick and choose among forms of theory and limit theory to one form, or to those forms of interest to researchers. The reason for this is simple: each of the critical forms serves to discipline the systematic forms and the empirically relevant forms. It is one thing to say that one is testing hypotheses about charisma, and another to do so. Making up a substitute "measurable" concept of charisma and pretending it is the same is not an advance. It is usually a retrogression. But without some actual knowledge of the complex history and reception of the concept one is unlikely to be able to do anything else. To ask "what Weber meant" is merely a disciplined way—disciplined by the need for fidelity to the texts and to history—of asking what basic social science concepts mean. Merton's famous paper on *anomie* (1938) was a clear case of substituting a novel concept of *anomie* for Durkheim's (Besnard 1987). Perhaps it was in some respects an advance. It launched a thousand empirical studies. But if one thought one understood the problems with the concept by merely reading Merton, one would have been deluded.

The favored forms of theory writing are partly a matter of academic conventions, partly of personal preference and capacity. Professors in the German sociological world of the interwar period were experts at inventing systems organized around key concepts—an inheritance of the neo-Kantian conception of "science." Parsons's theory of action was one of the last gasps of this particular style. But one damn system after another was a poor formula for dialogue, and these systems are long forgotten. Some theorists do their best thinking through commentary on other thinkers. And in any case there are lessons to be learned from the thinkers of the past. The fact that Bruno Latour could be bothered to write a brilliant defense and reconstructive analysis of Gabriel Tarde is a case in point (Latour and Lépinay 2009). Tarde indeed provides something missing from actor network theory, namely a way of thinking of actors other than in terms of the model of the rational actor.

I have been assuming that one's capacity to make explicit theory depends in large part on what one knows, what one has available to make mental associations with, what is tacitly there to work with. But what we know depends on what we have read and assimilated, and how it is assimilated. Our acquisition of knowledge is largely based on blind choices, choices, for example, to invest in understanding a thinker whose views we, by definition, do not yet understand; and forced choices, made for us by syllabus and reading list writers, the expectations of editors, and so forth. And there are quite different kinds of engagement with texts. It is one thing to quote Weber as an authority for one's own views, which one imagines to be similar enough for no one to notice the differences, and quite another to engage critically with Weber—to test the coherence of his views at every step, to attend to his critics.

These investments are costly. We are cognitively limited. So we must choose whom to invest in reading, and how to read them. For the non-theorist, the consumer of theory, this is a problem. When what is needed is a simple framework for the presentation of a case study, the wrong kind of theory is not going to be useful. Reading a lot of theory is not going to be helpful either. A fashionable framework, such as Bourdieuvian analysis, actor network theory, or some synthesis like neo-institutionalism is going to serve the purpose. But the theorist needs to be more strategic in his or her choices. And the strategies are going to vary, as are the choices. To gain some comparative advantage it is useful to avoid the herd. But to challenge one's own thinking comprehensively, it is better to engage in detailed explication and critique of thinkers one is not particularly sympathetic toward. And the classics are the most challenging thinkers of all.

Bildung: High Theory and Its Peculiarities

With considerations like these we have already turned to a different question: what makes a theorist? The answer to this question can be given historically, if one looks at paradigmatic theorists and sees what they did that made them the thinkers they were, and what made them unlike the thinkers who do not fit the criteria. Here of course one must make judgments, judgments on which there may be little agreement. But for myself at least, I see some bright lines between levels of "theorists," and at least some indications of what makes a real one.

Let me begin with a story: Friedrich Hayek, at the time of a bitter political controversy over "planning," the method of governance of Stalin and Hitler, and Roosevelt as well, wrote a book on the intellectual genealogy of the planners, *The Counter-Revolution of Science* (Hayek [1955] 1972). The book is a deeply thought-through analysis of such figures as Comte and Saint-Simon. It would be wrong to think of it merely as a critique or polemic, though it is certainly a statement that defines an enemy. Hayek, in fact, took one of his most distinctive ideas from the study of Comte: "spontaneous order." The term is in the title of one of the chapters of Harriet Martineau's great translation, *The Positive Philosophy of Auguste Comte* ([1855] 1896, vol. 2, Chap. V). Hayek's own thought was to focus on this problem, and it was a metaphor that guided him even into his startlingly original thoughts on cognitive science in *Sensory Order: An Inquiry into the Foundations of Theoretical Psychology* (Hayek 1952).

What this illustrates is the value of taking on adversaries with whom one is not only unsympathetic but hostile, and taking their thought with the utmost seriousness. But it also illustrates the need to cross boundaries. Would Hayek have arrived at his ideas on this subject without encountering Comte? Perhaps. Perhaps Comte merely articulated something he had tacitly been groping toward. But reading Comte, becoming acquainted with Comte, and going through the discipline of writing a whole book in which Comte and his line were analyzed in detail enabled Hayek to problematize, in a new way, the issues of the moment in which he was living. He did so by seeing these issues not merely as a practical problem of governance, but as a conflict in social theory itself, between conceptions of how the economy and social life are ordered.

Obviously much of contemporary social theory is conventionally leftist, not to say politically correct. Why even bother to mention Hayek, an antediluvian ideologist of the Right and the founder of the Mount Pelerin Society, the intellectual godfather of neo-liberal economic policy and its extension to social policy, who is not even a credentialed member of the relevant disciplines? The question is of course rhetorical: the answer is "for the same reasons that Hayek took on Comte." Understanding the intellectual genealogy of the present is one of the principal methods that social theorists have. Doing so requires that Hayek be taken as seriously as Hayek took Comte. Hayek took Comte seriously because he took his enemies seriously. And the enemies were ideological: the planners and advocates of planning who, at a certain moment in the history of (especially British) science had generated a powerful argument against liberal democracy in favor of rule by experts and a kind of syndicalism (Bernal 1939; cf. Turner 2008). There were ideological or passionate reasons for this response. But the results were of larger significance, and today it is only the historian who can reconstruct these motives.

What kind of "theory" are we talking about here? Obviously it is something radically unlike what I have called mundane theorizing, and it is unlike the examples of synthesis and system-building I have mentioned, though perhaps closer to system-building. What marks it out, to be not very precise about it, is a willingness, even a compulsion, to take on all comers, or at least those whose thought challenges and provides an alternative to one's own— within, of course, the human practical limits of what one can reasonably read, understand, and reflect on. Almost by definition, someone operating under this compulsion cannot be a disciplinary scholar: the rivals and alternatives are likely to come out of other fields. Nor can the horizon be the present: the most fully articulated alternatives may be in the past. And because the peaks of theory are few, this will almost certainly be the case. Moreover, the genuine alternatives will take the form of similarly full-blooded non-disciplinary thought, aspiring to coherence in more or less the same range of topics. We can call this "theorizing in the large sense." Theorists at this level, not to be confused with the professionally successful theorists, are the ones who are willing to do precisely this—and to do it as a part of a lifelong quest to challenge their own views by grappling with the views of others, whether they are the views of those they think of as with them, or those they think of as enemies. To do this is to grow into something quite different. But what is it that they are growing into, and how?

I should add a consumer warning here. This is not career advice. Career advice would use a different metric of success. And it is perhaps unavoidable, though not especially useful, to make this distinction explicit. The realities of academic careers are simple enough: academic life is clientelistic, and advancement and influence depends on finding friends and followers; it is caste-like in most disciplines, and this is especially true of sociology; opportunities to publish theory are limited, especially in prestigious journals, and reviewing is generally hostile unless one is in a club; stepping outside the boundaries is risky and rarely rewarded; feeding the audience what it wants, and in easily digestible pieces that have the appearance of originality, is the best way to get an audience; violating the norms of political orthodoxy or responding to criticism from those beneath you, violating the norms of caste, is the easiest way to lose one's caste status and the automatic audience that goes with caste membership.

The rules for becoming a public intellectual or intellectual celebrity are different still: no one's career depends on taking you seriously because you have published in the right journals. Luck, good prose, a pleasing enough speaking presence, and a perfect political attunement to audiences, however, help. Plato talked about this kind of speech in the *Republic*, attributing it to the Sophists (Book VI, 493b-c). He said that it

> . . . is just like the case of a man who learns by heart the angers and desires of a great, strong beast he is rearing, how it should be approached and how taken hold of, when—and as a result of what—it becomes most difficult or most gentle, and, particularly, under what conditions it is accustomed to utter its several sounds, and, in turn, what sort of sounds uttered by another make it tame and angry. When he has learned all this from associating and spending time with the beast, he calls it wisdom and, organizing it as an art, turns to teaching. Knowing nothing in truth about which of these convictions and desires is noble, or base, or good, or evil, or just, or unjust, he applies all these names following the great animal's opinions—calling what delights it good and what vexes it bad.

Perhaps this is too harsh. But it is incontrovertible that being a public intellectual requires pandering.

For the rest of us, Weber's message is still relevant: intellectual life now is possible almost exclusively in the form of academic careers. That is unavoidable. But it is still possible to live and work in a way that keeps these demands in perspective, and to read and assimilate what you decide is important, rather than what is decided for you. It is more difficult to produce and publish in this way. But it is not impossible. So let us leave the questions of careers to the careerists. Disciplines are good for one thing at least: discipline. But theorizing in the large sense requires discipline, too. There are many means of self-discipline and external discipline that impinge on the theorist: the most basic is the problem of writing. Making a coherent text out of the jumble of tacit and explicit thought is the basic work of the theorist. But the choices of what to invest in and how to treat what one reads are the conditions for having theoretical ideas in the first place. And these choices are likely to have the greatest impact on one's development as a thinker. They can also go wrong, especially when they are aligned with the demands of careers. Following the herd, or caving in to the demands of journal reviewers, which is the same thing, is the sure road to mediocrity. Even in the domain of the interpretation of texts, originality is hard to come by. The problem is to find the balance that allows one to say something original, make it intelligible to an audience, and to actually reach that audience, which is a condition of conversation and dialogue, and thus further development.

As I have hinted, one of the best means, and perhaps an essential one, is to master the work of a great thinker and to comprehend that of several others. Classical sociology gives us at least two. Weber and Durkheim, as well as at least the specter of Marxism, if not Marx himself. Of the three, Weber is the most challenging: a kind of permanent other to the idea of social theory itself. Raymond Aron, Frank Knight, Hans Kelsen, Talcott Parsons, Edward Shils, and countless others constructed their own systems by reacting to and reformulating Weber. One could not imagine Jürgen Habermas, Carl Schmitt, or indeed the early Frankfurt School, without this great other as a kind of permanent skeptical interlocutor sitting on the theorist's shoulder, like a conscience to struggle with. But to have this kind of relation to Weber requires effort.

To reject Weber, which is perhaps the best discipline for a social theorist, one must understand him. And one must do this on one's own, by reading the texts, puzzling over them, recognizing the way they fit together, and resolving the issues that are produced by other Weberian texts. One needs to have personally acquired knowledge of "what Weber meant," knowledge tested against one's own thinking: to think with to think against, in the Heideggerian phrase. One can of course be helped by the reflections of others. But even the best interpretation will not speak to the full range of your own responses to the original texts. When Habermas works through the texts of Weber, or John McCormick (2007) does, the result is idiosyncratic and personal. But this is not a bad thing, and to some extent it is inevitable: we can understand only on the limited basis of what we already understand. The text is a kind of record of an agonistic engagement—a dialogue. You grow by trying to answer the questions that Weber poses for you. What you reject you must justify against Weber. You must engage in a kind of inner dialogue, a struggle, with Weber. And one must be open to the outcome of this agonistic encounter: one must be willing to be overcome by Weber, or to understand the merits of his views, and reformulate one's own in light of this. It is perhaps unsurprising that many interpreters "go native" on their subjects, recognizing after a struggle the coherence and validity of views they originally came to Weber in order to dispute and reject.

One can strive to overcome this idiosyncratic character, and to write historically and philosophically, from the more general point of view of an imagined audience or from the point of view of the historical context (which one must reconstruct). But one never escapes the limits of one's own knowledge and the limits of what is tacitly available to oneself in thought. These limits, however, are at least in part the limits of circumstance, limits that we can escape by our own choices. We can read more. We can learn other things that illuminate the texts. We can do this consciously or unconsciously. We can gain new angles on the texts simply by being open to topics that we would not have previously recognized as relevant. To learn about mirror neurons is to learn something about empathy that illuminates some of the central passages in Weber, passages that a pre-cognitive science form of psychology did not prepare us to understand. But there is no guide for finding these potential connections, and no method for putting the parts together. Of course, finding gaps in a thinker's reasoning, finding places where concepts no longer apply in the same way or warrant the same inferences, are basic components of critique, and consequently a starting point for the finding of new connections. Learning something new is valuable to the extent that it can be used—critique makes a space in which it can be used.

Grandiosity

It takes a certain amount of nerve or chutzpah to take on a classic. But it takes a certain set of qualities to theorize at all in "the large sense," at the level of, or in common, with the great thinkers. And here there must also be some qualifications. Some theorists do in fact write in a whole range of fields, as Hayek did, and engage in print with thinkers across this range. But others, while they engage with and are deeply influenced by their encounter with these thinkers, say little in print that directly discusses them. There is a gap between reading and writing: a "mundane" theorist in print may be a "theorist in the large sense" in reading and thinking. The wider reading is submerged. In some sense, one's reading must always range more widely than one's writing. There are exceptional figures, such as Michael Polanyi, who seem to have read everywhere and written everywhere, but even for them it is likely that they read in areas where they didn't publish. In the case of a thinker like Shils, who notoriously did "read everything," the range of his writings was relatively small, the range of his opinions large, and his desire to make the opinions hang together and to take on all comers intense. But there are certainly synthetic thinkers in given disciplines, as well as technical appliers of rational choice methods and the like, who do not do theory in the large sense.

Wanting to do theory in the large sense, being caught up in the undeniable romance of thinking with the great thinkers, is something different: it is a desire to think across a large range, though not necessarily to write across it. There is no structured career ladder, or protocol. Nor is apprenticeship very useful. Disciplines give some feedback, but the concerns of disciplines are different. One can say something about who has a vocation for sociology, or organization theory. Perhaps there is something to be said about who has a vocation for theory in the large sense. Weber gave a list of three qualities of the person with a vocation for politics. One could infer a similar list from the comments I have made here.

One can also see a central danger or flaw associated with this kind of theory, which follows from the lack of checkpoints and steps. Samuel Stouffer, on the evidence of his letters of recommendation, was a shrewd judge of character, and one of his terms has stuck with me. He described the social psychologist, methodologist, and science studies thinker (among other things) Donald Campbell, then a graduate student, as "a bit grandiose." This was indeed true—in the best possible way. And it was this quality that enabled Campbell to be a theorist in a field that resisted theory. Campbell as an assistant professor became a friend and dialogue partner of Michael Polanyi. This is something that a less grandiose person would not have bothered with. It was a relationship that benefited both of them. But grandiosity, especially combined with other traits, can be fatal. Vanity is the occupational hazard of academics in the first place. It is the dysfunctional sibling of grandiosity. And while a bit of vanity is probably a useful trait, it can easily careen into something worse, especially when combined with grandiosity. There are endless examples of ambitious thinkers who venture into areas in which they are not technically competent and wind up making fools of themselves. It is a good test of one's competence to "pass" as a member of a different discipline. Michael Polanyi could do this in economics and philosophy—despite having been a physical chemist with a medical degree. Charles Taylor, today, passes in fields as diverse as political theory, philosophy, and religion, as well as sociology, and communes with such equally grand figures as Habermas.

But grandiosity is a dangerous thing. Vanity is one bad thing to combine it with. But there are others. Christian Fleck describes Max Horkheimer's experiences as a powerful figure in New York in the 1940s in these terms:

> Here, the art of networking in terms of arrangements and intrigues, exercised on an almost daily basis, and the contemptuous judgments of others that verge on social denunciation, are bound up with a specific attitude of grandeur and an almost paranoiac suspicion of everyone and everything. After the Holocaust, all this coalesced into a habitus of persecution that made Horkheimer all but unfit to cope with reality, as he was no longer able to assess the true dimensions of the danger. (C. Fleck 2011: 249)

Having a public audience, and a large topic in which it is interested, accelerates one's self-delusion about one's own wisdom and merit, and therefore about who one's enemies are. If vanity is one dysfunctional sibling of grandiosity, paranoia is another.

Some kind of grandiosity is necessary for the budding theorist to break with the limitations of a disciplinary situation and the expectations of others, in order to think originally. But one needs a strong stomach for abuse. Contemptuous denunciation is part and parcel of rivalries and hostilities at this level. One can use them profitably, as a means of intellectual growth, by figuring out what parts of this kind of response to take seriously. Or one can respond by avoidance. It is said that Horkheimer and Adorno decided to return to Germany because of Shils's critique (1954) of *The Authoritarian Personality* (Adorno et al. 1950). If this is true, it represents a failure: the critique went to the heart of issue of the biases and ideological blindness of the text. They would have done better to respond seriously.

If we combine two of these inevitable features of theorizing in the large sense, the cognitive limits of our capacity to absorb and the problem of grandiosity, we can see a real danger, a danger in what is the signature feature of, and constraint on, theorizing in the large sense: our choices of what to absorb are necessarily idiosyncratic. Once a thinker goes beyond a disciplinary canon, the choices become limitless and each thinker will make different ones, live in a different knowledge world, and develop his or her own idiolect. Their peers become foreigners. Because time and attention are limited, they will develop, and indeed must develop, reasons for ignoring what they ignore, as Horkheimer did—wholesale reasons that dismiss whole kinds of philosophy or social science, or whole class and ideological categories. And they will need the grandiosity—or paranoia—to keep believing that what they are doing, this highly idiosyncratic thing, is the right thing. At some point, the feedback they get doesn't help: they are either understood, and not confronted critically, or misunderstood, so that the criticism is misdirected. These are the ingredients for something going badly wrong: a life wasted on the wrong books, the wrong track, and nothing to show for it besides compliments that one pays to oneself, or are paid to you by your admirers, who are, because of the peculiarities of theoretical idiolect, not your peers.

What I have described here is not a business for everyone. But who is it for? Who has a calling for theory in the large sense? We can get a start on an answer to this question if we grasp that the particular strange passions of theorists and their quirks are by-products of the very qualities that mark out the "real" theorist, by which I mean simply the theorist who is engaged at this highest level of theorizing. The three qualities of mind that the theorist must have in order to rise to the level of "beyond ideologist," beyond mundane theorist, beyond synthesizer, and to the level of notional rival to the classic thinkers, are these:

1. Theoretical empathy: The theorist must be able to see the point of other thinkers' theorizing, to understand it from the inside, and to follow the reasoning of others, even when and indeed especially when this reasoning fails. For the social theorist, always skirting the boundary with ideology itself, there is perhaps even more: unless one can grasp the passionate foundation of ideological thinking, of such things as class rage or the sense of fury at the overweening self-regard of the

masters of the nanny state, one cannot understand one's peers and rivals.

2. Sensitivity to inferential gaps in the thinking of others and to the failure of concepts to apply. The users of theory are engaged in mastering a vocabulary and applying it. The theorist looks at this process from the other end: inventing a vocabulary when the old one doesn't apply. To put this brutally, theory, as opposed to dogma, depends on a shrewd sense of when a theory or core concept, such as "modernity," no longer applies. Usually this is not a matter of a failure of the main concepts of the theory. It is normally the folk concepts of the social world the theorist shares with the audience for theory, or the concepts that constitute the subject matter, that lose their grip. We notice, for example, that terms like "obligation" have disappeared from the normal speech of non-academics and non-lawyers, and recognize that this means there is trouble with a picture of the social world that assumes a social order made up of these things. The moment when our concepts no longer fit the relevant facts, or support the relevant inferences, is the moment at which discovery and problematization become possible. Similarly for inferential gaps: a concept like "socialization" is a black box that no one knew how to open up, or saw any need to open. But when cognitive science and child development studies show how it can be done, what was a black box becomes a gap: a part of the theory that needs to be filled in with something more than a conventional term with no content. The theorist is someone who is always sensitive to the fact that the floor might disappear from under any of his concepts, and must be able to respond by stepping back and rethinking. Without this sensitivity, theory collapses into a form of systematic theology, as it did for the last half of the career of Talcott Parsons.

3. Ruthlessness in criticism: Theorizing promises one thing first and foremost, gains in coherence, whether it is through the building of systems or the making of connections between different domains or lines of reasoning in order to strengthen both. The underside of this is false gains in coherence. When a solution is neat, one must still ask whether it has been purchased by fraud, whether the new concepts that make something cohere are bogus and produce only apparent coherence. The same ruthlessness applies to the received tradition, which is full of puzzling ideas that may on inspection turn out to

be empty. But most important, the ruthlessness of criticism must be applied to one's own views. Indeed, a life in theory is a life of giving up, qualifying, and abandoning one's starting points, beliefs, and convictions.

These qualities are of course shared with other intellectual pursuits, though perhaps not quite in this combination. But they are not those of a mundane theorist or synthesizer. One can be perfectly good at these kinds of theorizing without exercising any of these traits very often, or in combination. Conventions of correct form and vocabulary can be a guide. And one can be a good empirical researcher without exercising any of them, other than a kind of "criticism" for failing to accord with the conventions one has been taught. The theorist in the large sense cannot leave these qualities aside, ever. They are the motive force for what one does, the source of the irritants that compel the quest for coherence itself.

Living this life makes the theorist an oddity, and the theorist into a person with some very odd relations with peers and rivals. The theorist needs to be respectful of rivals and peers, in order to have the theoretical empathy necessary to understand them in the first place, and at the same time to have a kind of casual contempt for them and their works, in order to motivate the thinking up of alternatives. Descent into paranoia and megalomania, in the manner of Horkheimer, or of Talcott Parsons, is an extreme form of this contempt, uncorrected by theoretical empathy for one's rivals and enemies. But there are many other instances in which megalomania or vanity has combined with a dismissive response to any criticism. Some of this resulted from oversensitivity to criticism. The defensiveness and intellectual closure, combined with extravagant praise of one's diminished circle of allies, that one finds in Merton's letters, especially after 1968, makes for painful reading, more painful when compared to Merton at his undeniably brilliant best as the ruthless critic of Mannheim (Merton [1941] 1968). Yet Merton had respect for the people he regarded as theorists, even those he considered his enemies, and drew a sharp line between theorists and what they do and empirical researchers and what they do. Stephen Cole recalls Merton telling him the following:

> Steve, how many people are capable of doing empirical tests; hundreds or thousands? How many people are capable of devising theory—only a handful. Testing this theory would not be a worthwhile expenditure of my

time [implicit: it might be a worthwhile expenditure of your time because you could not write theoretical papers like I can]. (Merton quoted by Cole 2004: 835)

The vanity goes with the territory. In the case of Merton, perhaps it was justified. But there is another side of this as well: Merton's recognition and acknowledgment of others as theorists, including those he disagreed with or had nothing in common with. This is the "handful." He had, in fact, a warm correspondence with some who would normally be regarded as his opposites, such as Bourdieu, and was routinely a reference for Karl Polanyi as he applied for fellowships, and for Kurt Wolff in the early part of his career. And he had a wary knowledge and grudging respect for others he assumed were his critics and enemies. This is characteristic: theorists know one another as theorists, and not only when they are friends, but also when they despise each other. And they know also that despising has to go along with responding to criticism and to the implicit criticism posed by an alternative view, even if the "response" is simply to find a reason to dismiss it that is never articulated, much less published.

Weber ended his vocation lectures with words, not quite of discouragement, but of sobriety and disenchantment. There is plenty of disenchantment in the life of theory. It is illustrative that as chair of a theory prize committee one year, I was unable, without diplomatic intervention, to get a majority of the committee members to declare a single one, out of a dozen or so theory books (all published by prominent presses and almost all by prominent authors), "minimally acceptable." The seeker after personal validation, needless to say, will get nothing here. Rejection is the norm. Misinterpretation is the common fate. The paranoia of Horkheimer, the rages of Gouldner, the megalomania of Parsons, the vanity of others too numerous to mention, and the risk of falling into an abyss of eccentricity are everpresent dangers. The unending challenges and contestation that is the lot of theory make this an unappetizing life for most people. But for the person with the right qualities, in the right balance, the pleasures of making things fit together outweigh all of this.

7   The Counterfactual Imagination

Roland Paulsen

> Thinking means venturing beyond.
> —*Ernst Bloch*

IN THE RECURRING DEBATES ON EMPIRICISM IN SOCIAL SCIENCE, two types of human activity—both practiced on a daily basis by all and sundry—have continually been juxtaposed and differentiated from each other: *theorizing* and *observing*. Which activity should come first? Do the two presuppose each other? Is there a danger in having too much of one or the other? Particularly inflamed is the question of social science's relation to axiological neutrality. From Comte onward, positivist and functionalist currents have insisted on equating the study of society with the study of nature. In Comte's formulation of the discipline, sociology should be no less exact than natural science. Comte also believed that the doctrines of sociology should be imposed on the population by the state (in a so-called "sociocracy") with the purpose of eliminating the "anarchy of opinions" and guaranteeing "resignation" to the invariability of social laws (see Gane 2006: 6ff; Marcuse 1941: 340ff; S. Turner 2007). Whether or not there are any social laws, how sociology affects patterns of behavior, and if sociologists have any responsibility to intervene and question our ways of living remain central issues that tend to come to life whenever it is felt that the discipline must be reinvigorated. As from the 1970s, "the crisis of sociology" has been attributed both to its politicization (see Cole 2001; Horowitz 1993) and to its lack of political relevance (see Burawoy 2005; Gouldner 1970).

Although the distinction between theorizing and observing is easy to make analytically, in practice the two often intertwine. In this chapter, the reader is offered several examples related to a cognitive phenomenon known as *counterfactual thinking*. Swedberg mentions counterfactuals as a useful "heuristic device to construct an explanation" (2012: 27). For instance, to determine the importance of a historical event one might counterfactually imagine what would have happened if it never had taken place. In this way the factual state of affairs—"what is" or "what has been"—can be questioned, defamiliarized, evaluated, and analyzed more imaginatively than when only theorizing from the available facts. I argue that we all know how to do this. In fact, the reader might even have counterfactual thoughts at this very moment (e.g., "instead of reading this text, I could/should/might just as well do *x*"). I also argue that that there are social phenomena, notably different types of emotions, causal events, and power, that will go unnoticed unless we use our counterfactual imagination.

This text derives its raison d'être from the fact that even if we all have the capacity to think in counterfactual terms, this capacity can and needs to be developed and refined. For instance, it is a well-known phenomenon that people, particularly after traumatic life events, get caught in counterfactual thought loops (e.g., "if it were not for x, y would not have happened," or "if only I had done z to prevent w"), where only a fraction of the relevant counterfactuals are considered (see Byrne 2005: 14). The same mistake can also occur when theorizing social or historical events.

A typical example was provided when a car bomb detonated in Oslo on July 22, 2011, killing eight people. On the same day, leading terror experts in Scandinavia publicly offered their explanations of why this was an Islamic attack on the Western world. Several observations were presented to back up their theory: some persons with connections to al Qaeda had recently been identified in Norway; Norwegian Muslims were indignant about the Muhammad caricatures published in Denmark; the Taliban movement wanted revenge for Norway's involvement in Afghanistan. Before it became known that the bomb was part of a terror attack by a Norwegian ultranationalist who, including the subsequent gun rampage, managed to assassinate seventy-seven people, the speculations circulating in mass media almost exclusively emanated from the counterfactual that this was a case of Islamic terrorism (see Sandvik and Aune 2011). Why could the "experts" not imagine other alternatives?

In political debates, we often see a similar lack of imagination. Take the employment issue: right-wing commentators argue that cutting taxes will create more jobs; left-wing commentators argue that public spending will create jobs. The arguments for each strategy abound, but they all point toward the same counterfactual ideal: a society with endless economic growth, in which all (who can) work eight hours a day or more. Is there no alternative?

What I propose is not only that the counterfactual imagination is desirable when theorizing the social; if we want to produce more than pure descriptions or sheets of data, it is quite unavoidable. Social scientists often use counterfactuals without reflecting on their decision to do so. In this chapter, I offer five examples of counterfactuals that are of particular importance at different stages of the theorizing process. I also suggest how they might be used more imaginatively. Starting with the concept of *everyday counterfactuals* and some findings in cognitive psychology, I demonstrate how counterfactuals are part of everyday life and why social life is impossible to understand unless we take into account the practice of contrasting facts with counterfactuals. I then move on to develop Swedberg's notion of counterfactuality as an explanatory device and how counterfactuals influence our view on the contingency of history. *Historical counterfactuals* help us discern the significance of historical events and the causal links that bind them together. I argue that "what could be"—the unobservable and yet utterly present dimension of human existence—may sometimes be hard to distinguish from the observable "what is" when studying certain social phenomena. A clear example is the use of *power counterfactuals*. To be able to observe power at all, one must imagine how those subject to power would behave differently if it were not for the exercise of power. I also give two examples of how the counterfactual dimension plays a crucial role in the initial phase of the theorizing process when we decide what to theorize. When we define a social problem of a certain kind, we also imagine that it could be otherwise. Social scientists can be very involved in providing solutions to problems—solutions that remain counterfactual until implemented. *Instrumental counterfactuals* are solutions that leave the dominating power structures unaltered. *Utopian counterfactuals* are solutions that challenge the dominating power structures.

Everyday Counterfactuals

With reference to Weber, Durkheim, and Tocqueville, Swedberg argues that "empirical data should drive the theorizing process" and that this fact-oriented way of theorizing makes sociological theorizing different from the purely philosophical (Swedberg 2012: 9). But how can we decide *which facts* are worth dwelling on? Mills's ambition to "translate personal troubles into public issues" is a valuable guideline (Mills [1959] 2000: 187). In this section I provide a brief account of the role of counterfactuals in our conception of the first part of Mills's formula: "personal troubles."

In daily life, facts that people find the most enervating are often the ones that allow them to imagine *counterfactual alternatives* to reality—i.e., "what could have been" or "what could be." This "Not-Yet" of Bloch ([1959] 1986), or "negation" of Hegelians such as Marcuse ([1968] 2009) has over the past three decades been subject to experimental study in cognitive psychology. "If only . . . " scenarios have been proved to play a key part in everyday life. They emerge at a young age (usually 3 to 4 years); they have been observed in most cultures, and during some periods of life may seem irresistible and occupy most of our thoughts. In *The Rational Imagination*, Byrne argues not only that counterfactuality is more central to cognition than what cognitive scientists have earlier supposed, but also that the counterfactual imagination has a rationality of its own, an interpersonal logic that has been observed in many experiments: "One of the more surprising aspects of the counterfactual imagination is that there are remarkable similarities in what everyone imagines" (Byrne 2005: 3).

The experiments usually confront the respondents with a scenario that leads to a certain outcome while instructing them to think about how things could have been different. A typical example is offered in Girroto et al. (1991), where the scenario is about a Mr. Bianchi who, on his way home from work, is delayed by a tree trunk on the road, which leads him to take a detour during which he decides to have a beer in a bar. When he arrives home, Mr. Bianchi finds his wife suffering a heart attack on the floor. He tries to help her, but it is too late. In the months that follow he is haunted by counterfactual "if only . . . " mutations. When respondents were asked what they believed he would regret the most (e.g., not leaving work earlier, the falling tree, going to the bar), most answered that Mr. Bianchi would say, "If only I had not stopped for that beer." This example supports the rule that counterfactual thoughts are more likely to concern *controllable actions* rather than uncontrollable events.

Another characteristic of counterfactual thinking is the tendency to mentally mute *actions* rather than inactions in cases of both bad and good outcomes (Landman 1987). In response to Comte's fear about an "anarchy of opinions," it might also be added that people tend to keep in mind *few* counterfactual thoughts rather than the infinite plethora of imaginable alternatives

(Byrne 2005: 22ff). Even more important observations have been made about what people do *not* imagine. "Miracle counterfactuals," such as "if only Mr. Bianchi had had wings," are almost unheard of. Likewise, people do not go beyond natural laws when they consider alternative outcomes; they do not say, e.g., "if there had not been gravity the tree would not have fallen over the road" (McMullen and Markman 2002).

Everyday counterfactual thoughts tend to *focus on the possible*, things that might have happened or might still happen. In a replication of the scenario with Mr. Bianchi and his dying wife, respondents were confronted with different scenarios in which the delay was due to Mr. Bianchi's checking in on his aging parents to see if they were well, buying a newspaper, or stopping for a hamburger. Whereas only 12 percent of the participants imagined an alternative to visiting his parents, 22 percent focused on his decision to stop for a burger (McCloy and Byrne 2000). Counterfactual thoughts are thus immersed in *ethical considerations*.

The counterfactual imagination is a reality without which social life would be impossible to understand. Many of our most fundamental emotions, such as regret, guilt, shame, relief, hope, and anticipation, are counterfactual emotions. They originate from unactualized possibilities—and yet they are undeniably there. In this sense, even from a phenomenological standpoint, it might be argued that the "possible worlds" of Lewis—i.e., "entities that might be called 'ways things could have been'"(1973: 91)—are just as real as the actual world; sometimes they might even appear more real. As Sartre ([1960] 2004), Bloch ([1959] 1986), Marcuse (1941), and others have argued, the human being is first and foremost a creature that projects itself into potentiality. In sociology, however, this directedness tends to be ignored. As Skjervheim contends, "the dominating sociological portrayal of man is 'man without transcendence,'" a man "subordinated to social facticity" (1971: 59). As we shall see, there are, even so, important exceptions.

Historical Counterfactuals

The most frequently recurring form of counterfactual in social science is indisputably the historical counterfactual—i.e., the retrospective consideration of *what could have been*. In *Unmaking the West*, Tetlock et al. (2006) apply some of the psychological observations already mentioned to their own profession: individuals cannot live without counterfactual thought experiments, and neither can historians. The explanatory power of counterfactuals has been widely acknowledged, even by marked empiricists such as Popper (see Ferguson 1999: 80). In Swedberg's words, "the very notion of explanation is closely linked to the idea of counterfactuals, since there can be no explanation without the existence of a change to some initial stage, be it actual or theoretical" (Swedberg 2012: 27).[1] The notion of causality involves at least two assumptions: (1) that x caused y, and (2) that y would not have happened if it were not for x (with other things the same). If we can imagine y without x, the impact of x on y must be reassessed.[2] Accordingly, the counterfactual scenario of what might have happened if Bismarck had decided not to go into war tells us, as Weber ([1922] 1949: 164) says, "what causal *significance* is properly to be attributed to this individual decision in the context of the totality of infinitely numerous 'factors.'"

Weber early recognized the centrality of historical counterfactuals (he used the term "objective possibility") to historical analysis. "If history is to be raised above the mere chronicle of notable events and personalities," he wrote, "it has no alternative but to pose such questions" (Weber [1922] 1949: 164). Before any of the psychological studies referred to above were conducted, Weber also pointed out that counterfactuals are part of everyday life. A "temperamental young mother," tired of the mischief of her child, might decide to give "it a solid cuff" (this is the example he gives) and then, "sicklied o'er with the pale cast of thought," ponder whether she would have done the same thing if the antecedent quarrel with the cook had never occurred (ibid.: 177). The scientist asks the same type of questions, with the difference that the action must be interpreted from the outside since it rarely is part of one's subjective experience.

Weber notes that causation and objective possibility mostly have been treated by jurists, particularly by jurists specializing in criminal law. Although "anthropocentrically" oriented—i.e., centered on the objective possibilities of the *individual*, the causal significance of human action lies at the heart of penal guilt. The complex task of reconstructing the intent of the offender demands that we look into the objective possibilities at the time the crime was committed, and evaluate, with regard to ethical values, "the *subjectively* conditioned capacity of foresight into the effects" (Weber [1922] 1949: 169). In historical analysis, guilt and subjective intentions are not our main focus; there is a historical *interest*—different from the interests in causality of the judge, the physician, the artist—that helps the historian to discriminate between relevant and irrelevant facts, Weber argues. The historian is interested in the "general significance" of Caesar's death, the political effects and possibly structural issues that preceded it, not "in the details of the event—unless they are important either for the 'particular characteristic features' of Caesar or for the 'characteristic features' of the party situation in Rome" (ibid.: 170).

Long before other historians formulated the problem, Weber here offers helpful instructions on how to identify historically relevant counterfactuals among the infinity of objective possibilities that each moment represents. In his widely read *What Is History?*, Carr criticizes the "unhistorical" tendency to let the "imagination run riot on all the more agreeable things that might have happened," and in the attempt to "get rid of this red herring once and for all," Carr argues that it risks reducing history to mere speculation in trivialities. His main example is the Pascalian counterfactual relating to Cleopatra's nose: had Antony not been so bewildered by Cleopatra's nose, he might have kept his nerve at the Battle of Actium. Does this mean that historians should consider whether Cleopatra's nose caused the downfall of ancient Egypt and changed the course of history (Carr 1962: 98)?[3] In Weber's words, the possible effects of Cleopatra's nose must be regarded as a "chance causality," completely inaccessible to our knowledge in the same way that we cannot know how the exact shaking of a dice box will affect the number of eyes we throw. "We are justified," as Weber puts it, "in asserting that the physical style of the thrower has no influence *'stateable in a rule'* on the chances of tossing a certain number of eyes" (Weber [1922] 1949: 182). Weber's rule of thumb when we assess the causal significance of a historical fact is whether its counterfactual modification requires us to imagine a different chain of events: "in the event of the exclusion of that fact from the complex of the factors which are taken into account as co-determinants, or in the event of its modification in a certain direction, could the course of events, in accordance with general empirical rules, have taken a direction in any way different in any features which would be decisive for our interests?" (ibid.: 180). The answer can only be formulated in terms of probability, Weber says. Even though we reject the naturalistic notion of hard determinism we can never know what impact so-called butterfly effects might have on history, but since the available facts surrounding the Battle of Actium would not have to be modified in the counterfactual world where Cleopatra's nose was shorter, it seems *improbable* that Cleopatra's nose caused the defeat of Egypt.[4]

Besides helping us understand causal links between events, historical counterfactuals may also reveal the contingency of the past that often is lost in hindsight. According to Tawney, much of our naturalization of the past is due to the dominant form of history writing: "Historians give an appearance of inevitableness to an existing order by dragging into prominence the forces which have triumphed and thrusting into the background those which they have swallowed up" (Tawney [1912] 1967: 177). This tendency has not only been observed among historians. In a classic experiment on hindsight bias, Fischhoff (1975) told random participants about the Indian battles between the Gurkhas and the British. One set of participants was told that the Gurkhas had won, another that the British had won, and a third set was told nothing about the outcome. The participants who thought they were informed about the correct outcome were not only convinced that "their" outcome was more plausible; they also stated that they knew the (false) outcome even before participating in the experiment—an effect that Fischhoff calls "creeping determinism" (Fischhoff 1975: 297). Hence, what we understand as facts about the past may deeply affect how we perceive it and effectively bias what we once thought was probable and even possible. This is a well-replicated phenomenon and also a well-documented one. As Tetlock et al. comment: "Few in the early 1980s predicted the rise of the East Asian 'tigers' or the collapse of the Soviet Union, yet virtually everyone today who claims professional competence in such matters can muster half a dozen 'fundamental' or 'structural' causes why these outcomes had to happen roughly when and how they did" (Tetlock et al. 2006: 25).

Historical counterfactuals can and have been used with the explicit ambition to question the impact of the anonymous "forces of history" and to stress the contingency of the past (that nothing is predetermined). Yet it has been a very criticized type of theorizing. Carr, again, calls the reflection on these "might-have-beens of history" a mere "parlour game" (Carr 1962: 97), and he goes on to state: "History is, by and large, a record of what people did, not of what they failed to do: to this extent it is inevitably a success story" (ibid.: 126). Another example of the reluctance to historical counterfactuals can be found in Thompson's *The Poverty of Theory*, where the "counterfactual fictions," among a range of other theoretical notions from "the sociological section," are deemed "*Geschichtenscheissenschlopff*, unhistorical shit" (Thompson [1978] 1995: 145). The fact that so many historical counterfactuals have been presented just to produce humorous effects, or to demonstrate the author's capacity of wishful thinking, has probably contributed to the unscientific aura of counterfactuals in the field of history. According to Hawthorn, "most historians and social scientists, if they have considered counterfactuals at all, have done so only nervously, in asides" (Hawthorn 1991: 4). But even among the critics of counterfactual theorizing, historical counterfactuals have not been avoided in the conduct of actual historical analysis.[5]

While some have questioned the contingency or "arbitrariness" of history that counterfactuals presume, others associate counterfactual thinking with the neglect of individual agency. In *The Explanation of Social Action*, Martin offers an interesting critique of what he calls "third-person" explanations— theories that ignore or even distort first-person accounts while claiming to tell the "real truth." According to Martin, these explanations now dominate social science: "Social science rejects the possibility of building on first-person explanations because, to be blunt, it distrusts persons and their cognitions" (Martin 2011: 23). Although this is still a relevant critique of most social science (particularly of the "Freudo-Durkheimian" *von oben*-orientations), I cannot see why the use of historical counterfactuals must lead to this type of scholarly arrogance (cf. ibid.: 32–73). Martin confuses the use of counterfactuals in the context of discovery (when we use them to discern facts that we think should be further studied) with their use in the context of justification (when counterfactuals take the place of empirical research and laws of mechanical causality are assumed to be more important than individual motives (see Chapter 1 in this volume). The argument that focus on causality tends to obscure how motivation is at the core of social action has no clear link to counterfactual theorizing as such. Motives are often analyzed counterfactually, and there is nothing in the counterfactual as such that must result in reducing people's "*own* answers" to "rationalizations, justifications and so on" (Martin 2011: 72).

Here, it should be recognized that counterfactuals can be used very differently in relation to empirics. Among historians who are explicit in their use of counterfactuals, it has even been argued that for counterfactuals to have any value, they must somehow be empirically grounded. According to Ferguson, historians "should consider as plausible or probable *only those alternatives which we can show on the basis of contemporary evidence that contemporaries actually considered*" (Ferguson 1999: 86). In addition to Weber's criterion of plausibility *on the basis of* accessible empirics, Ferguson says that "we can only legitimately consider those hypothetical scenarios which contemporaries not only considered, but also committed to paper (or some other form of record) which has survived—and which has been identified as a valid source by historians" (ibid.: 87). This documentation criterion would yield even more to "observation" as Swedberg (2012: 9) uses the term, but it would also leave out the mass of thoughts unwritten and then forgotten.

Other methodologists argue that we can evaluate historical counterfactuals on more theoretical grounds based on clarity, logical consistency, historical consistency, theoretical consistency, and projectability (see Mahoney 2004: 92). Historical counterfactuals may also be useful beyond all empirical criteria. Lebow, for instance, advances the case for what he calls "miracle counterfactuals" with the following example: "If the population of the southern Sudan were Caucasian and Christian, would the West have intervened earlier or more effectively?" According to Lebow: "Miracle counterfactuals help us work through moral and scholarly problems" (Lebow 2007: 161). Here the utility of the counterfactual is more a question of pedagogical effectiveness than of empirical relevance. I would say that merely posing the question is of little use if we aspire to more than provocation.[6] Lebow's counterfactual could easily be backed up by comparing the case of Sudan with other instances of civil war where the population was "Caucasian" and Christian. All this, however, including Ferguson's search for documented counterfactuals, takes place in the sphere of justification. To be able to study and evaluate counterfactuals empirically, we must first discover them—i.e., *theorize*.

As we shall see, counterfactual theorizing in sociology can never be driven to such an extreme as in history. The popularity of historical counterfactuals as a fictional genre would be difficult to achieve for their sociological counterpart since the narrative aspect of sociological counterfactuals is very different. On the other hand, sociological counterfactuals are not restricted to yesterday's "what could have been"; they may also include existing institutions and "what can still become" of the future.

Power Counterfactuals

Just as some of our emotions emanate from counterfactuality, power can only be understood in the light of repressed counterfactuals. In *Power — A Radical View*, Lukes makes the following point: "Any attribution of the exercise of power . . . always implies a relevant counterfactual to the effect that (but for *A*, or but for *A* together with any other sufficient conditions) *B* would otherwise have done, let us say, *b*" (Lukes 2005: 44). Accordingly, *observing* the exercise of power requires the capability to imagine the counterfactual alternatives (*b*) that are prevented. Lukes criticizes sociological research that focuses too much on observable conflict and in some cases even makes it a defining characteristic of power. Observable conflict is only the tip of the iceberg, Lukes argues, and it is up to the sociologist's imagination to discover the "relevant counterfactual" in cases where the conflict is either hidden or latent. If we accept Luke's "third dimension" of power—the assumption that power may manipulate what we want while leading us astray from our real interests—it may indeed become "extraordinarily difficult to justify the relevant counterfactual" (ibid.: 49). This work, however, takes place in the context of justification and involves both empirical evidence and value-based arguments. Discovering whether there might be any hidden power to prove is a matter of counterfactual theorizing.

What cognitive psychologists call "upward" or "better-world" counterfactuals are subject to reflection and reasoning. Unlike in experimental psychology, the sociological study of power may reveal relevant counterfactuals that until then were unthought of. The perception of *relative deprivation*, the discrepancy between that which is and that which could and should be, has mainly been studied as an alien mechanism of the psyche, as a dangerous motor force for collective violence that seems to follow certain rules (cf. Gurr 1970). Likewise, the opposite phenomenon of "adaptive preference formation" or "sour grapes" has by its main theorist been ascribed "a strictly endogenous causality" (Elster 1996: 116)—a trick of the mind. Given Elster's definition of the term, this may very well be, but in his critique of Lukes and the assumption that rulers have the power to induce certain beliefs and desires in their subjects, Elster argues something more, namely that the intentional manipulation of thoughts and needs is impossible and that resignation and conformity are "essentially by-products" (Elster 1983: 116). In response to Elster, Lukes points out that power does not always have to take the form of deliberate intervention. Power relations can be unintended and even unconscious to both the "subjects" and the "rulers." But this does not rule out the possibility that resignation can be intentionally induced (Lukes 2005: 136).

The "exogenous" view of resignation defended by Lukes leaves open for sociological intervention an analysis of power relations in which the conflict is unobservable or veiled in formal consensus. Even if this, as Lukes argues, "is inherently controversial and involves taking sides in moral and political controversies" (Lukes 2005: 111), it is necessary for any critical study of power. This also counts for the intimately related illumination of relative deprivations. Since Davies's (1962) hypothesis of the "J-curve," a number of not-so-surprising correlations between counterfactual thinking and feelings of relative deprivation have been recognized in social psychology. For instance, we know that the perceived normality of a certain event, and whether people consider this event fair to them as individuals rather than as members of a certain group, tends to reduce counterfactual thoughts and thus social resentment (Olson and Roese 2002). However, as theorizing sociologists we are able to problematize concepts such as "normality," "fairness" and "group." We can *encourage* "upward counterfactuals"— i.e., thoughts about how the situation could have been better, not just different; it is within the range of our discipline to unveil the *fait accompli* and to question the supposed sourness of grapes (not to mention the alleged sweetness of lemons). The so-called "Tocqueville effect," that "social frustration increases as social conditions improve," appears, just like the related J-curve theory, to promote a historicist view of why people revolt. But it should be noted that Tocqueville also formulated his theory as follows: "the inevitable evil that one bears patiently seems unbearable as soon as one *conceives the idea* of removing it" (in Swedberg 2009: 260, emphasis added). He also distinguished *hope* as the crucial (and quite exogenous) mechanism involved in social change. Both hope and ideas of removing "the inevitable evil" can be generated and nurtured by good sociology.

Instrumental Counterfactuals

I now turn to two distinct ways of engaging in counterfactual theorizing of the critical type described above. I call one of them "instrumental" and the other one "utopian." The utopian approach that Erik Olin Wright has put forward may be regarded as a reaction to empiricist sociology. "[W]hat is pragmatically possible is not fixed independently of our imaginations, but itself shaped by our visions," Wright (2010: 6) writes. As many have argued, these visions are, however, remarkably missing from contemporary sociology. "The suppression of normativity and utopianism in sociology is, arguably, due to this quest for respectability through recognition as a science," Levitas (2010: 538) writes. In an answer to a harsh review of Wright's *Envisioning Real Utopias*, Burawoy (2011) similarly argues: "These days, social scientists are concerned with what is, perhaps with that has been, but very rarely with what could be."

In a strict sense, this last assertion, which comes close to what I am trying to say here, deserves some elementary remarks. As I mentioned earlier, counterfactuals appear in most historical accounts as explanatory thought experiments. These do not have to be motivated by ambitions to pursue critical analysis; "what could be" is not necessarily a radical concept, or even a political one. However, even critical counterfactuals are not that rare anymore. In an early critique of empiricist sociology, Marcuse argues that "the elimination of transitive meaning has remained a feature of empirical sociology" ([1964] 2008: 117). Even if that was true in the 1960s, it certainly is not today. A major part of sociology might very well have been instrumentalized to "social technology" (see Carleheden 1998), but even in the administrative evaluations of policy sociologists, there usually are some suggestions of how things might be changed for the better—i.e., an account "beyond descriptive reference to particular facts," as Marcuse puts it ([1964] 2008: 109). It might also be argued that even in the most descriptive statistics of, say, criminality, there is a "hidden 'it should be otherwise'" of the same type that Adorno (1980: 194) attributes to "even the most sublimated work of art." But the difference between instrumental counterfactuals and utopian counterfactuals is that whereas utopian counterfactuals oppose the dominating power structures as such, instrumental counterfactuals "*appeal* to the powerful," as Mills ([1959] 2000: 193) phrases it; in other words, they conform to instrumental rationality.

Instrumental counterfactuals have been fiercely debated, but under different names. They are at the core of what Rancière calls *la police*, the consensus-oriented form of "symbolizing the common" in which the community is represented as "an ensemble of well-defined parts, places and functions," as opposed to *le politique*, which denotes the antagonistic representations of this very common, "not a quarrel over which solutions to apply to a situation but a dispute over the situation itself" (Rancière 2010: 6). Before Rancière introduced the concept of "post-politics," Marcuse captured its essence in *One-Dimensional Society*, where "the therapeutic character" of modern politics is criticized on similar grounds. Marcuse also extended this critique to the type of sociological "operationalism" in which "conceptual thought is methodically placed into the service of exploring and improving the existing social conditions, within the framework of the existing societal institutions—in industrial sociology, motivation research, marketing and public opinion studies" (Marcuse [1964] 2008: 10). Of course, neither industrial sociology nor any of the other subdisciplinary specializations of sociology mentioned in the quote has to be therapeutic in Marcuse's sense, but the argument certainly extrapolates to "the applied sociology of the research technician" criticized by Mills ([1959] 2000: 76), and to the "policy sociology" defined by Burawoy as "sociology in the service of a goal defined by a client" (Burawoy 2005: 9).

While Burawoy argues that there is a "reciprocal interdependence" of policy sociology and his other types of sociology, others still adhere to the Marcusian critique. Echoing Rancière, Graeber (2004: 9) contends that "policy' is the negation of politics; policy is by definition something concocted by some form of elite, which presumes it knows better than others how their affairs are to be conducted." Although instrumental counterfactuals leave this elite unchallenged, they may often be wrapped in radical rhetoric. This is particularly true for identity politics, in which the counterfactual imagination is limited to the benefaction of separate social groups. "It is a good cause to be working with gay rights," as Chomsky (2009) puts it, "but even if gays had hundred percent rights, the institutional structure of oppression, the core of it, would remain unchanged." This does not mean, however, that instrumental counterfactuals are of no use or should be avoided when theorizing.

Utopian Counterfactuals

If it is true, as Elster (1996: 116) argues, that "what brings about the resignation—if we are dealing with sour grapes—is that it is good for the subjects," then it is also true that well-founded utopian counterfactuals have the capacity to make these grapes seem less sour. In her article on H. G. Wells and the institutional development of early British sociology, Levitas (2010: 530) gives a lively account of Wells's ambitions as a sociologist and "the implications of a hundred yeas of suppression of utopianism and normativity within the discipline." Wells, who besides his literary accomplishments was a deeply engaged sociologist and even aspired to the London School of Economics Chair of Sociology, believed utopian counterfactuals to be intrinsic to the practice of sociology. In *The So-Called Science of Sociology*, he asserts: "There is no such thing in sociology as dispassionately considering what *is*, without considering what is *intended to be* . . . Sociologists cannot help making Utopias; though they avoid the word, though they deny the very idea with passion, their very silences shape a Utopia" (in ibid.: 537).[7]

Sympathetic to this idea, Levitas argues that utopian sociology is not primarily about realizing whatever utopia one chooses to address, but more of a perspective that improves observation. With reference to Bloch, she argues that future possibilities are always present and must therefore be included in the representation of that which is. "Some commentators would say that utopias are *always* primarily about the present" (Levitas 2010: 542). This has also been suggested by Gorz: "It is the function of utopias, in the sense the term has assumed in the work of Ernst Bloch or Paul Ricoeur, to provide us with the distance from the existing state of affairs which allows us to judge what we *are* doing in the light of what we *could* or *should* do" (Gorz 1999: 113).[8]

A counterfactual that might illustrate this point is the ideal speech situation of Habermas. Even though there is empirical evidence of forums that come close to this ideal (see Habermas 1989), it is essentially an ideal to seek guidance from rather than to achieve: "in theoretical, practical, and explicative discourse . . . the participants have to start from the (often counterfactual) presupposition that the conditions for an ideal speech situation are satisfied to a sufficient degree of approximation," Habermas (1984: 42) says. Without this particular counterfactual in our mind it would, in other words, be impossible to engage in understanding-oriented interaction, according to Habermas. As Power puts it, the ideal speech situation has a "reconstructive-transcendental" dimension and a "critical-reflective" dimension: "the former argues for the counterfactual conditions of possibility of knowledge practices, while the latter seeks to anchor these conditions within an understanding of actual social and institutional structures" (Power 1996: 1006).[9]

It is important to note that opening up sociology for utopian counterfactuals does not necessarily imply any disregard for facts. In *Counterfactuals*, Lewis provocatively admits that he believes that "there are [counterfactual] worlds where physics is different from the physics of our world, but none where logic and arithmetic are different from the logic and arithmetic of our world" (Lewis 1973: 88). Along with Swedberg, I take the view that whereas philosophers can theorize exclusively in their minds, e.g., concentrating on logical counterfactuals as in the case of Lewis, and historians can construct miracle counterfactuals to understand causal links between events of the past, sociologists cannot leave the empirical facts behind (cf. Swedberg 2010: 7).[10] Just as everyday counterfactuals tend to be grounded in actual experience, utopian counterfactuals must be based on facts. In *The Principle of Hope*, Bloch partly defines hope as the emotion that "will not tolerate a dog's life which feels itself only passively thrown into What Is" (Bloch [1959] 1986: 3). He sees hope as an essential ingredient of everyone's life, not least in the form of daydreams of which one part is "just stale, even enervating escapism, even booty for swindlers, but another part is provocative, is not content just to accept the bad which exists, does not accept renunciation" (ibid.). Emanating from wishful thinking and other forms of everyday counterfactuals, hope must be *educated*, Bloch asserts. He discerns four "layers of the category possibility." From the "formally possible," which completely disregards the given reality and reflects the predicaments of Thomas More, Fourier, and Saint-Simon, he gradually makes it to "the dialectically possible" in which there is a firm relationship to reality that gives the counterfactual enough weight to oppose the actual and expose the possibilities that can be found in the concrete historical situation (ibid.: 223ff).

In *Envisioning Real Utopias*, Wright (2010) gives more tangible guidelines for evaluating utopian counterfactuals. When developing, using, and criticizing counterfactual "alternatives," one might evaluate them according to three different criteria: desirability, viability, and achievability. While the desirability criterion raises normative questions, the questions of viability and achievability are particularly apt to sociological theorizing, where the counterfactual imagination must be anchored in the available empirics. Wright gives a number of examples of which type of empirics to make use of: on the issue of direct democracy he describes the system of participatory budgeting developed in Porto Alegre; on the issue of workplace democracy and worker-owned co-operatives, he gives the example of Mondragón in the Basque region of Spain. These micro-scale utopias can provide rich information about problems that are likely to occur if any of the ideals were to be realized. But they are also likely to encourage the imaginations of both sociologists and non-sociologists to make use of utopian counterfactuals. When outcomes "almost occur," when we miss a plane by some minutes, or when a basketball team loses on the last shot, winning the game and boarding the plane become much more salient comparisons that intensify the resentment (Kahneman and Varey 1990). It is not hard to imagine that the utopian seeds Wright writes about may have the same effect. They are, in other words, not substitutes for the counterfactual imagination, but tools for it. From Mondragón we can learn how a worker co-operative functioned during a particular historical period (from 1956 to today) in a particular geographic area (starting in the Basque region and then spreading throughout the country), but we cannot learn how this type of co-operative would work among other co-operatives of the same type, in another time, in different industries, or in other parts of the world. For this, counterfactual theorizing will still be required.

"The dialectically possible" of Bloch points beyond mere facts. As Reed suggests, the "discovery of utopian possibility would be stronger if it was informed not only by fact, but also by some sort of explanation" (Reed 2011: 87), which in its turn would demand what Reed calls an "interpretative epistemic mode" in which "the primary focus of the investigator is on the arrangements of signification and representation, the layers of social meaning, that shape human experience" (ibid.: 10). At this point, however, we have moved to the sphere of justification where the utopian counterfactual is *emerging* from our analysis rather than *initiating* it. What I suggest here is somewhat less ambitious, namely that we spend time thinking (and reading) about utopian counterfactuals and how societal institutions should and could develop. Instead of letting taken-for-granted notions of "good society" influence our paths into research, such reflection would help us theorize more autonomously and ask questions that are politically relevant and perhaps even new.

Conclusion

Among the available tools for sociological theorizing, I have elaborated on the use of counterfactuals. The counterfactual imagination is part of everyday life. Everyone who can think also uses counterfactuals. These counterfactuals are not necessarily groundless: they tend to follow regular patterns; they have a rationality of their own. Counterfactuals can be of explanatory use, as in the field of history when one imagines what would have happened if a certain event had never taken place. In sociological theorizing, they can also be of critical use in addressing present conditions and power structures.

Theorizing critically means that "upward counterfactuals" are of particular value. Instead of just asking "What if?" the question that really interests us is: "Would it be better if?" Two things should be noted about this question: First, whether consciously or not, it is frequently used in sociological theorizing. In any study of oppressive power, this question has been posed somewhere along the road (usually at the beginning). To be able to observe power we must imagine how the oppressed part would have behaved differently if it were not for the exercise of power. If it can be assumed that there would be no difference, then it is reasonable to deduce that there is no power relation. Second, the question "Would it be better if?" can be educated. "Better" may refer to a situation in which a certain power structure remains unchanged or is even strengthened (as in the case of instrumental counterfactuals); it may also refer to the subversion of power structures (utopian counterfactuals). How far into counterfactuality one should go depends on normative judgment and the available facts (especially positive examples and how transferable they are).

As Swedberg (2012: 18) points out, theorizing is a skill that needs training. It is also a reflexive activity. The counterfactuals involved in any theorizing should be recognized and actively evaluated. It could be argued that this would be superfluous in a strictly analytic study, but since counterfactuality—not to mention intentionality—is part of social reality, excluding it from the analysis will make it unempirical. Not considering counterfactuals is also an ideological move. According to Skjervheim, all social analysis can serve either to negate the existing states of affairs or to legitimize them (Skjervheim 1971: 56). To negate them is not always preferable—Hitler also had his unrealized dreams. The Stoics, Spinoza, and some Buddhist currents would perhaps argue that it never is. But then one should be conscious of why relevant counterfactuals have been excluded from the analysis, and able to defend the decision. Most often counterfactuals are excluded without comment, as if doing so were the most natural thing in the world. A typical example, presented by Marcuse in *One-Dimensional Man*, is how "democracy" should be analytically defined. As soon as we restrict the criteria to the empirically observable (that there should be at least two competing candidates and that the competition should pervade the entire constituency, that the election should be free and preceded by vigorous efforts from both parties to win, that there should be formal freedom of speech, equality before the law, etc.), we become unable to judge the given state of affairs from a point of view other than that of the given state of affairs. Consequently "the analysis is 'locked'; the range of judgment is confined within a context of facts that excludes judging the context in which the facts are made, man-made, and in which their meaning, function, and development are determined" (Marcuse [1964] 2008: 119). The exclusion of counterfactual criteria means that there is no competing ideal that may urge existing institutions to develop and refine themselves.

By the same token, it may ultimately be argued that counterfactual theorizing is an indispensable part of democratic society. Mills contends that the first requirement of publics and parties for a fully democratic society is that "within them ideas and alternatives of social life are truly debated" (Mills [1959] 2000: 190). Theorizing sociologists cannot do the work for others, but they can encourage people to take part. Learning how to think, Swedberg (2011: 15) asserts, should be part of the educational system, as a foundation for the democratic process and as a tool for individuals in their own struggle with personal troubles. In these days, when "it is easier to imagine the end of the world than to imagine the end of capitalism" (Jameson 2003: 76), we are in desperate need of well-grounded counterfactuals. In *Capitalist Realism: Is There No Alternative?*, Fisher remarks that precisely because our imagination currently suffers a crisis, "even glimmers of alternative political and economic possibilities can have a disproportionately great effect" (Fisher 2009: 80). The promise of an imaginative sociology—with the capacity to spark the imagination of the public—can only be grasped in counterfactual terms.

8 The Work of Theorizing

Karl E. Weick

Concepts are a magnificent sketch map for showing us [that] our bearings can never fitly supersede perception.
—*William James (1996: 100)*

LTHOUGH THE NAME TALCOTT PARSONS IS PRACTICALLY SYNON-
ymous with theory (e.g., "Toward a General *Theory* of Action"),
Parsons made an effort to articulate the work of theorizing itself. The Carnegie Corporation, which funded his "Theory Project," kept asking Parsons,
"How do you make theory happen?" and "What procedures do you use to
produce your 'results"? Parsons's straightforward answer was that the group's
procedures were "essentially those of cogitation in relation to many types and
fields of empirical knowledge. The cogitation was partly individual, in the
solitude of the study, partly *a deux* in prolonged and intimate discussions,
partly in informal groups of two, three, or four, and partly in formal meetings
of eight to fifteen persons ... The relevant individuals 'racked their brains' as
best they could and attempted to mobilize their empirical knowledge in relation to the theoretical problems" (Isaac 2010: 304).

Parsons tried to make the activity of theorizing more tangible by describing it as an "event" similar to fieldwork during which tables and diagrams
were created in order to "reify the occurrence of theory" (Isaac 2010: 305).
He described theorizing using a strategic rhetoric of "breakthroughs," unexpected results, happenings, and advances (Isaac 2010: 309). And the product
of theorizing was described as a tool to accumulate and organize data (e.g.,
the five dichotomies of the pattern-variable scheme could be applied to any
kind of action [Isaac 2010: 307]). What is noteworthy in Parsons's discussions
is that he doesn't confuse the achievement (theory) with the working itself

(theorizing). The importance of this distinction has been argued by Gilbert Ryle (1979): seeing is a result reached, whereas peering and scrutinizing is the work; judgment is a result, pondering is the work; imagination is the achievement, conjecturing and supposal and guessing are the work.

Parsons's description, crafted in the late 1940s, can be viewed in the context of the other chapters in the current volume. Do those chapters suggest that Parsons's portrait of theorizing is dated, inapplicable to current work, misleading? Not especially. The connotations of "cogitating" and "racking one's brain" are certainly wide ranging, but they include many of the basics that are presumed in most of the chapters, basics such as pondering, relating to empirical knowledge, talking to oneself and others, and problem solving.

I want to reflect in more detail on why the phrase "racking one's brain" is an apt description for theorizing. "Racking" is an appropriate descriptor because it preserves the effortful struggles in theorizing between such dualities as variation and retention, living forward while understanding backward, perception and conception, and concreteness and abstraction. My intent is to make the process of theorizing more explicit so that the tensions created by these dualities can be preserved and managed rather than simplified away. I suggest that the management rather than the dismissal of tensions generated during the process of theorizing helps people create theories that are fuller explanations of everyday life and more prescient (Corley and Gioia 2011).

To develop the argument, I initially provide an informal understanding of "racking one's brain," embed that in Kierkegaard's well-known aphorism about understanding, and exemplify both using a sample of John Steinbeck's reflections on his expedition to the Sea of Cortez. Following this introduction, I discuss the dualities mentioned above and conclude with suggestions for theorizing that manage rather than dismiss the field of tensions inherent in theory work.

Theorizing as Racking One's Brain

In an earlier work I suggested that the process of theorizing embodies "disciplined imagination" (Weick 1989). My touchstone then was the idea that theorizing is a mini-evolutionary system of conceptual trial and error that unfolds in a manner analogous to artificial selection. The phrase "disciplined imagination" preserves some of the tension that is present during theorizing, but its connotations have remained undeveloped. The discussion in 1989 was built around the importance of heterogeneous thought trials, the diagnostic value of the reaction "That's interesting" (Davis 1971), and the possibility that the discovery of something "interesting" reveals weakly held assumptions that may have biased what people thought they saw earlier. The reaction "That's interesting" reveals these biases, and altering them may lead us to see differently. Imagination was treated as an activity that occurs when "we order and collect immediate sense impressions into objects and ideas that we understand, which have meaning beyond mere physical stimuli. We form in our minds a picture of reality that is capable of repeating complex relationships actually existing in the world" (Engell 1981: 120).

My intent then, as it is now, was to argue that theory cannot be improved until we improve the theorizing process, and we cannot improve the theorizing process until we describe it more explicitly and operate it more self-consciously (Weick 1989: 516). The earlier image of artificial selection involving thought trials made the work of theorizing more visible, but only in a rather general way. Furthermore, the importance of language was neglected. Both then and now my intent was also to write in the "spirit" of Parsons, since "disciplined imagination" is simply another way to describe "racking one's brain."

Informally, "to rack one's brain" is to think deeply with sustained effort in ways that may spill over into emotional discomfort. These connotations have their origin in a medieval torture device called the rack. People were tied to a rack by their arms and legs. The limbs were then steadily pulled until they tore away from the body. Initially, the word "rack" was used widely to indicate all sorts of things that produced anguish, pain, and stress. It is generally agreed that the first recorded use of "rack" to refer to brains is in William Beveridge's Sermon XXII delivered circa 1680. The relevant passage reads, "When we have as much as we at first desired, we are but where we were, our minds being no more satisfied than they were before, but rather much less . . . And hence it is that men take so much pains, and undergo so much trouble for this world; *they rack their brains*, they perplex their mind, they break their sleep, they tire their bodies, they hazard their lives for it . . . [and would] rather "lose their souls" than not gain what they desire of this world" (Beveridge 1862: 412–13).

To portray theorizing as "the anguish of the theorist" may sound awfully melodramatic, but there is a grain of truth to that phrase. Theorizing is an activity that involves "monstrous abridgements, but each is an equivalent for some partial aspect of the full perceptual reality" (James 1996: 96). As abridging increases during theorizing, and moves farther and farther from perceptual reality, the tension created by opposing pulls between the concrete and the abstract often grow stronger and more discomforting.

Theorizing as Reciprocal Tension between Living Forward and Understanding Backward

A significant source of tension lies in Kierkegaard's description of life as something that is lived looking forward and understood looking backward. "It is quite true what philosophy says; that life must be understood backwards. But then one forgets the other principle: that it must be lived forwards. Which principle, the more one thinks it through, ends exactly with the thought that temporal life can never properly be understood precisely because I can at no instant find complete rest in which to adopt a position: backwards" (Kierkegaard 1843, Journal IV A, cited in Cohen and Cohen 1954). A similar description is often found in other discussions of human struggles. For example, William James (1975: 107) says, "[W]e have to live to-day by what truth we can get to-day, and be ready to-morrow to call it falsehood . . . When new experiences lead to retrospective judgments, using the past tense, what these judgments utter *was* true, even tho [sic] no past thinker had been led there." Clifford Geertz comments on the gap this way: "The after-the-fact, ex post, life-trailing nature of consciousness generally— occurrence first, formulation later on—appears in anthropology as a continual effort to devise systems of discourse that can keep up, more or less, with what, perhaps, is going on" (Geertz 1995: 19).

Living forward is a blend of thrownness, making do, faith, presumptions, routines, expectations, alertness, and actions, all of which may amount to something, although we seldom know what that something will be until it's too late to do much about it. Unsettled, emergent, and contingent living forward contrasts sharply with our backward-oriented theoretical propositions that depict that living as settled, causally connected, and coherent after-the-fact. Productive theorizing to deal with this tension lies in work that narrows the gap between, in Heidegger's words, the ready-to-hand stance of the actor and the present-at-hand stance of the detached spectator.

Heidegger's (1962) terminology depicting three modes of engagement is especially helpful in maintaining awareness of the tension between forward living and backward understanding. The basic idea is that the starting point in any investigation should not be the assumption that people are detached, contemplative, and theoretical, but rather that they are involved, concerned, and practical (Stenner 1998: 61). People engaged in practical activity are concerned with projects and action in context, and their concerns shift as their needs shift. What practical activity does *not* consist of is a separation between subject and object. Instead, it consists of "absorbed coping," which Heidegger describes as a *ready-to-hand* mode of engagement. When people act in this engaged mode, they are aware of the world holistically as a network of interrelated projects, possible tasks, and "thwarted potentialities" (Packer 1985: 1083) rather than as an arrangement of discrete physical objects such as tools. Equipment is known by its uses and the way it fits into the world (e.g., there is hammering, not a hammer).

If an ongoing project is interrupted, then experience changes into an *unready-to-hand* mode. Problematic aspects of the situation that produced the interruption stand out in the manner of a figure-ground organization, but people still do not become aware of context-free objects. "Particular aspects of the whole situation stand out but only against a background provided by the project we are engaged in and the interests and involvements guiding it" (Packer 1985: 1084).

The third mode of engagement, which again involves a shift of experience, is *present-at-hand*. This mode occurs when people step back from their involvement in a project and reflect on it using analyses that are general and abstract and context-free. It is not until this stage that tools, artifacts, and objects emerge as independent entities, removed from tasks, endowed with distinct measurable properties of mass and weight, that are manipulated by distinct subjects. This is the mode of theoretical reflection, which is important in the present context because of Heidegger's (1962: 99) claim that "the ready-to-hand is not grasped theoretically at all." It is that disturbing possibility that lies at the core of the present analysis.

If we tie Heidegger's distinctions back to Kierkegaard's concern over living forward and understanding backward, then Kierkegaard's concern could be restated thusly: philosophers may be right that life is understood using present-to-hand images, but what they forget is that these images are supposed to explain ready-to-hand living. The potential for better theorizing lies in closer scrutiny of those moments where backward and forward views meet, namely, unready-to-hand moments. These are moments when practitioners are interrupted and discover relevancies that had been invisible up to that point. And these same unready-to-hand moments are opportunities for theorists to get a richer glimpse of what those ongoing practitioner projects were and what their relevancies looked like to engaged people.

A good example of managing the forward-backward tensions of theorizing is found in John Steinbeck's reflections on his empirical work with Ed Ricketts in *Sea of Cortez*. One such reflection involved a fish called the Mexican Sierra (Steinbeck and Ricketts 1941: 2–3).

> The Mexican Sierra has 17 plus 15 plus 9 spines in the dorsal fin. These can easily be counted. But if the sierra strikes hard on the line so that our hands are burned, if the fish sounds and nearly escapes and finally comes in over the rail, his colors pulsing and his tail beating the air, a whole new relational externality has come into being—an entity which is more than the sum of the fish plus the fisherman. The only way to count the spines of the sierra unaffected by the second relational reality is to sit in a laboratory, open an evil-smelling jar, remove a stiff colorless fish from the formalin solution, count the spines, and write the truth. . . . There you have recorded a reality which cannot be assailed—probably the least important reality concerning either the fish or yourself. It is good to know what you are doing. The man with his pickled fish has set down one truth and recorded in his experience many lies. The fish is not that color, that texture, that dead, nor does he smell that way. (Steinbeck and Ricketts 1941: 2–3)

Steinbeck does not so much dismiss spine counting as put it in perspective. What Steinbeck suggests is that it's good to know the degree of abridging that occurs between spine counting backwards and fishing forward. It is certainly true that a spine count provides one truth that "cannot be assailed." The same can be said more generally for denotations that strip away associations.[1] But equally true, denotations that cannot be assailed may also be some of the "least important realities." A spine count is not a falsehood, but it is a severe abridgment of lived experience. To gain access to Steinbeck's "more important realities" is to re-examine the way theorizing moves between perception and conception.

Theorizing as Reciprocal Tension
between Perception and Conception

Consider the perceptual flux that we start with. "Perceptual flux . . . means nothing . . . [I]t is always a much-at-once, and contains innumerable aspects and characters which conception can pick out, isolate, and thereafter always intend. It shows durations, intensity, complexity or simplicity, interestingness, excitingness, pleasantness or their opposites. Data from all our sense enter into it . . . " (James 1996: 49). William James continues and in doing so pinpoints an activity that is central to racking one's brain. "The intellectual life of man consists almost wholly in his *substitution* of a conceptual order for the perceptual order in which his experience originally comes" (James 1996: 49–51). When we substitute a conceptual order for the flux of experience, the experience becomes less than the sum of its parts.[2] The flux "tends to fill itself with emphases, and these salient parts become *identified* and *fixed* and *abstracted* so that experience now flows as if shot through with adjectives and nouns and prepositions and conjunctions" (James 1987: 783, emphasis added). Think of the perceptual order as living forward and the conceptual order as understanding backwards.

Substituting can be visualized by means of the metaphor of a sieve:

> The result of the thoughts' operating on the data given to sense is to transform the order in which experience *comes* into an entirely different order, that of the *conceived* world . . . The conceptual scheme is a sort of sieve in which we try to gather up the world's contents. Most facts and relations fall through its meshes, being either too subtle or insignificant to be fixed in any conception. But whenever a physical reality is caught and identified as the same with something already conceived, it remains on the sieve, and all the predicates and relations of the conception with which it is identified become its predicates and relations too; it is subjected to the sieve's network, in other words. (James 1981: 455)

During the activity of theorizing people may change the mesh of the sieve, recapture facts and relations that fall through, be sensitive to the subtle, doubt the insignificance of what has fallen through, and rethink the predicates and relations that comprise the mesh.

Theorizing as Reciprocal Tension between Concrete and Abstract

Although "substituting" is an apt general description of what theorists do when they theorize, the artist Robert Irwin provides a more detailed description of the changes that are involved in substituting. He suggests that the changes involve six stages: perception, conception, form, formful, formal, and formalized.[3] The progression "is not so much temporal progression as a phenomenological one. At any given moment, for any given individual, all six stages are operating simultaneously, and yet the earlier phases exist prior to the later ones in the sense that they ground them, they constitute the source out of which the more compound stages emerge" (Weschler 1982: 183). These stages differentiate and make more explicit specific changes that occur when, as James put it, concepts are substituted for perceptions. The stages also make the nature of racking one's brain more explicit.

Keep in mind that these substitutions are activities of imagination in tension with diffuse perceptual flux. This may seem like an odd positioning of imagination in the process of theorizing. Recall, however, the earlier description that imagination occurs when "we order and collect immediate sense impressions into objects and ideas that we understand, which have meaning beyond mere physical stimuli. We form in our minds a picture of reality that is capable of repeating complex relationships actually existing in the world" (Engell 1981: 120).

As abstractions compound, each step of compounding involves an active condensation of a previous perceptual whole. As Irwin puts it, "Wortz's law applies, as a complement to the gestalt conception of the world: 'Each new whole is *less* than the sum of its parts'" (Irwin 2011: 172). Each new re-presentation of an earlier level involves a complete transformation in all dimensions, which means the new form is never the same as the one that previously existed (Irwin 1977: 26). Each new whole is built by dropping details of experience. The six stages and five "transformations" involved in moving from one stage to another are briefly summarized as follows.

The first stage, *perception*, is described as "an originary pre-mediated perceptual field." Perception is treated as tactile, shifting, and dependent on non-objective factors such as presumptions and intentions (Irwin 2011:

181). Perception is the field across which thinking lays designs. In this pre-abstraction stage, "It is as if all of our senses were collectively running their hands over the world . . . [P]eople know the sky's blueness even before they know it as 'blue' or 'sky' (Irwin 2011: 170). We saw a similar "originary" starting point earlier in William James's description of "perceptual flux."

Undifferentiated perception begins to take on meaning in Irwin's second stage, *conception*, where people, still privately and individually, isolate *unnamed* zones of focus. Rather than register wholes, the emphasis now is on punctuation and on molding experience "into a systematic experience of cognizance." In this stage of abstraction individuals transform tactile flux into pictures, symbols, and perspectives. This is intuitive thinking, a byproduct of which is differentiation of an "I" that conceives from an earlier "being" that perceived. In other words, identity begins to emerge at the stage of conception.

In the third stage, *form*, these unnamed zones of focus begin to be named, and earlier individual perception now assumes a more public character. This is the stage of labeling. "Nounmaking is necessary for human sensemaking" (Bakken and Hernes 2006: 3). Mental forms are re-presented in physical form as things (objects), actions (behavioral form), and symbols (language form). Now people distinguish and name objects and place them into action. There is a change from private access to public access along with some surrender of the unique, idiosyncratic experience. Irwin calls this loss of information "active condensation" (Irwin 1977: 26). In stage 3, privately accessed subjective impressions are transformed into publicly accessed objective impressions. It is this stage where Wallace Stevens's description of opposed pulls between connotation and denotation in words and languages is especially salient.[4]

In the fourth stage, which Irwin calls *formful*, the named things are deployed relationally and are arranged in terms of dimensions like hot-cool, loud-soft, up-down. People begin to search for evidence of consistencies in performance (Irwin 1977: 27). They begin to measure and compare, which means that they begin to develop an expectation of what is usual, what can be compared with what, and what judgment means. With consistency come norms and standards. And with standards come abstractions in the form of principles, routines, and rules of procedure.

In Irwin's first four stages there is some fluidity in the process of abstracting. People still are able to reverse, redo, and relabel the abstractions they have in hand. This fluidity protects against committing Whitehead's fallacy of misplaced concreteness: "This fallacy consists in neglecting the degree of abstraction involved when an actual entity is considered merely/ so far as it exemplifies certain categories of thought. There are aspects of actualities which are simply *ignored* as long as we restrict thought to these categories" (Whitehead 1979: 7–8, emphasis added). This is the message of the Mexican Sierra floating in formalin. Don't freeze actual situations and occasions, "the throbbing life of work, relations and emotions" (Hernes 2007: 40).

In the fifth stage, which Irwin labels *formal,* patterns of relations begin to harden and become reified into uncontestable entities. For example, the form-ful relation of up-down now gets reified into the more formal relationship of superior to subordinate, master to slave, ruler to ruled. In the formal stage, abstractions are objectified with specified boundaries. Irwin describes the for-mal stage as, in one sense, the most productive stage. At this stage criteria for valid thinking become articulated, and logic as correct inference begins to be balanced against and separated from reason. We reason but we don't logic; we use logic. "Reason is the processing of our interface with our own subjective being. The inductive source of reason is self, the deductive source of reason is world presence. Logic is the processing of our interface with our objective constructs, our social being. The inductive source of logic is its axioms, the deductive source is its boundaries" (adapted from Irwin 2011: 176).

Irwin describes the sixth and final stage, *formalism,* as "objective form rei-fied into transcendent *truth* . . . [B]efore we know it we find ourselves attend-ing to the schema rather than to that which it is a schema of" (Irwin 2011: 177, emphasis in original). At this stage of abstraction, predicates become uncontestable and are misread as the nature of the object itself. Categories of thought and analysis are treated "as if they were real substance. Human beings living in and through structures become structures living in and through human beings" (Irwin 2011: 179). Hindsight associated with Kierkeg-aard's understanding backwards could be inadvertent formalization.

For our purposes, what is attractive about Irwin's thinking is that it marks off explicit degrees of abstracting, renders theorizing more controllable, and implies the value of more deliberate self-conscious work within each layer.[5]

Theorizing as Testing a Substitution

Before discussing implications of the ideas mentioned, we examine briefly an example that incorporates many of the distinctions mentioned so far. In the archives of Houghton library at Harvard University is William James's own annotated copy of his two-volume masterpiece *Principles of Psychology*. Between pages 1130 and 1131 is a slip of paper with a note that is not in James's handwriting. The note is signed by Russell T. Greene '96, who was a graduate student at the time the note was written.

Here's what the note says. "The following incident occurred to the knowledge of my brother who is with the Forbes Lithographic company in whose factory it transpired. The foreman of the works at Chelsea was showing some ladies a machine which he said had recently cut off a finger of one of the operators. He described somewhat carefully just how the accident had happened. The story had such an effect on one of the ladies that she could not resist the impulse to thrust in her finger which was immediately cut off."[6] One is reminded of Erving Goffman's (1974: 30) statement that "we can tolerate the unexplained, but not the inexplicable." That's where theorists come in.

The chapter subheading on page 1131 where the note was inserted reads "Ideo-Motor action." The basic notion is that "human actions are initiated by nothing other than the idea of the sensory *consequences* that typically result from them" (Stock and Stock 2004: 176, emphasis added). James phrases the notion in the form of a question: "Is the bare idea of a movement's sensible *effects* its sufficient mental cue, or must there be an additional mental antecedent, in the shape of a fiat, decision, consent, volitional mandate, or other synonymous phenomenon of consciousness, before the movement can follow?" After reviewing the evidence, James concluded that an idea issues directly in an act when there is *"the absence of any conflicting notion in the mind.* Either there is nothing else at all in the mind or what is there does not conflict" (James 1987: 1132, emphasis added)

When perceptions and conceptions are joined, the tension of theorizing becomes evident. We see some of this tension when James connects the note with the idea of ideo-motor action. This connecting involves the combination of a cue [the note], a frame [ideo-motor theory], and a connection [at least in the mind of James]. This threefold structure is the root act of connecting when people try to make sense of puzzles (Weick 1995: 110).[7] This moment of theorizing can also be interpreted as an explicit effort to avoid what Kant warned against, namely, perception that is blind because it is isolated from conception and conception that is empty because it is isolated from perception. The note could have been inserted between any two pages in the 1295 pages of the *Principles* book with potentially quite different interpretations of what the note seemed to contain and which ideas seemed more or less useful to understand it.

We also see part of the tension between perception and conception when we realize how little we know about the incident itself. As the note seems to indicate, the foreman who conducted the tour described the actions and consequences of the accident in detail. What does "detail" mean here, and what was the context (e.g., noise) of the tour? Assume that he did describe the details clearly. Those details should be fresh in the minds of the women. This freshness calls into question the abstract condition that there is an "*absence* of any conflicting notion in mind." The question becomes, "*What* was fresh in the woman's mind? To work on issues such as these is to give the past its present. To do this is to rack one's brain and to work from the more *formal* ideo-motor theory toward Irwin's *formful* relations, *forms* encased in public words, and *concepts* that focus attention (e.g., the content of the foreman's talk, the consequences envisioned).

All of these activities that move from highly abridged abstractions toward those that are less abridged tend to follow one of Irwin's favorite maxims, Paul Valery's statement that "seeing is forgetting the name of the thing seen" (Weschler 1982: 180). The naming that transforms originary seeing into consensual seeing (e.g., ideo-motor) may introduce order into social life, at least life among theorists. But the conceptions that accomplish this often come to "mean something wholly independent of their origins" (Irwin 1977: 25). It is this potential for theories to become divorced from their origins that predisposes authors toward theories that contribute little to understanding. That's why the preservation and management of tensions seems crucial. Compounding may be inevitable, but it need not conceal its origins.

Implications for the Practice of Theorizing

The preceding discussion of moments and processes in the construction of theory has been articulated in an effort to help theorists be more deliberate, more thoughtful, and more aware of what is occurring as they move from the concrete to the abstract, from the particular to the general. I adopted Parsons's homely image of "racking one's brain" because that activity seems to be missing from some of the more dispensable theories. Theorizing is tough. And it is even more difficult when the processes associated with cumulative, reciprocal work are invisible and non-recurrent. John Dewey was aware of this when he argued that the opposite of theory was not practice, but fancy. "[F]lights of fancy and inventions of the imagination are not theories. A theory in a particular case is simply a thoroughgoing analysis of it . . . The alternative to theory as 'thoroughgoing analysis' is not practice, but sentimentality, instinct, authority, laziness, stupidity, or, perhaps more positively, flight of fancy. That there is practice that relies on such substitutes for thoroughgoing analysis, however, is a notorious fact" (Hickman 1990: 112). The shortcoming of this description is that Dewey should have said "analyzing" rather than "analysis" to reflect that the process is ongoing. The full-length book *Sea of Cortez* (Steinbeck and Ricketts 1941) is an example of more thorough analyzing because it includes marine biology, ecology, evolution, anatomy, synthesis, and conjecture.

If nothing more, "compounded abstraction" is a reminder of how we lose contact as we formalize, how editing is inevitable, how we can control the speed of the progression among stages, how abstract forms may be reversible, how we can discover at least the possibility that "it could be other" (i.e., a different whole). Awareness of what we are doing can also allow us to alter the sequence of theorizing (e.g., we start with stage 4, then move to stage 2, and then to stage 3; i.e., we first explicate relations and then draw boundaries and search for descriptive labels).

If we use Irwin as a template to guide the work of theorizing, then we are more likely to register more of the experience. Labels are more nuanced, differentiated, creative, contextually embedded and abridge less as we move from stage 2 to stage 3. Stage 4 may involve a fair amount of RE-connecting that was momentarily lost in the discreteness created by labels in stage 3. The prescriptive counsel is, slow down when you get to stages 3 and 4. Retrace your steps. You already have imposed considerable discipline by these stages.

By now it may seem like the sole message of this essay is, leave nothing out. Every move away from perception while theorizing seems to raise a red flag. And the farther one moves from perception the greater the danger and, oddly enough, the more insignificant the product. Thus, theorizing and description seem to be synonymous. To describe, however, is to condense, and theorists and non-theorists alike confront that reality. To theorize is to be more conscious of your abridging and more deliberate in its deployment. What did you partition? What did your nouns, relations, logic, reason, and truths leave out? Would earlier changes alter subsequent abstractions and abridgements?

The continuing pull of fuller description creates a significant source of tension in theorizing. If, as Kierkegaard contends, we understand backwards then we need to give back to the past its present. The rationale for doing so was articulated by the Australian anthropologist and historian Greg Dening.

> To give back to the past its present is to slough off certainties and to *imagine* people looking at possibilities. We are comfortable in our view of the past. The past happened in a totally particular way in space and time. That is its realism. All the possibilities of what might have happened are reduced to one. The energies of historical enquirers are focused on discovering what that one possibility was. But by that we have not re-presented the past. To do that we have to enter into the experience of those actors in the past who, like us, experience a present as if all the possibilities are still there. If a historian's ambition is to describe how people actually experienced their lives, then that historian has to slough off many certainties. To give back to the past its present, one has to be a little humble about what one can know. (Dening 1996: xv–xvi, emphasis added)

The picture of theorizing that has been created so far suggests several tactics that theorists can employ. A sample is listed below:

1. To gauge progress in theorizing, keep working to increase the present meaning of lived experience. To increase present meaning is to multiply sensed distinctions and extend significance.

2. Mobilize empirical knowledge in relation to the theoretical problems as Parsons tried to do.

3. The reaction "That's interesting" is a clue that weakly held assumptions have been disconfirmed, and that the assumptions in question may have created blind spots in previous trial-and-error conceptualizing.

4. Having accepted that you abridge perceptual reality when you theorize, invoke James's assessment and ask yourself, are those abridgments "monstrous" given what you started with? That's a subjective assessment. But so too is the abridging.

5. In your efforts to theorize about "temporal life," accept that you'll always be behind. As Geertz (1995: 19) put it, consciousness is life-trailing "occurrence first, formulation later on," which means that theorizing is "a continual effort to devise systems of discourse that can keep up, more or less, with what, perhaps, is going on." Theorizing is

about conceptual substitutes that keep up, which suggests that process imagery, gerunds, recurrent cycles, feedback loops, and sequences are tools for enacting a theorizing frame of mind.

6. Interruptions, surprises, disconfirmations, the unexpected all qualify as moments of unready-to-hand engagement where flow and flux become disassembled in context and provide clues as to plausible variables, patterns, dimensions, configurations that are implicit in ready-to-hand engagement. The unready-to-hand is a source of potential conceptual substitutions.

7. Pay attention to breakdowns (e.g., Patriotta 2003). As John Dewey puts it, "In every waking moment, the complete balance of the organism [system] and its environment is constantly interfered with and as constantly restored . . . Life is interruptions and recoveries . . . At these moments of a shifting in activity, conscious feeling and thought arise and are accentuated." (Dewey 2002: 178–79, emphasis added). Interruptions are occasions when feelings, thoughts, and shifts in activity are accentuated and made more visible and more available for abstracting as part of the work of theorizing. Interruptions turn streaming experience inside out and create a context for discovery. This suggests that the growing body of work on interruptions in organizational performance is important for its ability to expose key interactions, processes, and routines that hold organizations together (see, e.g., Perrow 1984; Roe and Schulman 2008; Roberts 1990; Vaughan 1996; Perin 2005; Weick et al. 1999).

8. In John Steinbeck's words, it's good to know what you are doing. To foster such knowledge, visualize a continuum anchored at one end by a fighting, colorful, straining Mexican Sierra and at the other end by an evil-smelling dead Mexican Sierra in a jar of formaldehyde. Spine counting is impossible and trivial at the fighting end, effortless at the formaldehyde end. That is roughly the same continuum that extends from Irwin's "perception" to his "formalization" and "formal." Once you locate your work somewhere on either end of the continuum, rethink where you are by moving both one step to the right and one step to the left. Those are moves of theorizing that add and subtract abridgments. As you move, ask yourself what has happened to the controlling idea that you started with. Do other conceptual substitutions seem more suitable, more useful, more probable as interpretations of ready-to-hand engagement?

9. To move closer to perceptual flux and a fresh start, practice a kind of conceptual amnesia that is implied in Paul Valery's words, "seeing is forgetting the name of the thing seen" (Weschler 1982: 180). When you forget names, you fall back on rough unnamed zones of focus and much-at-onceness. If you also enlarge your repertoire of forms, descriptions, and words, then you may change your thinking. That change is likely if you recall one form of sensemaking that occurs during theorizing, a form that is summarized as "How can I know what I think until I see what I say?" What you say colors what you think. And if you forget prevailing names and change what you say, then the resulting thoughts may be more original. This may be what is happening when Parsons and his associates practiced "cogitation in relation to many types and fields of empirical knowledge."

10. An awareness of the work of theorizing can often be fostered by viewing it metaphorically. I have used such images as performing artificial selection, moving toward or away from a pickled fish in a jar, editing perceptual flux, and the image of sifting by means of a sieve. The image of sifting captures several components of theorizing, and it is well to recall them so that they can be managed with more agency. Most facts and relations that fall through the mesh of a sieve would seem to be too subtle or too insignificant to matter. But subtle or insignificant relative to what? That's one question. Another is, are there other predicates and relations that link those objects that remain on the mesh? To theorize is to change the mesh of the sieve and re-examine what previously fell through.

11. To imagine is to condense, abstract, and create a gestalt that is different from and probably less than what you started with. To imagine is to re-present and transform earlier perceptions. While imagination is often viewed as an asset in theorizing, especially in pursuit of originality, it can also create costly abridgments.

12. Irwin's fifth stage, "formal," appears to contain a cue that tracks where one is in the theorizing process. The cue resides in the transition between reason and logic or, as Irwin puts it, we can reason but we can't logic. Reason is subjective, logic is objective. A common move in theorizing is to shift from explanations of reasoning to more formal descriptions of "the logic of" some event, performance, or routine. The result is a tidy but substantial substitution.

13. Take Kant seriously and connect perceptions to conceptions to avoid blindness, and connect conceptions to perceptions to avoid emptiness. Linear, one-directional movement from perception to formal statements commits both lapses and produces blind, empty abstractions.

14. Weaken hindsight. Better theories, defined as explanations that narrow the gap between understanding and living, can be crafted if hindsight is neutralized. Thinking is less likely to be dominated by hindsight and backward understanding if the observer looks back at history without a clear outcome in hand. This suggests that theorists should engage in retrospect only when they are aware of multiple contradictory outcomes of the history that they are examining, or when they have access to no outcomes at all. Furthermore, if people carried out projects in a forward-looking way, and then used project-sized units of analysis to look backward, the gap between present and ready-at-hand might be narrowed.

Conclusion

The preceding effort to draw out and animate the process of theorizing is filled with glosses, many of which gloss pragmatists. It is fitting to end with John Dewey's own "categorical imperative" since it reads like a version of Parsons's preoccupation with "cogitation" and "racking one's brain." "Progress means increase of present meaning, which involves multiplication of sensed distinctions as well as harmony, unification . . . If we wished to transmute this generalization into a categorical imperative we should say: 'So act as to increase the meaning of present experience' (Dewey 1922: 283). The hallmark of such increases tends to be discomfort. Once we accomplish something, such as an increase in present meaning, new "struggles and failures are inevitable. The total scene of action remains as before, only for us more complex, and more subtly unstable . . . [Next steps] can be derived only from study of the deficiencies, irregularities and possibilities of the actual situation" (Dewey 1922: 288–89).

Every day we theorize and engage in "disciplined imagination" as we substitute conceptions for perceptions and move haphazardly or deliberately toward truths that work. Substituting has been depicted as working within constraints imposed by the process of compounding abstractions, a process that moves farther and farther away from originary perceptions. Theorizing viewed as a progression from perception to the formal creates cumulative losses along the way. This is old news. But its inevitability, significance, and malleability may be more controllable than we realize. To theorize with disciplined imagination is to *move* between more and less abstraction, between more and less familiar storylines, and with close attention to precisely what is being imagined.

And to theorize with disciplined imagination is to remain connected to the human condition. Earlier I cited Greg Dening's comment about giving to the past (backward understanding) its present (forward living). When Dening died in 2008, his obituary, written by Dipesh Chakrabarty, included this passage: "As Dening said in his semi-autobiographical *Beach Crossings: Voyaging across times, cultures and self* (2004), in life as in work 'the gamble is being yourself' . . . He believed in the gerund form over the plain noun, for life was in the living of it, not in the word 'life.' Nouns froze things too much for his taste" (*Sydney Morning Herald*, April 11, 2008).

Unreflective compounding of abstractions, too, can freeze things too much. Moments of interruption, when things we need are unready to hand, uncover the gambles, foster theorizing, and live on in gerunds. The work of theorizing forces us to keep asking Peter Reason's (1996: 24) question, "Does abstraction help us understand our world better?"

9 Susan Sontag and Heteroscedasticity

James G. March

PETER HANDKE BEGINS HIS NOVEL *SHORT LETTER, LONG FAREWELL* with a note to the narrator from his wife: "I am in New York. Please don't look for me. It would not be nice for you to find me" (Handke 1974: 1). As it turns out, his wife is not in New York; she seems to be pursuing him more than he is looking for her; and when they finally get together, the encounter, though not entirely nice, is prelude to grace. The novel examines how a man and a woman make each other simultaneously more understandable and more appreciated, the simple terror and joy of the contradiction between an understanding and an interpretation of life. By an understanding of life I mean the comprehension of human action in causal terms. We gain understanding through observation and inference. The formal technology of observation and inference is well known. In the past sixty-five years, our understandings of individual behavior have been improved by that technology in the biological, behavioral, and social sciences. In terms of both scientific knowledge and engineering applications, we know more than we used to know. For example, we know more about voting behavior, population biology, problem solving, organizational decision making and learning, small group interactions, consumer behavior, risk taking, social mobility, and the engineering of individual change than we did at the end of the Second World War.

The technology of observation and inference is not limited to science. We have accepted it into the jargon of mundane curiosity. We attempt to learn from our experience by forming causal hypotheses and testing them against observations. We confront each other with arguments couched in the terminology of evidence and inference. Our journalism, conversations, and daily efforts to change the world use empirical observations and causal speculations as a route to a theory of life.

By an interpretation of life, I mean an appreciative comprehension of the human condition, the terms of commentary on life. The disciplines of interpretation are criticism, aesthetics, and rhetoric. Their engineering forms are the arts, psychotherapy, journalism, consciousness-raising, history, awareness, social criticism, ethnography, and ideology. Our interpretation of life has been affected perceptibly by such disparate things as great literature and art, the theater of the absurd, psychoanalysis, Zen, Marxist social philosophy, and film criticism.

The search for an interpretation of life can be seen in current best sellers at the local bookstore and the outpouring of blogs on the Internet. We have commentary on life that innocently recapitulates the history of ideas as a basis for critiques of modern existence. Like those of understanding, these esoterica of interpretation are mirrored in ordinary life. The search for identity is the pursuit of an interpretation of destiny without necessarily conceding its existence. The search for ideology is a claim of meaning in social life. With an enthusiasm stimulated by the struggle, we seek not only pleasure and pain but also their justification and elaboration. We learn to interpret ourselves in a way dimly illuminated by our intellectual traditions.

The contradiction between understanding and interpretation has a distinguished history. One of the more persistent themes of intellect is the creative antithesis between the causal description of existence and the mystery of its interpretation. It fills our philosophy: Kierkegaard, Hegel, Kant. It fills our poetry: Wordsworth, Goethe, Neruda. It fills our science: Da Vinci, Darwin, Marx. It fills our prose: Dostoevsky, Vesaas, Fontane.

Despite the elegant pedigree, a contradiction between understanding and interpretation is not easily sustained. In science, for example, we are corrupted into a form of resolution by both our philosophy and our technology, although philosophical and social critics of science often treat conventional descriptions of scientific method as a more powerful and pervasive ideology in science than it actually is. The ideology of science claims primacy for understanding. The philosophy of science and formal treatises on method rarely wander far from the dicta of logical empiricism and a handsomely austere conception of meaning. Working scientists, on the other hand, rarely worry about the philosophy of science, often do not learn its niceties, and follow them only haphazardly. This is, I believe, true even among working social and behavioral scientists, who tend to take the philosophy of science more seriously than do other scientists. As a result, science as practiced is consistently less peculiar than science as talked about.

Nevertheless, the critics have a point. Among those of us seeking some systematic understanding of human existence and behavior through observation and causal inference, there is sometimes an implicit assumption that an understanding of life preempts an interpretation of it. For example, the current cliché for the irrelevance of interpretation is evolution. The argument is simple:

> An understanding of biology limits the claim to centrality by the individual human organism and the ideas that individuals espouse. The organism is a temporary carrier of genes, part of a natural selection process measuring changes in hundreds of generations and in shifts in the gene pool. The individual organism neither changes nor acts in a significant way; it participates in the adaptation of the species by contribution (through reproduction) to the genetic characteristics of the next generation; but that participation involves no elements of choice and no particular significance for the individual organism or for the interpretations of life that humans find compelling.

Thus one distinguished biologist has suggested, without apparent humor, that Camus's ignorance of biology led him to fail to recognize the absurdity of life.

Such excursions of behavioral scientists into metaphysics are often pretentious, but they are mercifully uncommon after adolescence. The more common posture is not to reduce metaphysics to science but to treat commentary on the aesthetics of life as a domain of intelligence irrelevant to scientific comprehension. The tendency takes two major forms: The first is intellectual imperialism. The imperialist position claims the nature of life as properly a domain of observation. At any point in time, some aspects of that investigation remain a mystery. The parts that are mystery are left temporarily in the hands of the interpretations of art, literature, religion, and metaphysics. Those parts are gradually claimed by observation so that the domain of art, literature, religion, and metaphysics is continually being reduced.

The second position is one of intellectual specialization. The specialist imagines the nature of life as a causal phenomenon to be properly the domain of observation. The nature of life as a metaphysical interpretive construct is conceded to metaphysics and the arts. The two domains are viewed as intrinsically incomparable. Neither contributes to the other; neither is more important than the other.

Both arguments are reflected in ordinary conversations and in formal treatises. Both are, I think, wrong. Interpretation and understanding are not well defined as residuals of each other, nor do they sit in simple parallelism, separated by a division of labor. They form a dialectic of comprehension, each apparently in opposition to the other but developing in consequence of that opposition into compound forms that elaborate each without resolving the contradiction.

The issue is related to, but not identical to, the standard portrayal of differences between science and the humanities. The dialectic between understanding and interpretation is a dialectic within science, within engineering, within literature, and within art rather than a difference among them. It is a dialectic within individual scientists and artists, and describes the most distinguished among them.

Among modern behavioral scientists, for example, three names stand out as premier contributors to our comprehension of the nature of the social existence: Darwin, Marx, and Freud. Each spoke in a language of science and observation; each was a distinguished scholar; but each was a poet of interpretation as well as an architect of knowledge. In fact, when we speak of Darwin, Marx, or Freud now, we are likely to comment more on the brilliance of their insights than on the impressiveness of their observations or the clarity of the links between the two. The assessment implicit in such comments is misleading, for it tends considerably to underestimate the extraordinary observational and inferential skill of all three. Nevertheless, it is instructive that the most important contributors to modern behavioral science are noted for their aesthetics.

Against this history, our technical development of the tools of comprehension is not balanced. We have developed and taught the technology of observation and inference sufficiently to ensure that a well-trained person of modest abilities can make significant contributions to our understanding of behavior. The technology of interpretation is not as well developed; what we know about it is not normally taught in science or to scientists in a form meaningful to them.

Consider the array of technologies that any reasonably competent behavioral scientist can learn efficiently in almost any reasonably respectable graduate program and can be expected to use relatively correctly in reporting results in almost any reasonably recognized journal: Test and questionnaire construction; sample design; experimental design; estimation; hypothesis testing; multivariate analysis; reliability and validity of instruments; machine manipulation of data; difference and differential equations; linear algebra; decision theory; coding and counting; probability; computational methods of theoretical representations.

It is an impressive achievement to be able to say, as I think we can, that the observational and inferential competencies of the average advanced graduate student in the average program in social and behavioral sciences now easily exceeds the competence of most of the best students in the best programs sixty-five years ago. Or that the average observational and inferential power of an article published in a major journal sixty-five years ago is substantially lower than that found in a journal published today.

Multiple regression, the prototypic contemporary scientific mousetrap, illustrates the case. Although there are students of the social behavioral sciences who do not know (or even care) what multicolinearity, specification error, and heteroscedasticity are, such competencies are widely shared, routinely taught, and relatively intelligently used by people who are not intellectual giants.

On the other hand, we do not know how to teach or think about interpretation in a way that makes likely the systematic development or application of interpretive skills in science. We have been reluctant to try to reduce the genius of interpretation to the elementary techniques it might involve. To suggest that we can simulate Darwin, Marx, or Freud by some technocracy of aesthetics is lightheaded. But if we can recognize the importance of interpretation to comprehension, we may be prepared to develop it.

Partly we are ignorant. The study of criticism is older and grander than the study of empirical inference. It calls forth great names in philosophy and the arts. It is a demanding and subtle literature buried in a rich context of issues. Those of us who want to speak science intelligently will have to come to a better comprehension of that literature and the issues to which it is addressed.

Partly we are unimaginative. We have a too restrictive definition of technology. It is not clear in what ways a technology of interpretation would resemble our technology of understanding. We have enough experience with substantial differences among the forms of contemporary science to be wary of assuming that a new extension would necessarily look like any of them. We will need some new ideas before converting the awareness of interpretation into technique.

In the end, however, it is the philistines who confirm the power of intellect. If we are going to use the intelligence of art and literary criticism constructively and routinely in science, we will have to make criticism accessible to fools, in the same way (and with the same risks) that experimental design and statistics make inference accessible to fools.

The problems of science are significant, but I mean them to be illustrative of broader problems of human sensibility. The simple difficulties of comprehending life—in science, the arts, literature, business, school, government, family—are partly difficulties of maintaining a serious contradiction between observation and construction. Those difficulties are amplified by the disparity between our everyday familiarity with the methods and spirit of observation and inference and our everyday ignorance of the procedures and spirit of criticism, rhetoric, and aesthetics.

Despite heroic aspirations, or perhaps because of them, I suspect we should start with ambitions somewhat more modest than the construction of a new aesthetics of existence. There are mundane problems familiar to us where the difficulties are joined well in an ordinary way, and where our efforts might be sustained both by experience and by necessity. Two such domains, "consciousness-raising" and "social evaluation," illustrate the possibilities.

Consciousness-raising is a general metaphor for any deliberate procedure by which individuals substitute one world view for another. The metaphor suggests spiritual excavation. It normally proclaims some process by which pre-existing interests, beliefs, values, and perspectives within an individual are brought to awareness and substituted for prior illusionary conceptions. Although the behavioral situation appears often to be one in which some individuals persuade other individuals to change perspectives, the change is identified as uncovering a pre-existing truth with the help of a neutral external agent; and the separate standing of the reality discovered makes the change a monument to autonomy rather than dependence. In that sense, the process is analogous to the process and pretense of science. But the technology appears to be quite different.

Consider most forms of psychotherapy. The relation between the therapist, the patient ex ante, and the patient ex post is seen as one in which the therapist helps the patient to uncover previously hidden self-perceptions and to use such insight as a basis for personal reinterpretation.

Consider political consciousness-raising (or ethnic, or national, or sexual). The relation between the political activist, the citizen ex ante, and the citizen ex post is one in which the activist is seen as exposing the objective reality of the unfortunate (or fortunate) state of the citizen and allowing the citizen to become personally self-aware of his position.

Consider product advertising. The relation between the advertiser, the consumer ex ante, and the consumer ex post is one in which the advertiser presents himself as helping the consumer to identify a need previously unrecognized or an answer to that need previously unknown.

Psychotherapy, political consciousness-raising, and advertising are not the same. They differ in their ideologies, procedures, and consequences. They share, however, an approach that is distinctly different from that of conventional science: They focus on the terms of interpretation of life, the aesthetics of life, rather than the understanding of life in strictly observational terms. As a result, the conventional terms of science do not always seem to help them.

Social evaluation has a similar problem, but a different recent history. The evaluation of social actions (or experiments if we use that term loosely) represents an important part of social history and philosophy. After the Second World War, however, a more narrow conception of evaluation arose. We have tried a number of relatively specific social experiments. For example, in the United States we have tried early childhood special education, school vouchers, prepaid medical care, food stamps, clean prisons, affirmative action. The efforts to learn something of value from these experiments has stimulated an incipient field of social evaluation.

The standard technology of evaluation is well known. It involves establishing the objectives of the experiment, then comparing those objectives with independently developed measures of performance while controlling for extraneous considerations. Much of the paraphernalia is borrowed from the methodology of experimental design. The effort has clarified our understanding of social action and encouraged a number of new efforts intended to correct apparent defects in the tested programs.

There are, however, numerous ways in which such procedures appear to be ineffective, wrong, or deeply unsatisfying. For example, consider a common feature of many histories of evaluation: The better the technical quality of the evaluation, the more likely it appears to be that the social experiment will be seen as deficient in the sense of failing to make a significant difference in outcomes. This tendency seems to be independent of the type of experiment, the apparent sophistication of the ideas in the experiment, or the degree of commitment to the experiment, although each of those is sometimes cited as a possible explanation in individual cases.

Evaluation, as a field of social engineering, has discovered the absurdity of life and the complications of certifying systematic improvement in it. Understandably, this had led to a search for new experiments offering new hopes not yet dashed, and to some modest rediscovery of the philosophic implications of hopelessness. It has also led to a more narrow concern with our inclination to identify the problem of social criticism as a problem in experimental design. Such concerns bring some students of evaluation to an interest in procedures for articulating an interpretation of life.

Consciousness-raising and social evaluation are techniques of considerable practical interest. There are other similar areas, like planning, program design, and political leadership. Each involves the relatively inelegant necessities of addressing actual problems. But each is also a domain for the possible exploration of key questions in the intellect of interpretation.

In fact, the inadequacies of our current modes of interpretation in science, policymaking, social design, and ordinary life are in danger of becoming a new orthodoxy in social thought. We have proposals for criticism in the classroom and rhetoric in planning. We have rediscovered classical historiography and classical ethnography. We have reasserted the aesthetics of formal modeling.

Since I share both the diagnosis of our problems and, to the limits of my character, enthusiasms for the possible alternative perspectives, I would not want the rising popularity of such sentiments to condemn them to banality. But to avoid banality means two things. It means to retain an awareness of the contradictory complementarity between understanding and interpretation. To urge development of a usable coda for interpretation is not to reject modern techniques for observation and inference but to seek a comparable development in another aspect of intellect. Neither exists well without the other, and to pose their contradiction is to seek not to choose between them but to strengthen their dialectic.

Avoiding banality also means moving to specifics of technique. To seek a concrete description of interpretation is to risk subsuming passion in the mechanics of copulation, but I think it may be feasible in modest ways. And I suspect it is necessary. The idea is limited: I think it is possible that some serious effort by students of human behavior and institutions on the one hand,

and students of criticism on the other might, help illuminate each. I think they share a limited set of relatively well defined problems. I do not think either tradition provides suitably sensible answers to the practical problems of interpretation. And I think significant people in both traditions know it. The idea is neither grand nor original; but it requires some work.

The work may perhaps be justified by some minor madness that allows contemplating the day when a routine evaluation of a curriculum would be as intelligent as Susan Sontag's writing on pornography or photography, or the day when a legislator looking at an evaluation of a favorite program says, as T. S. Eliot once did of the analysis of one of his poems by a critic: "[It] was an attempt to find out what the poem meant—whether that was what I had meant it to mean or not. And for that I was grateful" (Eliot 1961: 125–26).

This is not the place to try to detail systematically what an agenda might be; nor am I confident that such an agenda could be constructed easily now. Consider, however, four simple items that appear to be important to confronting interpretation in the engineering of life and also appear to touch major issues of relevance to criticism:

1. The role of *ambiguity* in purposive action. Experience with planning, awareness, and evaluation has led many participants to note the complications of ambiguity: ambiguity with respect to intentions, with respect to meaning, with respect to goals, with respect to experience. These ambiguities are neither well comprehended nor well tolerated within most of our present modes for improving human action. The role of ambiguity in interpretation is an important theme in criticism; it needs to become similarly important in the prosaics of social engineering.

2. The role of *contradiction* in intelligence. Conventional models for individual and social intelligence build on simple ideas of coherence. They treat contradiction as a pathology to be resolved, through choice, or mediation, or reconstruction, by the calculation of "trade-offs." Even in the domain of social conflict, where there is greater acceptance of the necessity of conflict, there is little attention to it as a central process. The role of contradiction in comprehension is a common concern of criticism in terms that might be made useful to engineering.

3. The role of *context* in meaning. Much social engineering seems to depend on being able to limit contextual issues to a few key

variables. This has led to considerable difficulty, apparently due to the fine-grained detail of historical, cultural, institutional, and personal contexts in which things occur and are given meaning. The micro structure of a variety of simultaneous contexts is not easily accommodated within our conventional thinking in social engineering; it is an important theme in some forms of criticism.

4. The role of *affirmation* in construction. Many contemporary efforts to achieve social change presume that change is most easily caused by inducing overt dissatisfaction with present existence. It begins with a presumption of neutrality or antipathy. Such a style is also common in serious criticism of poetry or art, but it plays a lesser role. The critic more commonly looks for interpretations that discover aspects of an artistic expression that make it more interesting or more beautiful than when first observed, or developing the uncertainties of simultaneous attraction and repulsion. Truly distinguished pieces of criticism are almost always ones in which a critic enlarges our appreciation of the beauties and complexities of art that is loved by providing enriched interpretations.

The idea of making a technology of criticism is ridiculous on the face of it. Most great critics have themselves been artists. They exhibit not a set of procedures but a complicated mosaic of cultural and intellectual exposure. Efforts to capture the rules of criticism seem usually to result in platitudinous silliness or patent obscurantism.

But such a portrayal of interpretation is trite enough to be wrong. To elaborate perspectives of criticism toward ambiguity, contradiction, context, and affirmation into technologies for behavioral science, social engineering, and everyday life is a fantasy. And since it will not be easy, it is, according to some views of such things, worth imagining.

Afterword

Neil Gross

"G ENIUS WITHOUT EDUCATION IS LIKE SILVER IN THE MINE," RECORDS *Poor Richard's Almanack.* Is theoretical promise without education similarly ore-like? The contributors to this volume think so. Although they differ in their understanding of what theory in the social sciences entails and in their sense of what makes for high-quality theoretical work, all share with Richard Swedberg a belief that it is possible to identify certain mental habits or techniques associated with theoretical creativity, and to stir up more of it by making such techniques part of the theorist's education.

Swedberg is right that there has been surprisingly little written on the practicalities of theorizing. That alone makes the volume a welcome contribution. My main goal in this short concluding essay is to pull out a few of the themes that echo among the chapter contributors in the hope of distilling some of the book's lessons. I also raise three critical questions that will perhaps point the way toward future scholarship, building on the good work of Swedberg and his colleagues. One question has to do with whether self-reflection on the part of theorists is the best way to understand theorizing; another concerns the network structure of sociology; and the last returns to Franklin's aphorism. Theoretical genius may need to be honed, but the silver has to be in the ground in the first place, and I discuss the possibility that unless a reconfiguration of theory takes place—of the sort that none of the chapter authors seems to be contemplating—we may see a decline in theoretical interest in the years to come.

First, though, what binds together these wonderfully eclectic papers, written by sociologists, economists, and organizational scholars? An interest in theorizing theory, of course, but what else? One thing worth noting is that many of the chapters draw inspiration from the intellectual tradition of classical American pragmatism. This is not entirely surprising given the list of contributors; several of the authors are already well-known champions of pragmatist ideas. Could there be a more direct line of influence between pragmatism and the contemporary social sciences than that which runs through Karl Weick and his notion of sensemaking, for example—the attempt on the part of actors in and out of organizations to devise tentative, provisional, and experimental answers to the question, "What's going on here?" when the usual smooth course of action is disrupted (Weick 1995)? It is not pragmatism's general orientation that informs most of the chapters, however. Instead, the emphasis is on Charles S. Peirce's notion of abductive reasoning as applied to social-theoretical work. To be sure, abduction cannot be neatly hived off from pragmatism's philosophical anthropology. As Swedberg recognizes in his opening discussion, for Peirce it is only in moments of genuine doubt that scientists, with some surprising fact at hand, begin to make guesses about what produced the fact, in so doing employing in a disciplined way the capacity for creativity and experimentation that is part of human kind's evolutionary heritage. Yet the main pragmatist focus of the volume is on what it means for social theorizing to view abduction as an operation distinct from induction and deduction.

For Swedberg, the implications are clear. The fence that Hans Reichenbach saw separating the contexts of discovery and justification must be torn down, not necessarily because, following a pragmatist epistemology, the truth-value of an idea must always be assessed in relation to the uses for which it is put and the problems it was designed to solve, but because—in a twofold operation—social scientists must study empirically how they formulate theories in order to produce better theories, while in other phases of inquiry allowing themselves full access to puzzling facts in response to which theories may be generated. (The analysis of such facts might otherwise be thought to lie within the realm of justification, but Swedberg urges that they be considered first during a "prestudy.") Swedberg makes additional suggestions for improving social theoretical abduction: gather any kind of information you can about a social phenomenon before forming intuitions and hunches; use metaphors, analogies, and typologies to guide your thinking; let yourself go and be creative, worrying about logical elaboration at a later stage of the game; and so on.

In their essay Isaac Reed and Mayer Zald also put abduction at the forefront. To the observation that scientists generate theories in the face of puzzles, Reed and Zald add that since a major source of puzzlement for social scientists is new developments occurring in the social world, theoretical energy in social science should be tied not simply to the volume of social dynamism—which is implied by every contextualist account stressing the origins of European and American sociology in modernization—but also to how that dynamism maps on to social scientists' guiding concerns, including ideological concerns. Unsettled times and unsettled sociological lives yield theoretical innovation. Abduction is no less important in Weick's chapter, where theorizing is treated as a form of sensemaking. Weick draws on the ideas of the artist Robert Irwin (among other sources) to suggest that elaborating a theory through abduction involves "compounded abstraction" in which, as one moves from concrete to abstract representations of objects, those objects are effectively transformed. Attending to the processual aspects of this—to the different moments of compounding—allows the analyst to slow things down, linger in particularly fruitful periods of conceptualization, and move back and forth as necessary between denotation and connotation. Is there not a kind of Peircean pragmatism apparent even in James March's paper? March insists on dissolving the dualism between observation and interpretation, as Peircean semiotics would. Furthermore, while denouncing metaphysical pretensions, he expresses a metaphysics of creativity himself when he makes a case that interpretive insight could improve social science theorizing by directing our attention to the ontological realities of ambivalence and contradiction, context and affirmation.

To see so many leading social scientists treat pragmatism as an intellectual resource is heartening. Pragmatist ideas have shaped work in the social sciences, and sociology in particular, since the early years of the twentieth century (Gross 2007). While pragmatism's fortunes in the discipline have risen and fallen, we are currently in the midst of an upswing, owing partly to generational change and the declining strength of theoretical movements of the 1970s and 1980s, and partly to the sustained efforts of Hans Joas at showing how pragmatist notions might be folded into sociological models of action, with wide-ranging theoretical consequences. That the volume's authors see value in pragmatism from another angle indicates not merely that they are participants in a broader movement, but that pragmatism has not yet exhausted its potential to enrich social science. The would-be theorist who masters the art of abduction is well on her way, and the chapters offer clues about how such mastery might be gained.

Abduction is not the only recurring theme. A second—crosscutting the first—is that good theorizing, based as it may be on inspiration and guess-work, is effortful activity. This is what stands out for me in the chapters by Vaughan, Paulsen, Knorr Cetina, and Turner. I say crosscutting because abduction plays a role in several of these essays as well. Citing Swedberg's interpretation of Peirce, alongside a paper about abduction in qualitative research by Stefan Timmermans and Iddo Tavory (2012), Vaughan describes abduction as "a series of mental processes: a continuing iteration and adjust-ment between alternative hypotheses, theory, and data to either refine, cor-rect, or expand a theory in new directions, narrow its scope, or define it as inappropriate. Abduction depends upon weighing anomalous findings against existing theories to construct new theories." The aspect of abductive reasoning of special interest to her is "analogical theorizing." Swedberg is also concerned with this, but Vaughan provides a thick, illustrative description by telling the story of her own research career around organizational devi-ance. It may have been productive for her, as a graduate student, to analyze how certain features of a drugstore chain's organizational setting conduced toward deviance—a Medicaid fraud scheme. But it was only when she read Robert K. Merton's theory of deviance in an analogical fashion that she was able to move her own theoretical understanding forward. Merton theorized deviance as a matter of structural imbalance between normative values and the means society makes available to different groups of actors to enact those values. Vaughan's realization was that organizational forms could be seen as like opportunity structures—a realization that led her to a respecification of her theory, and to search for cases from other empirical domains in which the subprocesses in her emerging account, such as "signaling," also loomed large. Consistent with Timmermans and Tavory's portrayal, here abduction requires hard work sustained over years: to be productive, analogical theoriz-ing must be cultivated, with insights derived from purposively looking else-where—beyond one's immediate topic and area of expertise—continually fed back into the development of a conceptual scheme.

Good theorizing is hard work in Paulsen's account too, but for a different reason. Little conscious effort is required for the construction of what Paulsen calls "everyday counterfactuals"—"what if" imaginings that underpin the life narratives people tell themselves, bursts of intersubjective agreement, opera-tions of collective memory, a range of emotions. But theorists' counterfactu-als are of a different order, and Paulsen reviews some of the methodological suggestions offered over the years to improve counterfactual reasoning around historical events, power, policy analysis, and the envisioning of theoretical utopias. Perhaps the biggest lesson of the paper is that since counterfactuals are inevitable in social science theorizing, theorists could improve the quality of their fare if they attended to them more closely.

Knorr Cetina's chapter proceeds along similar lines. Theorizing involves intuition, she claims. But the cognitive processes drawn upon to generate theoretical insight are different than those we mobilize when we make snap judgments in our daily lives: the former are back-of-consciousness processes that work slowly, stewing over a problem—even over the identification of a problem—until a possible solution pops into view. For Knorr Cetina, a theorist and ethnographer, repeated contact with a field site long after an initial data-gathering period has ended is essential for keeping her theoretical "processor" running smoothly. So is the minimization of distraction.

Theory is effortful activity for Turner as well. While all of the chapters in the volume touch on the humanity of the theorist, Turner's may be the one with the most pathos. Theory is a noble pursuit, Turner wants to say, requiring passion and commitment, but it is not apt to lead to disciplinary fame and fortune in the empiricist sociological world of today, especially if one is intent on producing not "mundane theorizing," in which theories are extended by accounting for anomalies, but theory of a more elevated sort in which the aim is to develop novel ways of grasping how and why elements of the social world "hang together" as they do. Professional perseverance and a willingness to remain at the margins of the field are essential here, as is a kind of simultaneous worldliness and unworldliness. Coming up with solutions to theoretical puzzles is often a matter of being able to tacitly make useful associations, and this requires both practical knowledge of social settings—Turner's example is how knowledge of gambling inadvertently helped him make sense of the social psychology of charisma—and an extraordinarily wide base of learning that goes beyond what the average sociologist knows to encompass philosophy, history, literature, art. Doing good theory, Turner argues, is not a matter of following procedural rules, but of cultivating oneself in the manner of the theorist, ignoring disciplinary and subdisciplinary boundaries and resting secure in the knowledge that while intellectual fads and fashions may come and go, social theory is an important scholarly dialogue and tradition that stretches across the ages.

Finally, many of the chapters share the view that an adequate understanding of theory is the first step toward better theorizing. One sees this perhaps most clearly in the chapter by Daniel Klein, where he insists that for an economic model to count as a theory three questions must be answerable: "Theory of what?," "Why should we care?," and "What merit in your explanation?" Most model-building exercises in economics, at least in the leading journal that Klein examines, do not answer all three questions, and Klein suggests that theoretical economics and the social sciences as a whole would be improved if theorists "disciplined" themselves more around such basic definitional matters.

Thought-provoking essays, these. No doubt they will push young and established theorists alike to higher levels of reflexivity. This is a good thing. My own assessment of the state of theory today is not as pessimistic as that of Swedberg or Turner. It seems to me that a good deal of interesting and sophisticated conceptual work is now being done that aims to provide us with tools for better explanation of complex social outcomes, patterns, and events. This work may not always be social theory in Turner's broad sense, but what makes it something different—its close connection to empirical research, its more restricted range of ontological and intellectual reference, its bundling with post-positivist assumptions about the nature and aims of social science—also reflects its strengths. Still, there is always room for improvement, and a volume of papers reflecting on how theorists theorize is likely to spark new ideas.

As important as the chapters may prove to be in this respect, however, it is obvious that Swedberg and the other authors regard them not as providing the last word on theorizing but as opening contributions to a much needed, long-term conversation. In that spirit, I want to raise a few critical points that might seed future inquiries.

The first will come as no shock to anyone familiar with the research area known as the sociology of ideas, which studies the social processes, structural and institutional conditions, and practices that lead intellectuals to their knowledge claims. Perhaps the most fundamental methodological tenet of research here, adhered to by sociologists of knowledge, sociologists of science, sociologically savvy intellectual historians, and others, is that if you want to understand the social origins of knowledge you should *not* accept at face value the narratives that knowledge producers offer as to how their ideas took shape. Leaving aside general methodological debate about whether social actors are accurate reporters of their own experiences and behavior, there is good reason to believe that the epistemic cultures of most areas of knowledge production provide their practitioners with vocabularies of intellectual motive and normative narratives of creativity that systematically minimize and obscure the role of the social. One might expect the vocabularies and narratives employed by sociologists when talking about themselves to be more sociological—as they usually are. But sociologists too can show blindness, succumbing to the usual temptations of presenting their work as unfolding in a more linear, rational fashion than it actually did, or playing up their own intellectual virtues and playing down the role of social structure or social interest—or invoking structure in order to show their ideas in a favorable light, as happens when scholars depict their thought as having emerged with an air of inevitability out of some historically significant social context (for example, as having been stimulated by the author's participation in a heroic social movement). Part of the problem is that knowledge producers are simply too close to their own work to have any perspective.

It is not that sociologists of ideas think autobiographical accounts useless: among other things they can help researchers fill in factual blanks as they reconstruct biographical timelines. But we should not expect the self-reflections of intellectuals to correspond in any straightforward way with the behind the scenes practices that in fact led to the development of their ideas; or that self-reflections would properly register the impact of broader forces. To get at practices, for their part, we need close observational data, access to correspondence, interviews with colleagues and collaborators, studies of the technologies of knowledge making (which can often tell us something about their use)—and a theoretical sensitivity that alerts us to mundane ways of doing things that may be shared among actors occupying similar positions in social space. Structural analyses make their own demands.

Why does this matter for the purposes of this volume? Because, presumably, the best way to improve the theory-making practices of social scientists is to encourage them to follow the practices *actually* employed by successful theorists to good effect, not post hoc autobiographical reconstructions of those practices that might seem perfectly sensible—as do the practices and techniques discussed by the chapter authors—but may or may not bear much resemblance to the reality of knowledge production. In a recent edited volume, Charles Camic, Michèle Lamont, and I made the case that we would have a better grasp of the roots of social knowledge—of empirically warrantable claims made about the social world by academic and non-academic social scientists, policymakers, journalists, and others—if we spent more time analyzing practices in the manner of socio-historical work on the natural sciences (Camic, Gross, and Lamont 2011). One of the chapters in our volume was about social theory, in which Johan Heilbron (2011) attempted to pin down the distinctive research practices that eventually led Pierre Bourdieu to come up with such signature concepts as habitus and field. It strikes me that if one's goals for theory were applied rather than explanatory, and one sought to improve the quality of theorizing overall, one could do worse than to multiply the number of studies like Heilbron's, expanding the focus beyond successful theorists and theories to less successful ones (see the discussion in Baehr 2013) with the aim of cataloguing best and worst practices, and encouraging emulation or avoidance. It would be a fascinating exercise if the authors of the chapters in this volume allowed a sociologist of ideas to follow them for a year, watching them as they worked, as they browsed the library shelves, read and took notes, engaged in fieldwork, organized their files, interacted with colleagues, and produced paper drafts—and then if they allowed their practices to be described as they truly appeared, with no censorship or presentational varnish. If the descriptions of the sociologist of ideas were combined with self-reflections by the theorists, that exercise might take us some way toward understanding how good theory is made.

There is a second critical point I want to raise. I worry that some of the tips and techniques for better theorizing offered by the contributors do not square with social structure of the contemporary American social sciences. Although the authors differ in their view of how abductive reasoning works, most maintain that theoretical imagination is at its richest when thinkers are deeply immersed in the factual material of their projects, but are also able to pull from contributions made by other scholars in completely different areas of inquiry, theorizing by analogy, modeling processes in their domain on those found elsewhere, and so on. Here the contributors' claims do map onto work by sociologists of ideas. Andrew Abbott (2001), for example, has argued that academic knowledge production is fractal in nature: distinctions between subfields and disciplines or between bad work of the past and good work of the present or between one methodology and another get drawn and institutionalized, and then creativity—or what comes to be called creativity—happens as scholars bridge or transcend or flip the distinctions, bringing to the fore ideas that were previously marked as other in an endlessly repetitive cycle in which progress takes the form of marginally novel recombinations, and in which distinctions are drawn within distinctions. Similarly, Randall Collins

(1998) suggests that the truly creative philosophers of world history are distinguished primarily by their social network ties to other philosophers. On the one hand, they are connected closely enough to other leading thinkers—often through their mentors—that they are able to gauge accurately how any new idea will be seen by those whose judgment matters most from the point of view of status rewards. On the other hand, their network ties (along which ideas travel) are sufficiently diverse that they can fashion eclectic ideational assemblages, combining the perspectives of others in unusual ways as they work out their own philosophical systems.

So what is the problem? In a phrase, subdisciplinary specialization. Throughout the social sciences (as in the natural sciences and humanities) the number of recognized specialty areas has exploded. While it is common for social scientists to labor in two or three areas, there are strong incentives against locating oneself in more disciplinary pockets than this: doing so increases beyond a manageable level the amount of information that must be processed, the size of peer networks grows too large, carving out a professional reputation becomes more difficult (particularly for young scholars), and the risk rises that one will be seen as a dilettante. Accordingly, Erin Leahey (2007) has shown that subdisciplinary specialization is associated with higher productivity and salary levels. James Moody's (2004) work on collaboration networks in American sociology since the 1960s demonstrates that specialization does not result in the creation of small-world-like specialty area silos, in which practitioners are hunkered down and focused on narrow sets of issues: there is a fair amount of collaboration across areas, with the boundaries between them quite permeable—a network structure consistent with Abbott's theory of fractalization. Yet much of this boundary-spanning, Moody also shows, is taking place among scholars whose research is quantitative and for whom area-neutral quantitative methodologies become the basis for collaboration and commensurability. My question is whether encouraging young scholars to hone their powers of abduction by reading broadly can do anything to counterbalance these social structural trends—trends that, while creating opportunities for theoretical growth in the form of bringing together ideas from adjacent subfields, would seem to push against more expansive forms of theoretical creativity by setting limits on the range of eclecticism. My guess is that the answer is no, it cannot. To put this differently, the best theorists may be generalists, and the social structure of the social sciences these days is at odds with generalism. Again, I am not as pessimistic as some of the contributors about what this means for the viability of theory; there is indeed productive theorization that can come from spanning a few sub-fields, at the same time that some locations in network space will continue to provide privileged vantage points for generalist analysis, with the two kinds of theory interacting in an intellectual division of labor. Yet I do think that ongoing pressures toward specialization mean that some contributors' proposals are overly sanguine. I love March's idea that we ought to do more to develop technologies of interpretation that could bridge interpretation and understanding, for instance. But—particularly at a moment when the humanities are in trouble institutionally—how many young scholars can realistically make careers for themselves by spanning the humanities and the social sciences in the manner March calls for? This relates to Turner's point: being a social theorist who does not respect conventional intellectual boundaries is no longer a strategy for career success, if it ever was.

Is there not, though, some kind of happy medium we could find between ignoring the fact of specialization and resigning ourselves to it? There is, and it is connected to my first point about studying practices: moving forward, we might consider focusing on how productive theorizing occurs *in the context of heightened specialization*; and we should encourage more of it, pushing the limits of the possible, given structural constraints.

Third and finally, I want to come back around to the silver in the mine. There is something significant about theorizing that remains unexplored in the book's chapters: in the social sciences anyway (perhaps less so in the humanities), theory is a gendered activity. By this I mean that, although there are obviously many female scholars who have made major contributions to theory, theory tends to be culturally marked as a male domain of intellectual labor and is a vocation that occupies more men than women. It is hard to find direct evidence that speaks to the cultural marking claim, but that men outnumber women in theory is apparent. Of the 1,399 members of the American Sociological Association who listed theory as one of their areas of interest in 2013, only 438—or 31 percent—were women, at a time when women made up 52 percent of ASA membership overall. Likewise, most of the articles submitted to *Sociological Theory* are by men. The idea that theory may be gendered is hardly novel (for example, see Lutz 1995). More generally, that specialty areas within occupations may come to be sex typed is well recognized by scholars of gender inequality. Explaining how theory became marked as a male pursuit and how that reputation continues to maintain itself despite challenges from feminist scholars and others are matters that will have to be left for elsewhere, but it seems to me there are implications for the future: unless theory can be recast to be as appealing to women as to men (there are some hints that this may be starting to happen now, such as extremely active participation by female sociologists in the ASA's annual Junior Theorists Symposium), we could well see declining theoretical interest over time, given that the number of women entering the social sciences continues to rise. For a follow-up volume to this one, it would be great to see a chapter on the practical challenges faced by theorists who are women in navigating a traditionally male preserve; or perhaps one by a female journal editor or ASA section officer describing her efforts to degender or regender theory or get more of the conceptual work done by female scholars in subfields such as sex and gender, culture, and political sociology to be recognized as theory proper. Making sure that a high proportion of people in the social sciences remain oriented toward theoretical matters is surely as important for our collective enterprise as sharpening powers of abductive reasoning.

Notes

Chapter 1

1. But even if there does not exist a distinct body of literature on theorizing, there do exist some writings that are very suggestive and helpful in this context. Among these, I especially recommend the works by Karl Weick, C. Wright Mills, Everett C. Hughes, James March, Andrew Abbott, and Howard Becker, all of whom are referred to in this introductory chapter. There are also a small number of very suggestive social scientists who write in what can be called a theorizing style, such as Thomas Schelling and Albert O. Hirschman. Philosopher Herbert Dreyfus also has much of interest to say on the topic of theorizing.

2. For clarification, it should be added that Popper is not talking of social science studies of creativity but of understanding how a creative insight is produced in the mind of the single researcher.

3. The quote comes from Karl Weick 1989: 516. See also Weick's article "What Theory Is *Not*, Theorizing *Is*" (Weick 1995).

4. According to Jennifer Platt, little is currently known about pilot studies (Platt 2011; cf. e.g. van Teijlingen and Hundley 2001). Nonetheless, pilot studies are often described as unofficial trial runs before the study itself is undertaken. One wants, for example, to see if some part of a questionnaire will work or not. An exploratory study, in contrast, is used when one knows very little about a topic but does not want to undertake a full study. "An exploratory paper", according to Robert Merton and Harriet Zuckerman, "can take us to a problematics of our subject: the formulation of principal questions that should be investigated with the rationale for considering these as questions worth investigating" (Merton and Zuckerman 1973: 497—98, 559). The prestudy differs from both the pilot study and the exploratory study in that it is an organic part of a full study. Its purpose is also primarily theoretical.

5. The quote comes from Doyle [1891] 2001: 14.

6. *Oxford English Dictionary*, Second edition, 1989; online version November 2010. http://www.oed.com:80/Entry/200430>; accessed on February 13, 2011.

Chapter 2

1. Some have called the appeal to intuition by scientists "the very cliché of creative genius." See Dietrich 2004. There are also Einstein quotes celebrating intuition. See "21 Awesome Quotes on Intuition," January 25, 2012. http://www.ideachampions.com/weblogs/ archives/2012/01/the_only_real_v.shtml (accessed October 13, 2012).

2. I don't personally differentiate discovery from what is called theory testing, since some testing should be built into the discovery; and intricate testing tends to need new theorizing, as fields like high energy physics show.

3. Kahneman quotes Herbert Simon who, after studying chess masters, found the feats of expert intuition to be rather less magical than we think. "The situation has provided a cue; this cue has given the expert access to information stored in memory, and the information provides the answer. Intuition is nothing more and nothing less than recognition" (Kahneman 2011: 11).

4. For an interesting but quite different attempt to deal with implicit knowledge in contrast to explicit knowledge that starts from Polanyi, see H. Collins (2010). Collins would probably classify what I do here under "somatic tacit knowledge," which means "knowledge that is tacit because of the way it is inscribed in the material of body and brain" (H. Collins 2010: 11, see also his Chap.5).

5. It is important to note that the modules appear not to function like isolated units but are rather like specialized circuits that, if damaged, create functional difficulties in other areas (Gazzaniga 2008: 127).

6. For example, Evans (2008) describes the intuitionist system as working unconsciously or as being preconscious: it is implicit, automatic, low effort, rapid, high capacity, and holistic, and it is the default process (most of the action is intuitive). In contrast, the reasoning system is conscious, controlled, high effort, slow, low capacity, inhibitory, perceptual, analytic, and reflective. On a functional level the intuitionist system operates in associative ways, and is domain specific, contextualized, pragmatic, engaged in parallel processing, and stereotypical; while the reasoning system operates in a rule- based, domain-general, abstract, logical, sequential, and egalitarian (not stereotyping) way.

7. This of course does not mean that emotions (or some neurological substrate related to what we call emotions) cannot become conscious. But initial processing of emotional content appears to occur "in various limbic system structures such as the amygdala." According to Damasio's model (1994), "the computational product of these limbic structures is used by the next levels of affective processing represented by the cingulate cortex and the ventromedial prefrontal cortex (Dietrich 2004: 748). The point here is that the neural circuits for the two types of information processing systems described in the literature appear to be located in different areas of the brain,

and have evolved at different times. This assumes some modularity of the brain, but modules are not like isolated units; for example, the electric currents for them appear to be scattered widely throughout the brain (Gazzaniga 2008: 127, cited in Franks 2010: 110).

8. The notion of a progressive research program dates back to Imre Lakatos (1970): Luhmann's system theory may be an example. There is surely ample evidence to counter the assumption that social systems are "closed" systems, but Luhmann pushed on—to me it seems, to positive effect.

9. There are, for example, questions about the evolutionary aspects of the systems—for instance, about the assumption that the intuitive system is evolutionary, ancient, and common to all mammals. Although this system appears to have "much in common with animal cognition, it looks very different" in a brain that also has the reasoning system (Evans 2008: 261). On a more philosophical level, Evans (2012) summarizes several "false beliefs and fallacies" of received views of dual process theories that they may have inherited, he says, from traditional studies of deductive reasoning.

10. It is an argument about ontology, but I do not want to address this on a philosophical level, where such questions properly belong.

11. The student I worked with was Klaus Amann. Laboratory studies seek to observe scientists in their "natural" environment, the laboratory, to learn something about scientific practice—for example, what social and other processes explain how scientists conduct experiments—or to convince themselves that they have obtained publishable findings.

12. What is demanding, surely, varies personally and perhaps even culturally, but this is included in the formulation offered.

13. There is, to my knowledge, evidence from cognitive neuroscience that social interactions are more costly than other tasks, but I do not have the reference.

14. I used to think of this as the curious, seemingly inexhaustible desire to look at things over and over again.

15. See, for example, Knorr Cetina 1999 (2003); Knorr Cetina and Bruegger 2002a; and Knorr Cetina 2012.

16. The pleasure may also have come from the fact that the discussions were spurred on by a best friend.

17. I am here neglecting other explanations for the presence of emotions in science. For example, science draws on a rhetoric of excitement that can be witnessed in grant proposals and public presentations of knowledge, and may be internalized by practitioners. On the other hand, one assumes that scientists working long hours for twenty years on complicated, hard-to-understand topics—as they do, for example, in high-energy physics—are not just rhetorically motivated. Most of those I interviewed seemed to emotionally "love" their objects (e.g., their detector) and their work.

Chapter 3

1. This section draws extensively from Vaughan (1992). For details, see original.

2. At the National Archives, Washington, D.C., were 9,000 pages of interview transcripts and 122,000 NASA documents and engineering analyses. Also, the official report contained two volumes totaling 5,000 pages of commission testimony (see Presidential Commission on the Space Shuttle Accident, 1986).

3. Personal interview by the author with James Smith, Chief Engineer, Solid Rocket Booster Project, June 8, 1992; quoted in Vaughan 1996: 118.

4. Prus (1987), Snow et al. (2003), and Zerubavel (2007) also support following Simmel's formal sociology to identify generic patterns across similar events in different social settings. Their approaches differ from what I propose, however. Analogical theorizing differs from all three in the emphasis on analogy, its presence in both the cognitive and material practice of analysis, the logic of case selection, and the emphasis on both analogies and differences, on structures in addition to processes, and on using a situated action frame.

Chapter 4

1. This is our own rendering of Peirce's concept, which in some versions includes future inquirers. See Peirce 1992a; Haskell 1984; see also L. Fleck [1935] 1979. Peirce connected individual thinking to the collective process by which truth is pursued, a theme that has long occupied sociologists of science but which has also been picked up by recent philosophers of science (Longino 2002; Farber 2005). Importantly, Peirce located the potential rationality of scientific inquiry—conceptualized broadly as the capacity, over the long run, of scientific knowledge to approach truth about the world *at the collective level.*

2. More specifically, this model has two key flaws, in our view. First, it ignores a dimension of theory growth and *decline* that Lakatos captures by distinguishing between progressive and degenerative problem shifts in research programs (Lakatos 1970: 116–20). The former is compatible with Berger and Wagner's approach to theory elaboration and growth, but they ignore the possibility that theories run out of gas, fail to attract enthusiastic pursuit, and increasingly make only marginal contributions. Second, and related, they treat theory development only as an intellectual and cognitive achievement, ignoring or leaving to others the issue of the mobilization of excitement and commitment of the scholarly community. This issue is central if one's purpose is to think about what contributes to the amount of theorizing at any point in time.

3. See also Neil J. Smelser (1997), "Sociology as Science, Humanism, and Art." Smelser also understands sociology to be subject to influences in a different way than most natural sciences, and he captures this via the "intractable dilemma" of "scientific dispassion versus interventionism," tracing this opposition through one hundred years of sociology. Here we wish to explore how this "dilemma" is in fact a source of collective energy for theorizing.

4. Zald paid little attention to defining the differences among the disciplines that constitute the humanities and no attention to the self-definitions of either the social sciences or the humanities. One can make an argument that some of the humanities disciplines, or parts of those disciplines, can be thought of as "quasi-sciences." Some philosophers do not consider themselves to be part of a humanities discipline. At the University of Arizona, the Philosophy Department is located in the Division of Social Science. Linguistics and social linguistics could easily be seen as part of the social sciences. Increasingly, philologists use precise models to describe when languages separated from other languages ages ago. One has to be careful about reifying the classification of social science, natural science, and humanities. To some extent it is a matter of administrative convenience as much as it is of fundamental within division homogeneity. The perception of fundamental differences ends up having political, economic, and intellectual consequences.

5. In cultural sociology, Ann Swidler has proposed that *unsettled times* are times in which totalizing ideological systems become particularly compelling (Swidler 2001).

Chapter 5

I thank Jason Briggeman and Hannah Mead for valuable copyediting and Deirdre McCloskey, Thomas Mayer, Niclas Berggren, Richard Swedberg, and two referees for helpful comments.

1. The paper is available at http://econjwatch.org/articles/model-building-versus-theorizing-the-paucity-of-theory-in-the-journal-of-economic-theory. It was published in 2007 in *Econ Journal Watch*, of which I am the chief editor and four others are co-editors. The journal's policy is that when an editor submits something to the journal it must be reviewed and approved by two other editors, as was the article in question.

2. When we commenced the project in late 2005, the most recent complete year published and available online for download was 2004.

3. The spreadsheet is available online at http://www.econjournalwatch.org/pdf/KleinRomeroAppendixMay2007.xls.

4. That article was Article #16 as listed in the spreadsheet.

5. For some of the articles failing *Theory of what?*, one may question whether they really even fashion themselves as explanations. While using some economic terminology ("congestion," "utility," "strategy," etc.), some are essentially mathematical (e.g., #3, 17, 18, 25, 26, 29) Also, one article (#20) reports the results of a classroom experiment that tries to recreate a pre-existing model; another (#54) designs an allocation mechanism as a kind of operations research problem. These endeavors do not qualify as explanations, but in fairness, they do not pretend otherwise. Still, such works will usually be termed "theory" within the academic culture.

6. The correspondence with Quiggin is available at http://econjwatch.org/articles/why-should-we-care-what-klein-and-romero-say-about-the-journal-of-economic-theory.

7. Another reaction to Klein and Romero (2007) came from Robert Goldfarb and Jon Ratner (2008). Although they share our concerns, they explore a diversity of understandings of the terms "model" and "theory" and criticize us by suggesting that we used definitions of those terms that are not definitive, and that, with other definitions, an investigation may well have deemed more of the *JET* articles to qualify as theory.

8. The most notable occasions of his doing so are Smith (1790: 17, fn * on 46, 163–65, 193, 306); and Smith (1977: 49).

9. Find review excerpts at http://econfaculty.gmu.edu/klein/Assets/curbRtsPraise.html.

10. The idea of private ownership could be extended also to the streets, an idea discussed in Klein (2012: Chap. 11).

Chapter 7

1. For a detailed account of counterfactuals and causal inference in quantitative sociology and the context of justification, see Morgan and Winship (2007).

2. In functionalist explanations, the logic is pretty much the same with the difference that we ask about function instead of causation with y representing the system and x the substructure. As Roy comments: "Historical logic and functional logic each are capable of generating counterfactual analysis but differ in how they identify counterfactual possibilities and how they explain actual outcomes. Functional logic considers the function played by a structure and proposes alternative structures that could play the same function, explaining actual events by showing how they fulfilled the function better than other alternatives" (Roy 2001: 309).

3. A recent example of the same argument has been provided by Martin, who applies what he calls "simple counterfactualism" to this scenario: "A lives in Africa approximately 500,000 years before the present. Then, 500,000 years after A dies, C, breaking in to what was believed to be an empty store, encounters B and kills him. DNA mapping indicates that A is a distant ancestor of B or C. Did A cause the death of B?" (Martin 2011: 38). According to Martin, "the counterfactual understanding of causality" (ibid.: 33) must lead to an affirmative answer: "[W]e cannot ask the question, What caused B's death? and bring in anything less than an infinite number of causes, with little way of telling them apart" (ibid.: 38). Contrary to how others (see below) interpret counterfactual theorizing, Martin seems to assume that it presupposes a deterministic world governed by causal mechanisms. Although this might be the case with some social scientists, my argument is rather that counterfactuals are of particular relevance to social science because of the endless possibilities of each moment that human agency entails. If things could not have been different, counterfactual thinking becomes a quite meaningless exercise.

4. Here there are several similarities to the statistical testing of the null hypothesis (which also can never be definitely proven or falsified), but also one notable difference. The process of theorizing is much faster than the methodological labor that

takes place in the context of justification. For instance, as soon as we can leave the issue of Cleopatra's nose behind, there should be no need for counterfactually testing the significance of any other features of her appearance. Weber argues that we tend to arrive rather intuitively at our main suspects and that this is natural in the early phases of theorizing, regardless of discipline: "[I]t is absolutely no different with the really great advances in knowledge in mathematics and the natural sciences. They all arise intuitively in the intuitive flashes of imagination as hypotheses which are then 'verified' *vis-à-vis* the facts" (Weber 1949 [1922]: 176). For more about this "scientific intuition" and how it may be trained and developed, see Swedberg (2012: 16–19).

5. For some of Carr's counterfactuals, see Tetlock et al. (2006: 32).

6. But this is not meant to belittle the value of provocations. Provocative counterfactuals can be very helpful not only in historical research, but also in philosophical thought experiments to test ethical maxims, and in critical social science to defamiliarize institutions of the present day. A brilliant example of the latter has been offered by Bentall (1992), who in an article in the *Journal of Medical Ethics* proposes that happiness be classified as a psychiatric disorder. Bentall consistently demonstrates how happiness is statistically abnormal, how it is associated with different debilitating abnormalities, and how it may reflect the abnormal functioning of the central nervous system. The objection that happiness is not negatively valued is dismissed as scientifically irrelevant. Only in the last sentence does Bentall suggest the purpose of his provocation, namely to illustrate the importance of openly declaring the relevance of values in psychopathology.

7. Again, Wells's view of sociology is the exceptional one. Weber, who made no secret of his use of historical counterfactuals, has been described as one of the main proponents of value-free science with a sharp distinction between "Is" and "Ought" (see Dahrendorf 1987; Marcuse [1968] 2009). Yet in Lassman and Speirs's (1994) account, Weber's intellectual principles did not prevent him from engaging in political issues and taking an interest in what I here call utopian counterfactuals. In Weber's article "Academic Freedom in the Universities," he rejects the scientific justification of political demands as "senseless arrogance." What a scientist *could do*, Weber argues, is to *analyze* political demands, trace the beliefs and value judgments that underlie them and "next, explore their historical origin; then investigate the practical preconditions for and probable consequences of their realization; and finally establish whether current developments are moving in the right direction for these demands or not, and why. These are all really 'scientific' questions" (Weber [1909] 2008: 73). In other words, Weber cannot support scientists' invention and propagation of utopian counterfactuals themselves; the rest of Wells's normative program could easily be squeezed into the Weberian framework.

8. This distance is not only a necessity for producing critical theory; it is first and foremost a perspective from which relevant research questions may be posed irrespective of what their answer might be (which indeed must be subject to scientific inquiry). Consider Bell and *The Coming of Post-Industrial Society* ([1973] 1999]) in which he asks whether the enormous growth in industrial productivity potentially could result

in "the end of scarcity." The end of scarcity, a society in which all our needs are satisfied without labor, is a utopian counterfactual of mythological proportions. It appears already in ancient Greece and most notably in the sixteenth-century myth of *Schlaraffenland* (see Bloch [1959] 1986: 357), but it is also a counterfactual that has become increasingly relevant insofar as there are economic facts and technological achievements that challenge us to ask whether we could work less and still enjoy material abundance. Unlike Marx, Russell, Keynes, and the whole school of critical theory, Bell answers the question in the negative. It would be hard to deny that Bell's analysis to a large extent legitimizes the existing state of affairs (see Paulsen 2010: 163–66), yet, pushed by the counterfactual notion of the end of scarcity, Bell provides highly valuable theories regarding the "new scarcities" of post-industrialism.

9. The ideal speech situation remains one of the few utopian counterfactuals of critical theory that are explicitly defined. As Power (1996) comments, critical theories often suffer either from being too descriptive, drawing their conceptual resources from existing institutions and thus losing their critical edge; or from being too external in the sense that they become elitist and lose resonance in the experience of the people for whom the critique is articulated. Illustrating the latter problem, Horkheimer and especially Adorno clung to the idea that "wrong life cannot be lived rightly" (Adorno [1951] 2005: 39) and that this alienation renders it impossible to even imagine how life could be lived rightly (see Jaeggi 2005; Adorno and Horkheimer [1956] 2010: 55–56). This left their critique on the frail fundament of "radical despair," which eventually led into the abyss that Lukács mockingly named *das Grand Hotel Abgrund*. Marcuse and Neumann, on the other hand, were much more open with their practical-political ideals, and yet these were only vaguely defined and never as explicit as in Bloch, Gorz, or even Sartre (cf. Alway 1995).

10. Another example of counterfactual thinking in which facts are deliberately "bracketed" can be found in the early phenomenology of Husserl. For Husserl, taking counterfactuality into account guarantees the universality of phenomenology. Removing perception from varying "factualness," such as the color, material, or location of a table, and entering the "realm of the as-if, which supplies us with 'pure' possibilities," is precisely what characterizes his *eidetic* analysis. The universal perception of the *epoché* "floats in the air, so to speak—in the atmosphere of pure phantasiableness. Thus removed from all factualness, it has become the pure '*eidos*' perception, whose '*ideal*' extension is made up of all ideally possible perceptions, as purely phantasiable processes" (Husserl [1931] 1982: 70).

Chapter 8

1. Stevens (1965: 13). See endnote 4.

2. "It is crucially important to recognize that in each step of the process [of compound abstraction] a complete transformation, *in all dimensions,* has been accomplished, that the new form is never the same as that which previously existed whole. While active condensation can be considered a gain using external criteria (for

example, expediency), this change in dimensions is not accomplished without loss (a loss, specifically, of information). Here Wortz's law applies, as a complement to the gestalt conception of the world: 'Each new whole is *less* than the sum of its parts" (Irwin 2011: 172).

3. As a side note, Irwin formulated his ideas about compound abstraction in a 1977 exhibition catalogue for the Whitney Museum. One body of work that he mentioned as moving away from uncontestable formalisms was "ethno-methodology," which he described as "now trying to account fully for the relativity of the observer/individual, the human element, represented in the unique perspective of the individual as the ultimate frame of reference" (Irwin 2011: 183).

4. See endnote 1. "A language [theory], considered semantically, *evolves* through a *series of conflicts* between the denotative and connotative forces in words; between an asceticism tending to kill language by stripping words of all association and a hedonism tending to kill language by dissipating their sense in a multiplicity of associations. These conflicts are nothing more than changes in the relation between imagination and reality" (Stevens 1965: 13, emphasis added).

5. The application of Irwin's scheme to organizational issues is illustrated in an analysis of sensemaking at NASA that resulted in the disintegration of the Columbia space shuttle over Texas (Weick 2005). The rapid compounding of abstraction produced formalized actions by higher-level NASA personnel who concluded that the apparent foam shedding fit the general category of an "in-family event that is well understood" (misplaced abstraction), while those lower in the hierarchy worried that the particulars of their perceptions, conceptions, and forms were indications of a far more serious problem that was an "out-of-family event not well understood."

6. The content of this note is found on p. 1476 of Volume 3 of *Principles of Psychology*, which was created in 1981 to include "Notes, Appendices, Apparatus, General Index" not found in the original two volumes published by Harvard University Press.

7. Magala (1997: 324) has described sensemaking as "inventing a new meaning (interpretation) for something that has already occurred during the organizing process, *but does not yet have a name* (emphasis in original), [and] has never been recognized as a separate autonomous process, object, event."

Chapter 9

This essay is based on some comments originally prepared for the Ford Foundation and subsequently presented as an invited address at the 1976 annual meeting of the American Educational Research Association in San Francisco. In the ensuing years, I have often shared the sentiments with colleagues and have occasionally shared the text but have never seen a good reason or had a good opportunity for more extensive circulation. I am grateful to Richard Swedberg for providing both reason and opportunity and for his comments on the essay. In addition, I am in debt to a number of friends who have talked or written on what I think is essentially the same topic, although they may not agree. Most notably, those are Sheila Cahill, Carol Clawson,

Michael Cohen, Elliot Eisner, Margaret Floden, Robert Floden, Martin Krieger, Susan Krieger, Gail McCutcheon, Clarissa McDaniel, Martin Rein, Terri Saario, Gail Stockholm, David Tyack, Elizabeth Vallance, and Stephen Weiner.

Afterword

Thanks to Isaac Reed and Iddo Tavory for helpful comments on this chapter.

Bibliography

Abbott, Andrew. 2009. "Organizations and the Chicago School." In *The Oxford Handbook of Sociology and Organization Studies*, ed. P. Adler, pp. 399–420. New York: Oxford University Press.

———. 2004. *Methods of Discovery: Heuristics for the Social Sciences*. New York: W. W. Norton.

———. 2001. *Chaos of Disciplines*. Chicago: University of Chicago Press.

Abolafia, Mitchel Y. 1996. "Hyper-Rational Gaming," *Journal of Contemporary Ethnography* 25(2): 226–50.

Adams, Julia. 2010. "The Unknown James Coleman: Culture and History in *Foundations of Social Theory*," *Contemporary Sociology* 39 (3): 253–58.

Adorno, Theodor W. [1951] 2005. *Minima Moralia: Reflections on a Damaged Life*. London; New York: Verso.

———. 1980. "Commitment." In Theodor W. Adorno, *Aesthetics and Politics*, ed. R. Taylor, pp. 177–96. London: Verso.

Adorno, Theodor W., and Max Horkheimer. 2010 [1956]. "Towards a New Manifesto." *New Left Review* 65 (Sept.– Oct.): 32––61.

Adorno, Theodor, Else Frenkel-Brunswik, Daniel Levinson, and Nevitt Sanford. 1950. *The Authoritarian Personality*. New York: Harper & Row.

Akerlof, George A. 1970. "The Market for 'Lemons': Quality Uncertainty and the Market Mechanism." *Quarterly Journal of Economics* 84(3): 488–500.

Alexander, Jeffrey C. 1995. "Modern, Anti, Post, and Neo: How Intellectuals Have Coded, Narrated, and Explained the 'New World of Our Time.'" In *Fin-de-Siecle Social Theory: Relativism, Reduction, and the Problem of Reason*, pp. 6–64. New York: Verso.

———. 1981. *Theoretical Logic in Sociology*. Vol. 1: *Positivism, Presuppositions, and Current Controversies*. Berkeley: University of California Press.

Allan, Kenneth, and Jonathan Turner. 2000. "A Formalization of Postmodern Theory," *Sociological Perspectives* 43(3): 363–85.

Alway, Joan. 1995. *Critical Theory and Political Possibilities: Conceptions of Emancipa-
tory Politics in the Works of Horkheimer, Adorno, Marcuse, and Habermas.* West-
port, Conn.: Greenwood Press.

Aufrecht, Monica. 2010. *Values in Science: The Distinction between the Context of Discovery and the Context of Justification.* PhD dissertation, University of Washington.

Bachelard, Gaston. [1934] 1984. *The New Scientific Spirit.* Boston: Beacon Press.

Baehr, Peter. 2013. "The Honored Outsider: Raymond Aron as Sociologist," *Sociological Theory* 31: 93–115.

Bail, Christopher. 2014. "The Cultural Environment: Measuring Culture with Big
Data," *Theory and Society.* v. 43.

Bailey, Kenneth. 1973. "Constructing Monothetic and Polythetic Typologies by the
Heuristic Method," *Sociological Inquiry* 14 (Summer): 291–308.

Baird, Benjamin, Jonathan Smallwood, Michael D. Mrazek, Julia W. Y. Kam,
Michael S. Franklin, and Jonathan W. Schooler. 2012. "Inspired by Distraction:
Mind Wandering Facilitates Creative Incubation," *Psychological Science* 23(10):
1117–22.

Bakken, Tore, and Tor Hernes. 2006. "Organizing Is Both a Verb and a Noun: Weick
Meets Whitehead," *Organization Studies* 27 (November): 1599–1616.

Becker, Howard. 1998. *Tricks of the Trade: How to Think about Your Research While
Doing It.* Chicago: University of Chicago Press.

Bell, Daniel. [1973] 1999. *The Coming of Post-Industrial Society: A Venture in Social
Forecasting.* New York: Basic Books.

Benson, J. Kenneth. 1977. "Organizations: A Dialectical View," *Administrative Science
Quarterly* 22(1): 1–21.

Bentall, Richard P. 1992. "A Proposal to Classify Happiness as a Psychiatric Disorder."
Journal of Medical Ethics 18(2): 94–98.

Berger, Joseph, and Morris Zelditch, eds. 2002. *Contemporary Sociological Theories:
New Directions.* New York: Rowman & Littlefield.

Berger, Joseph, David Willer, and Morris Zelditch. 2005. "Theory Programs and Theoretical Problems," *Sociological Theory* 23(1): 127–55.

Berger, Peter, and Hansfried Kellner. 1964. "Marriage and the Construction of Reality," *Diogenes* 46: 1–25.

Bernal, John Desmond. 1939. *The Social Function of Science.* New York: Macmillan.

Bernstein, Richard J. 1978. *The Restructuring of Social and Political Theory.* Philadelphia: University of Pennsylvania Press.

Besnard, Philippe. 1987. *L'anomie: Ses usages et ses functions dans la discipline soci-
ologique depuis Durkheim.* Paris: Presses Universitaires de France.

Beveridge, William. 1862. *Theological Works.* Vol. I. Oxford: John Henry Parker.

Bhaskar, Roy. 1979. *The Possibility of Naturalism: A Philosophical Critique of the
Contemporary Human Sciences.* Atlantic Highlands, N.J.: Humanities Press.

Black, Max. 1962. *Models and Metaphors: Studies in Language and Philosophy*. Ithaca, N.Y.: Cornell University Press.

Blalock, Hubert. 1969. *Theory Construction: From Verbal to Mathematical Formulations*. Englewood, N.J.: Prentice-Hall.

Blau, Peter M. 1964. *Power and Exchange in Social Life*. New York. Wiley.

Bloch, Ernst. [1959] 1986. *The Principle of Hope*. Cambridge, Mass.: MIT Press.

Blumer, Herbert. 1960. *Symbolic Interactionism*. Cambridge, U.K.: Cambridge University Press

Booth, Wayne C. 1974. *Modern Dogma and the Rhetoric of Assent*. Chicago: University of Chicago Press.

Bourdieu, Pierre. 2000. *Pascalian Meditations*. Cambridge: Polity Press.

———. 1990. *Outline of a Theory of Practice*. Cambridge, U.K.: Cambridge University Press.

———. 1988. *Homo Academicus*. Stanford, Calif.: Stanford University Press.

Brent, Joseph. 1998. *Charles Sanders Peirce: A Life*. Bloomington: Indiana University Press.

Bruun, Hans Henrik. 2007. *Science, Values and Politics in Max Weber's Methodology*. New expanded edition. Aldershot, U.K.: Ashgate.

Buechler, Steven M. 2011. *Understanding Social Movements: Theories from the Classical Era to the Present*. Boulder, Colo.: Paradigm Publishers.

———. 2004. "The Strange Career of Strain and Breakdown Theories of Collective Action." In *The Blackwell Companion to Social Movements*, ed. David Snow, Sarah Soule, and Hanspeter Kriesi, pp. 47–66. Malden, Mass.: Blackwell.

Burawoy, Michael. 2011. "Argument: Michael Burawoy and Russell Jacoby." *Dissent* (February).

———. 2005. "For Public Sociology," *Soziale Welt* 56(4): 347–74.

———. 1990. "Marxism as Science: Historical Challenges and Theoretical Growth," *American Sociological Review* 55: 775–93.

———. 1979. *Manufacturing Consent*. Chicago: University of Chicago Press.

Busso, Mauro. 2010. "Not So Dismal" [Interview with Paul Krugman], *Bloomberg Markets*, October 13.

Byrne, Ruth M. J. 2005. *The Rational Imagination: How People Create Alternatives to Reality*. Cambridge, Mass.: MIT Press.

Camic, Charles, Neil Gross, and Michèle Lamont, eds. 2011. *Social Knowledge in the Making*. Chicago: University of Chicago Press.

Campbell, Lewis, and William Garnett. 2001. *The Life of James Clerk Maxwell*. London: Macmillan.

Carchedi, Guiglielmo. 1987. *Class Analysis and Social Research*. Oxford, U.K.: Blackwell.

Carleheden, Mikael. 1998. "Another Sociology—The Future of Sociology from a Critical Theoretical Perspective." *Dansk Sociologi*, Special Issue.

Carr, Edward Hallett. 1962. *What Is History?* New York: Knopf.

Carruthers, Peter. 2009. "An Architecture for Dual Reasoning." In *Two Minds: Dual*

Processes and Beyond, ed. J. Evans and K. Frankish. Oxford, pp. 108–28., U.K.: Oxford University Press.

Carter, Rita. 1999. *Mapping the Mind.* Berkeley: University of California Press.

Castells, Manuel. 1996. *The Rise of the Network Society.* Cambridge, U.K.: Blackwell.

Chatterji, Shurojit, and Sayantan Ghosal. 2004. "Local Coordination and Market Equilibria." *Journal of Economic Theory* 114(2): 255–79.

Chomsky, Noam. 2009. "The Political Philosophy of Noam Chomsky," *Against the Grain,* radio broadcast, November 11.

Churchland, Patricia S. 2002. *Brain-Wise: Studies in Neurophilosophy.* Cambridge, Mass.: MIT Press.

Coelho, Philip R. P., and James E. McClure. 2008. "The Market for Lemmas: Evidence That Complex Models Rarely Operate in Our World." *Econ Journal Watch* 5(1): 78–90.

Cohen, Morris Raphael, and Fernand S. Cohen, eds. 1954. *American Thought: A Critical Sketch.* New York: Free Press.

Cole, Stephen. 2004. "Merton's Contribution to the Sociology of Science." *Social Studies of Science* 34(6): 829–44.

———, ed. 2001. *What's Wrong with Sociology?* New Brunswick, N.J.: Transaction.

Coleman, James S., and Thomas Hoffer. 1987. *Public and Private High Schools: The Impact of Community.* New York: Basic Books.

Collier, David, Jody Laporte, and Jason Seawright. 2008. "Typologies: Forming Concepts and Creating Categorical Variables." In *The Oxford Handbook of Political Methodology,* ed. Janet M. Box-Steffensmeier, Henry E. Brady, and David Collier, pp. 152–73. New York: Oxford University Press.

Collins, Harry. 2010. *Tacit and Explicit Knowledge.* Chicago: University of Chicago Press.

Collins, Randall. 1998. *The Sociology of Philosophies: A Global Theory of Intellectual Change.* Cambridge, Mass.: The Belknap Press of Harvard University Press.

———. 1989. "Sociology: Proscience or Antiscience?" *American Sociological Review* 54: 124–39.

Comte, Auguste. [1855] 1896. *The Positive Philosophy of Auguste Comte.,* 3 vols. Translated and condensed by Harriet Martineau. London: George Bell & Sons.

Corley, Kevin G., and Dennis A. Gioia. 2011. "Building Theory about Theory Building: What Constitutes a Theoretical Contribution," *Academy of Management Review* 36(1): 12–32.

Coslor, Erica. 2011. "Wall Streeting Art: The Construction of Artwork as an Alternative Investment and the Strange Rules of the Art Market." PhD dissertation, Department of Sociology, University of Chicago.

Csikszentmihalyi, Mihaly. 1990. *Flow. The Psychology of Optimal Experience.* New York: Harper & Row.

———. 1988. "The Flow Experience and Its Significance for Human Psychology." In *Optimal Experience: Psychological Studies of Flow in Consciousness,* ed. M. Csikszentmihalyi, pp. 15–35. Cambridge, U.K.: Cambridge University Press.

Dahrendorf, Ralf. 1987. "Max Weber and Modern Social Science." In *Max Weber and His Contemporaries*, ed. W. J. Mommsen and J. Osterhammel , pp. 574–80. London: Allen & Unwin.

Damasio, Antonio. 2012. *Self Comes to Mind: Constructing the Conscious Brain*. New York: Pantheon Books.

———. 2009. "Neuroscience and the Emergence of Neuroeconomics." In *Neuroeconomics: Decision Making and the Brain*, ed. P. W. Glimcher, pp. 209–13. Amsterdam: Academic Press / Elsevier.

———. 2003. *Looking for Spinoza. Joy, Sorrow, and the Feeling Brain*. Orlando, Fla.: Harcourt.

———. 1994. *Descartes' Error: Emotion, Reason and the Human Brain*. London: Vintage.

Daston, Lorraine, and Elizabeth Lunbeck, eds. 2011. *Histories of Scientific Observation*. Chicago: University of Chicago Press.

Davenport, Thomas H., and John C. Beck. 2001. *The Attention Economy: Understanding the New Currency of Business*. Boston: Harvard Business School Press.

Davies, James C. 1962. "Toward a Theory of Revolution," *American Sociological Review* 27(1): 5–19.

Davis, Murray S. 1971. "That's Interesting." *Philosophy of the Social Sciences* 1: 309–44.

De Neys, Wim. 2006. "Dual Processing in Reasoning: Two Systems but One Reasoner," *Psychological Science* 17(5): 428–33.

Dening, Greg. 2004. *Beach Crossings: Voyaging across Times, Cultures, and Self*. Philadelphia: University of Pennsylvania Press.

———. 1996. *Performances*. Chicago: University of Chicago Press.

Derrida, Jacques. 1988. *Limited Inc*. Evanston, Ill.: Northwestern University Press.

Dewey, John. [1922] 2002. *Human Nature and Conduct*. Mineola, N.Y.: Dover.

———. 1930. *The Quest for Certainty: A Study of the Relationship between Knowledge and Action*. London: Allen & Unwin.

Dietrich, Arne. 2004. "Neurocognitive Mechanisms Underlying the Experience of Flow," *Consciousness and Cognition* 13(4): 746–61.

Doyle, Sir Arthur Conan. [1891] 2001. *The Adventures of Sherlock Holmes*. London: The Electronic Book Company.

Deutsch, M., and R. M. Krauss. 1960. "The Effect of Threat on Interpersonal Bargaining," *Journal of Abnormal and Social Psychology* 61: 181–89.

Dreyfus, Hubert, and Stuart Dreyfus. 1986. *Mind over Machine: The Power of Human Intuition and Expertise in the Era of the Computer*. New York: Free Press.

Durkheim, Emile. [1895] 1982. *The Rules of Sociological Method*. Translated by W. D. Halls. New York: Free Press.

———. [1895] 1964. *The Rules of Sociological Method*. Translated by Sarah Solvay and John Mueller. New York: Free Press.

Eliot, T. S. 1961. *On Poetry and Poets*. New York, NY: Farrar, Straus and Giroux. Reprinting of "The Frontiers of Criticism" (1956).

Elster, Jon. 2010. "Obscurantisme dur et obscurantisme mou dans les sciences humaines et sociales," *Diogène* 1: 231–47.

———. 1983. *Sour Grapes: Studies in the Subversion of Rationality*. Cambridge, U.K.: Cambridge University Press.

Engell, James. 1981. *The Creative Imagination: Enlightenment to Romanticism*. Cambridge, Mass: Harvard University Press.

Engelskirchen, Howard. 2007. "The Aristotelian Marx and Scientific Realism: A Perspective on Social Kinds in Social Theory." PhD dissertation, State University of New York at Binghamton.

Epstein, Steven. 1996. *Impure Science: AIDS, Activism, and the Politics of Knowledge*. Berkeley: University of California Press.

Evans, Jonathan St. B. T. 2012. "Dual-Process Theories of Deductive Reasoning: Facts and Fallacies." In *The Oxford Handbook of Thinking and Reasoning*, ed. K. J. Holyoak and R. G. Morrisom, pp. 115–33. Oxford, U.K.: Oxford University Press.

———. 2008. "Dual-Processing Accounts of Reasoning, Judgment and Social Cognition," *Annual Review of Psychology* 59: 255–78.

Evans, Margaret. 1961. "A Biographical Profile of Robert K. Merton," *The New Yorker* 28: 39–63.

Fan, Jin, Bruce D. McCandliss, John Fossela, Jonathan I. Flombaum, and Michael I. Posner. 2005. "The Activation of Attentional Networks," *Neuroimage* 26: 471–79.

Farber, Ilya. 2005. "Reality, Truth and the Convergence of Inquiry in the Limit," *Transactions of the Charles S. Peirce Society* 41(3): 541–66.

Ferguson, Niall. 1999. *Virtual History: Alternatives and Counterfactuals*. New York: Basic Books.

Fischhoff, Baruch. 1975. "Hindsight Is Not Foresight: The Effect of Outcome Knowledge on Judgment under Uncertainty," *Journal of Experimental Psychology: Human Perception and Performance* 1(3): 288–99.

Fisher, Mark. 2009. *Capitalist Realism: Is There No Alternative?* Winchester, U.K.: Zero Books.

Fiss, Peer C., and Paul M. Hirsch. 2005. "The Discourse of Globalization; Framing and Sensemaking of an Emerging Concept," *American Sociological Review* 70: 29–52.

Fitzgerald, Tina, Alice Fothergill, Kristin Gilmore, Katherine Irwin, Charlotte A. Kunkel, Suzanne Leahy, Joyce M. Nielsen, Eve Passerini, Mary E. Virnoche and Glenda Walden. 1995. "What's Wrong Is Right: A Response to the State of the Discipline," *Sociological Forum* 10(3): 493–98.

Fleck, Christian. 2011. *A Transatlantic History of the Social Sciences: Robber Barons, the Third Reich and the Invention of Empirical Social Research*. Translated by Hella Beister. London: Bloomsbury Academic.

Fleck, Ludwik. [1935] 1979. *Genesis and Development of a Scientific Fact*. Edited by Thaddeus J. Trenn and Robert K. Merton, with a foreword by Thomas S. Kuhn. Chicago: University of Chicago Press.

Franck, Georg. 2007. *Ökonomie der Aufmerksamkeit*. Munich: C. Hanser Verlag.

Franks, David D. 2010. *Neurosociology: The Nexus between Neuroscience and Social Psychology*. New York: Springer.

Freese, Lee. 1981. "The Formalization of Theory and Method." In *The State of Sociology*, ed. James Short, pp. 60–78. London: Sage.

——, ed. 1980. *Theoretical Methods in Sociology: Seven Essays*. Pittsburgh, Penn.: University of Pittsburgh Press.

Frickel, Scott, and Neil Gross. 2005. "A General Theory of Scientific/Intellectual Movements," *American Sociological Review* 70: 204–32.

Friedman, Milton, and Rose Friedman. 1980. *Free to Choose: A Personal Statement*. New York: Avon Books.

Fromm, Erich. 1941. *Escape from Freedom*. New York: Rinehart.

Fuller, Steve. 2001. *Thomas Kuhn: A Philosophical History for Our Times*. Chicago: University of Chicago Press.

Gandhi, Leela. 1998. *Postcolonial Theory: A Critical Introduction*. New York: Columbia University Press.

Gane, Mike. 2006. *August Comte*. London: Routledge.

Gazzaniga, Michael S. 2008. *Human: The Science behind What Makes Us Unique*. New York: Harper Collins.

Geertz, Clifford. 1995. *After the Fact*. Cambridge, Mass.: Harvard.

——. 1973. "Thick Description: Toward an Interpretive Theory of Culture." *The Interpretation of Cultures*, pp. 3–31. New York: Basic Books.

Gentner, Dedre. 2003. "Analogical Reasoning, Psychology of." In *Encyclopedia of Cognitive Science*, Vol. 1, pp. 106–12. London: Nature Publishing Company.

——. 1983. "Structure-Mapping: A Theoretical Framework for Analogy," *Cognitive Science* 7: 155–70.

Gerhardt, Uta. 2011. *The Social Thought of Talcott Parsons*. New York: Ashgate.

Gibbard, Allan, and Hal R. Varian. 1978. "Economic Models," *The Journal of Philosophy* 75: 664–677.

Giddens, Anthony. 1987. *Social Theory and Modern Sociology*. Stanford, Calif.: Stanford University Press.

Gieryn, Thomas. 1982. "Relativist/Constructivist Programmes in the Sociology of Science: Redundance and Retreat," *Social Studies of Science* 12: 279–97.

Gigerenzer, Gerd. 2007. *Gut Feelings. The Intelligence of the Unconscious*. New York: Viking.

Girotto, Vittorio, Legrenzi, Paolo, and Rizzo, Antonio. 1991. "Event Controllability in Counterfactual Thinking," *Acta Psychologica* 78 (1–3): 111–33.

Gladwell, Malcolm. 2008. *Outliers: The Story of Success*. New York: Little, Brown.

——. 2005. *Blink: The Power of Thinking without Thinking*. London: Penguin Books.

Glaser, Barney, and Anselm Strauss. 1967. *The Discovery of Grounded Theory*. Chicago: Aldine Press.

Go, Julian. 2013. "Enter 'Postcolonial Theory,'" *Perspectives* 35(1): 1–2, 6.

——. 2008. "Global Fields and Imperial Forms," *Sociological Theory* 26(3): 201–29.

Goffman, Erving. 1974. *Frame Analysis*. New York: Harper Colophon.

———. 1961. *Asylums*. Garden City, N.Y.: Anchor.

Goldfarb, Robert S., and Jon Ratner. 2008. "'Theory' and 'Models': Terminology through the Looking Glass." *Econ Journal Watch* 5(1): 91–108.

Goldstone, Jack, and Bert Useem. 1999. "Prison Riots as Micro-Revolutions," *American Journal of Sociology* 104: 985–1029.

Goldthorpe, John. 2007. *On Sociology*. 2nd edition. Stanford, Calif.: Stanford University Press.

Gorz, André. 1999. *Reclaiming Work: Beyond the Wage-Based Society*. Cambridge, U.K.: Polity Press.

Gouldner, Alvin Ward. 1970. *The Coming Crisis of Western Sociology*. New York: Basic Books.

———. 1968. "Reciprocity and Autonomy in Functional Theory." In *Symposium in Sociological Theory*, ed. L. Gross, pp. 251–70. New York: Harper & Row.

Graeber, David. 2004. *Fragments of an Anarchist Anthropology*. Chicago: Prickly Paradigm Press.

Groopman, Jerome. 2007. *How Doctors Think*. Boston: Houghton Mifflin.

Gross, Neil. 2007. "Pragmatism, Phenomenology, and Twentieth-Century American Sociology." In *Sociology in America: A History*, ed. C. Calhoun, pp. 183–224. Chicago: University of Chicago Press.

Gurr, Ted. 1970. *Why Men Rebel*. Princeton, N.J.: Princeton University Press.

Habermas, Jürgen . 1989. *The Structural Transformation of the Public Sphere: An Inquiry into a Category of Bourgeois Society*. Cambridge, Mass.: MIT Press.

———. 1984. *The Theory of Communicative Action*. Vol. 1: *Reason and the Rationalization of Society*. London: Heinemann Educational.

———. 1971. *Knowledge and Human Interests*. Boston: Beacon Press.

Hacking, Ian. 2004. *Historical Ontology*. Cambridge, Mass.: Harvard University Press.

Hage, Jerald, ed. 1994. *Formal Theory in Sociology: Opportunity or Pitfall?* Albany: State University of New York Press.

Haidt, Jonathan. 2001. "The Emotional Dog and Its Rational Tail: A Social Intuitionist Approach to Moral Judgment," *Psychological Review* 108(4): 814–34.

Haidt, Jonathan, and Selin Kesebir. 2010. "Morality." In *Handbook of Social Psychology*, 5th edition, ed. S. Fiske and D. Gilbert, pp. 797–832. Hoboken, N.J.: Wiley.

Handke, Peter. 1974. *Short Letter, Long Farewell*. New York, N.Y.: Farrar, Straus and Giroux.

Hardin, Garrett. 1968. "The Tragedy of the Commons," *Science* 162(3859): 1243–48.

Haskell, Thomas L. 1984. "Professionalism versus Capitalism: R. H. Tawney, Emile Durkheim, and C. S. Peirce on the Disinterestedness of Professional Communities." In *The Authority of Experts: Studies in History and Theory*, ed. Thomas L. Haskell, pp. 180–225. Bloomington: Indiana University Press.

Hassin, Ran R., James. S. Uleman, and John A. Bargh, eds. 2005. *The New Unconscious*. Oxford, U.K.: Oxford University Press.

Hausman, Daniel M. 1992. *The Inexact and Separate Science of Economics*. Cambridge, U.K.: Cambridge University Press.

Hawthorn, Geoffrey. 1991. *Plausible Worlds: Possibility and Understanding in History and the Social Sciences*. Cambridge, U.K.: Cambridge University Press.

Hayek, Friedrich A. [1955] 1972. *The Counter-Revolution of Science*. Glencoe, Ill.: Free Press.

———. 1952. *Sensory Order: An Inquiry into the Foundations of Theoretical Psychology*. Chicago: University of Chicago Press.

Hechter, Michael, and Satoshi Kanazawa. 1997. "Sociological Rational Choice Theory," *Annual Review of Sociology* 23: 191–214.

Hedström, Peter, and Richard Swedberg. 1996. "Rational Choice, Empirical Research and the Sociological Tradition," *European Sociological Review* 12: 127–46.

———, eds. 1998. *Social Mechanisms: An Analytical Approach to Social Theory*. Cambridge, U.K.: Cambridge University Press.

Heidegger, Martin. 1977. "Science and Reflection". Pp. 154–82 in *The Question Concerning Technology and Other Essays*. New York: Harper.

———. 1962. *Being and Time*. New York: Harper & Row.

Heilbron, Johan. 2011. "Practical Foundations of Theorizing in Sociology: The Case of Pierre Bourdieu." In *Social Knowledge in the Making*, ed. C. Camic, N. Gross, and M. Lamont, pp. 181–224. Chicago: University of Chicago Press.

Hempel, Carl G., and Paul Oppenheim. 1948. "Studies in the Logic of Explanation." *Philosophy of Science* 15(2): 135–75.

Hernes, Tor. 2007. *Understanding Organization as Process: Theory for a Tangled World*. New York: Routledge.

Hickman, Larry A. 1990. *John Dewey's Pragmatic Technology*. Bloomington, Indiana: Indiana University Press.

Hilgartner, Stephen, and Charles L. Bosk. 1988. "The Rise and Fall of Social Problems: A Public Arenas Model," *American Journal of Sociology* 94(1): 53–78.

Hoffer, Eric. 1951. *The True Believer: Thoughts on the Nature of Mass Movements*. New York: Harper & Row.

Hollingshead, August B. 1949. *Elmtown's Youth*. New York: John Wiley.

Horowitz, Irving Louis. 1993. *The Decomposition of Sociology*. New York: Oxford University Press.

Howard, Gerald. 2007. "Reasons to Believe." *Bookforum* (Feb./Mar.). *http://www.bookforum.com/inprint/013_05/72* (accessed May 8, 2013).

Hoyningen-Huene, Paul. 1987. "Context of Discovery and Context of Justification," *Studies in History and Philosophy of Science* 18(4): 501–15.

Hughes, Everett C. 1984. *The Sociological Eye: Selected Papers*. New Brunswick, N.J.: Transaction Press.

Hume, David. [1748] 1955. *An Inquiry Concerning Human Understanding*. Edited by C.W. Hendel. New York: Bobbs-Merrill.

———. [1739/1740]. 1978. *A Treatise of Human Nature*. 2nd edition. Edited by L. A. Selby-Bigge and revised by P. H. Nidditch. Oxford, U.K.: Clarendon Press.

Husserl, Edmund. [1931] 1982. *Cartesian Meditations: An Introduction to Phenomenology.* Boston: M. Nijhoff.

Immordino-Yang, Mary Helen, and Kurt W. Fischer. 2010. "Neuroscience Bases of Learning." In *International Encyclopedia of Education,* 3rd edition, ed. V. G. Aukrust, pp. 310–16. Oxford, U.K.: Elsevier.

Irving, John. 1978. *The World According to Garp.* New York: E. P. Dutton.

Irwin, Robert. 2011. *Notes toward a Conditional Art.* Los Angeles: Getty Publications.

———. 1977. "Notes toward a Model." In *Exhibition Catalog for the Robert Irwin Exhibition, Whitney Museum of American Art, April 16–May 29, 1977,* pp. 22–31. New York: Whitney Museum of American Art.

Isaac, Joel. 2010. "Theorist at Work: Talcott Parsons and the Carnegie Project on Theory, 1949–1951," *Journal of the History of Ideas* 71(2): 287–311.

Jaeggi, Rahel. 2005. "'No Individual Can Resist': Minima Moralia as Critique of Forms of Life," *Constellations* 12(1): 65–82.

James, William. [1911] 1996. *Some Problems of Philosophy: A Beginning of an Introduction to Philosophy.* Lincoln: University of Nebraska Press.

———. 1987. *Writings: 1902–1910.* New York, Library of America.

———. 1981. *Principles of Psychology.* 2 vols. Cambridge, Mass.: Harvard University Press.

———. 1975. *Pragmatism.* Cambridge, Mass.: Harvard University Press.

———. 1950. *Principles of Psychology.* New York: Dover.

———. 1907. *Pragmatism: A New Name for Some Old Ways of Thinking.* New York: Longmans, Green.

Jameson, Fredric. 2003. "Future City," *New Left Review* 21: 65–80.

Kahn, Robert L., and Mayer N. Zald. 1990. *Organizations and Nation-States: New Perspectives on Conflict and Cooperation.* New York: Jossey-Bass.

Kahneman, Daniel. 2011. *Thinking, Fast and Slow.* London: Allen Lane.

Kahneman, Daniel, and Varey, Carol A. 1990. "Propensities and Counterfactuals: The Loser That Almost Won," *Journal of Personality and Social Psychology* 59(6): 1101–10.

Kant, Immanuel. [1784] 1970. "An Answer to the Question: 'What Is Enlightenment?'" In *Kant's Political Writings,* ed. Hans Reiss, pp. 54–60. New York: Cambridge University Press.

Katz, Jack. 2001. "Analytic Induction." In *International Encyclopedia of the Social and Behavioral Sciences,* Vol. 1, ed. N. J. Smelser and P. B. Baltes, pp. 480–84. Oxford, U.K.: Elsevier.

———. 1988. *Seductions of Crime.* Chicago: University of Chicago Press.

Kaufman, Scott B., and Jerome L. Singer. 2012. "The Creativity of Dual Process 'System 1' Thinking," *Scientific American.* http://blogs.scientificamerican.com/guestblog/2012/01/17/ the-creativity-of-dual-process-system-1-thinking/ (accessed February 4, 2013).

Kierkegaard, Søren. [1836] 1962. *The Present Age and of the Difference between a Genius and an Apostle.* New York: Harper & Row.

———. [1846] 1941. *Concluding Unscientific Postscript*. Princeton, N.J.: Princeton University Press.

Klein, Daniel B. 2012. *Knowledge and Coordination: A Liberal Interpretation*. New York: Oxford University Press.

Klein, Daniel B., and Pedro P. Romero. 2007. "Model Building versus Theorizing: The Paucity of Theory in the *Journal of Economic Theory*," *Econ Journal Watch* 4(2): 241–71.

Klein, Daniel B., Adrian T. Moore, and Binyam Reja. 1997a. *Curb Rights: A Foundation for Free Enterprise in Urban Transit*. Washington, D.C.: Brookings Institution Press.

———. 1997b. "Curb Rights: Eliciting Competition and Entrepreneurship in Urban Transit." *Independent Review* 2(1): 29–54. http://econfaculty.gmu.edu/klein/Pdf-Papers/CURB.PDF (accessed September 17, 2013).

Knorr Cetina, Karin. 2012. "What Is a Financial Market? Global Markets as Micro-institutional and Post-Traditional Social Forms." In *Handbook of the Sociology of Finance*, ed. K. Knorr Cetina and A. Preda, pp. 15–33. Oxford, U.K.: Oxford University Press.

———. 2009. "The Synthetic Situation: Interactionism for a Global World," *Symbolic Interaction* 32(1): 61–87.

———. 2003. "From Pipes to Scopes. The Flow Architecture of Financial Markets," *Journal Distinktion. Special Issue on Economic Sociology* 7: 7–23.

———. 1999/2003. *Epistemic Cultures. How the Sciences Make Knowledge*. Cambridge, Mass.: Harvard University Press.

———. 2002. "The Couch, the Cathedral, and the Laboratory: On the Relationship between Experiment and Laboratory in Science." In *Science as Practice and Culture*, ed. Andrew Pickering, pp. 113–38. Chicago: University of Chicago Press.

Knorr Cetina, Karin, and Urs Bruegger. 2002a. "Global Microstructures: The Virtual Societies of Financial Markets," *American Journal of Sociology* 107: 905–95.

———. 2002b. "Inhabiting Technology: Features of a Global Lifeform of Financial Markets," *Current Sociology* 50(3): 389–405.

Kornhauser, William. 1959. *The Politics of Mass Society*. Glencoe, Ill.: Free Press.

Kuhn, Thomas S. 1959. "The Essential Tension: Tradition and Innovation in Scientific Research." Reprinted in 1977 in *The Essential Tension: Selected Studies in Scientific Tradition and Change*, pp. 225–39. Chicago: University of Chicago Press.

Lakatos, Imre. 1970. "Falsification and the Methodology of Scientific Research Programmes." In *Criticism and the Growth of Knowledge*, ed. I. Lakatos and A. Musgrave, pp. 91–196. Cambridge, U.K.: Cambridge University Press.

Landman, J. 1987. "Regret and Elation Following Action and Inaction: Affective Responses to Positive versus Negative Outcomes," *Personality and Social Psychology Bulletin Personality and Social Psychology Bulletin* 13(4): 524–36.

Larkin, Jill, and Herbert Simon. 1987. "Why a Diagram Is (Sometimes) Worth 10,000 Words," *Cognitive Science* 11: 65–99.

Lash, Scott, and John Urry. 1987. *The End of Organized Capitalism*. Cambridge, U.K.: Polity Press.

Lassman, Peter, and Speirs, Ronald. 1994. "Introduction." In *Weber, Political Writings*, ed. P. Lassman and R. Speirs. pp. vii–xxv. Cambridge, U.K.: Cambridge University Press.

Latour, Bruno, and Vincent Antonin Lépinay. 2009. *The Science of Passionate Interests: An Introduction to Gabriel Tarde's Economic Anthropology*. Chicago: University of Chicago Press.

Laube, Stefan. 2008. "The Sounds of the Market: How Traders Keep the Pace with a "Silent" Market on Screen." Unpublished paper, University of Constance.

Lave, Charles A., and James G. March. [1975] 1993. *An Introduction to Models in the Social Sciences*. New York: University Press of America

Law, John. 2004. *After Method: Mess in Social Science Research*. London: Routledge.

Lazarsfeld, Paul F., and Morris Rosenberg, eds. 1972. *Continuities in the Language of Social Research*. Glencoe, Ill.: Free Press.

———. 1955. *The Language of Social Research: A Reader in the Methodology of Social Research*. Glencoe, Ill.: Free Press.

Leahey, Erin. 2007. "Not by Productivity Alone: How Visibility and Specialization Contribute to Academic Earnings," *American Sociological Review* 72: 533–61.

Lebow, Richard Ned. 2007. "Counterfactual Thought Experiments: A Necessary Teaching Tool," *The History Teacher* 40(2): 153–76.

LeDoux, Joseph E. 1996. *The Emotional Brain: The Mysterious Underpinnings of Emotional Life*. New York: Simon & Schuster.

Leijonhufvud, Axel. 1997. "Models and Theories," *Journal of Economic Methodology* 4(2): 193–98.

Lemert, Charles. 2000. "A Commentary on Allan and Turner. Sailing in Postmodern Winds: Formal Methods in Uncertain Worlds," *Sociological Perspectives* 43(3): 387–97.

Lenski, Gerhard. 1988. "Rethinking Macrosociological Theory," *American Sociological Review* 53: 163–71.

Levi, Edward. 1949. *An Introduction to Legal Reasoning*. Chicago: University of Chicago Press.

Levin, Peter. 2005. "Information, Prices, and Sensemaking in Financial Futures Trading." In *Qualitative Organizational Research: Best Papers from the Davis Conference on Qualitative Research*, ed. K. D. Elsbach, pp. 205–26. Greenwich, Conn.: Information Age Publishing.

Levitas, Ruth. 2010. "Back to the Future: Wells, Sociology, Utopia and Method," *The Sociological Review* 58(4): 530–47.

Lewis, David. 1973. *Counterfactuals*. Oxford, U.K.: Basil Blackwell.

Lindesmith, Alfred R. 1947. *Opiate Addiction*. Bloomington, Ind.: Principia Press.

Little, Daniel. 1986. *The Scientific Marx*. Minneapolis: University of Minnesota Press.

Longino, Helen. 2002. *The Fate of Knowledge*. Princeton, N.J.: Princeton University Press.

Loveman, Mara. 1998. "High-Risk Collective Action: Defending Human Rights in Chile, Uruguay and Argentina," *American Journal of Sociology* 104(2): 477–525.

Luhmann, Niklas. 1982. "The World Society as a Social System," *International Journal of General Systems* 8(3): 131–38.

———. 1981. "Kommunikation mit Zettelkästen. Ein Erfahrungsbericht." In *Öffentliche Meinung und sozialer Wandel. Für Elisabeth Noelle-Neumann*, ed. Horst Baier, pp. 222–28. Opladen: Wedstdeutscher Verlag.

Luker, Kristin. 2008. *Salsa Dancing in the Social Sciences: Research in an Age of Info-Glut*. Cambridge, Mass.: Harvard University Press.

Lukes, Steven. 2005. *Power: A Radical View*. 2nd edition. Basingstoke: Palgrave Macmillan.

Lutz, Catherine. 1995. "The Gender of Theory." In *Women Writing Culture/Culture Writing Women*, ed. R. Behar and D. Gordon, pp. 249–66. Berkeley: University of California Press.

MacIntyre, Alaisdair. 1984. *After Virtue*. 2nd edition. Notre Dame University Press.

MacKenzie, Donald. 2011. "The Credit Crisis as a Problem in the Sociology of Knowledge," *American Journal of Sociology* 116, 6: 1778–1841.

Magala, Slavomir J. 1997. "The Making and Unmaking of Sense," *Organization Studies* 18(2): 317–38.

Mahoney, James. 2004. "Comparative-Historical Methodology," *Annual Review of Sociology* 30(1): 81–101.

Manning, Peter K. 1979. "Metaphors of the Field," *Administrative Science Quarterly* 24(4): 660–71.

March, James G. 1970. "Making Artists out of Pedants." In *The Process of Model-Building in the Social Sciences*, ed. R. M. Stogdill, pp. 54–75. New York: Norton.

Marcuse, Herbert. [1968] 2009. *Negations: Essays in Critical Theory*. London: MayFly-Books.

———. [1964] 2008. *One-Dimensional Man: Studies in the Ideology of Advanced Industrial Society*. London: Routledge.

———. 1941. *Reason and Revolution: Hegel and the Rise of Social Theory*. New York: Oxford University Press.

Markovsky, Barry. 2008. "Graduate Training in Sociological Theory and Theory Construction," *Sociological Perspectives* 51(2): 423–45.

Martin, John Levi. 2011. *The Explanation of Social Action*. Oxford ; New York: Oxford University Press.

Marx, Karl, and Friedrich Engels. [1844] 1967. *The Communist Manifesto*. London: Penguin Books.

Maxwell, James Clerk. [1884] 1993. "Are There Real Analogies in Nature?" In *Truth versus Precision in Economics*, by Thomas Mayer, pp. 347–55. Hants: Edward Elgar.

McAdam, Doug. 1986. "Recruitment to High-Risk Activism: The Case of Freedom Summer," *American Journal of Sociology* 92(1): 64–90.

McCloskey, Deirdre N. 2000. *Economical Writing*. 2nd edition. Long Grove, Ill.: Waveland Press.

———. 1985. *The Rhetoric of Economics*. Madison: University of Wisconsin Press.

McCloy, Rachel, and Byrne, Ruth. 2000. "Counterfactual Thinking about Controllable Events," *Memory & Cognition* 28(6): 1071–78.

McCormick, John P. 2007. *Weber, Habermas and Transformations of the European State: Constitutional, Social, and Supranational Democracy*. Cambridge, U.K.: Cambridge University Press.

McMullen, Matthew, and Markman, Keith. 2002. "Affective Impact of Close Counterfactuals: Implications of Possible Futures for Possible Pasts," *Journal of Experimental Social Psychology* 38(1): 64–70.

Merton, Robert K. 1984. "Socio-Economic Duration: A Case Study of Concept Formation in Sociology." In *Conflict and Consensus: A Festschrift in Honor of Lewis A. Coser*, ed. Walter Powell and Richard Robbins, pp. 262–85. New York: Free Press.

Merton, Robert. [1941] 1968. "Karl Mannheim and the Sociology of Knowledge." In *Social Theory and Social Structure*, revised and enlarged edition, pp. 543–62. Glencoe, Ill.: Free Press.

Merton, Robert K. [1938] 1968. "Social Structure and Anomie." In *Social Theory and Social Structure*, revised and enlarged edition, pp. 185–214. New York: Free Press.

———. 1967. *On Theoretical Sociology*. New York: Free Press.

———. 1938. "Social Structure and Anomie," *American Sociological Review* 3(5): 672–82.

Merton, Robert K., and Elinor Barber. 2004. *The Travels and Adventures of Serendipity*. Princeton, N.J.: Princeton University Press.

Merton, Robert K., and Harriet Zuckerman. 1973. "Age, Aging, and Age Structure in Science." In *The Sociology of Science*, by Robert K. Merton, pp. 497–559. Chicago: University of Chicago Press.

Meyer, John W., and Brian Rowan. 1977. "Institutional Organizations: Formal Structure as Myth and Ceremony," *American Journal of Sociology* 83: 340–63.

Meyer, John W., John Boli, George M. Thomas, and Francisco O. Ramirez. 1997. "World Society and the Nation-State," *American Journal of Sociology* 103(1): 144–81.

Millett, Kate. 1971. *Sexual Politics*. Sheffield, U.K.: Equinox Books.

Mills, C. Wright. 1959. *The Sociological Imagination*. New York: Oxford University Press.

Monk, Ray. 1990. *Ludwig Wittgenstein: The Duty of Genius*. New York: Free Press.

Montesquieu, Charles de Secondat, Baron de. [1748] 1989. *The Spirit of the Laws*. Cambridge, U.K.: Cambridge University Press.

Moody, James. 2004. "The Structure of a Social Science Collaboration Network: Disciplinary Cohesion from 1963 to 1999," *American Sociological Review* 69: 213–38.

Morgan, Gareth. 1980. "Paradigms, Metaphors, and Puzzle-Solving in Organization Theory," *Administrative Science Quarterly* 2: 27–46.

Morgan, Stephen L., and Christopher Winship. 2007. *Counterfactuals and Causal Inference: Methods and Principles for Social Research*. New York: Cambridge University Press.

Naipaul, V. S. [1959] 2002. *Miguel Street*. New York: Vintage Books.

Nersessian, Nancy. 2008. *Creating Scientific Concepts*. Cambridge, Mass.: MIT Press.

Norris, Paul, and Seymour Epstein. 2011. "An Experiential Thinking Style: Its Facets and Relations with Objective and Subjective Criterion Measures," *Journal of Personality* 79(5): 1043–79.

Oakeshott, Michael. 1991. *On Human Conduct*. Oxford, U.K.: Clarendon Press.

Olson, James M., and Neal J. Roese. 2002. "Relative Deprivation and Counterfactual Thinking." In *Relative Deprivation: Specification, Development, and Integration*, ed. I. Walker and H. J. Smith, pp. 265–87. Cambridge, U.K.: Cambridge University Press.

Olson, Jr., Mancur. 1965. *The Logic of Collective Action: Public Goods and the Theory of Groups*. Cambridge, Mass.: Harvard University Press.

Packer, Martin J. 1985. "Hermeneutic Inquiry in the Study of Human Conduct," *American Psychologist* 40: 1081–93.

Patriotta, Gerardo. 2003. "Sensemaking on the Shop Floor: Narratives of Knowledge in Organizations," *Journal of Management Studies* 40(2): 349–76.

Paulsen, Roland. 2010. *Arbetssamhället: Hur Arbetet Överlevde Teknologin*. Malmö: Gleerups.

Peirce, C. S. 1992a. "The Fixation of Belief." In *The Essential Peirce*. Vol. 1, ed. Nathan Houser and Christian Kloesel. Bloomington, Ind.: Indiana University Press.

———. 1992b. "Some Consequences of Four Incapacities." In *The Essential Peirce*, Vol. 1, ed. Nathan Houser and Christian Kloesel, pp. 28–55. Bloomington, Ind.: Indiana University Press.

———. 1992c. "On the Logic of Drawing History from Ancient Documents: Especially from Testimonies." In *The Essential Peirce*. Vol. 2, ed. Nathan Houser and Christian Kloesel. Bloomington, Ind.: Indiana University Press.

———. 1992d/1998. *The Essential Peirce*. 2 vols. Bloomington: Indiana University Press.

———. 1992e. "Training in Reasoning." In *Reasoning and the Logic of Things*, pp. 181–96. Cambridge, Mass.: Harvard University Press.

———. 1934. "How to Theorize." In *Collected Papers of Charles Sanders Peirce*, Vol. 5, pp. 413–22. Cambridge, Mass.: Harvard University Press.

———. 1933. *Collected Papers of Charles Sanders Peirce*. Vol. 4. Cambridge, Mass.: Harvard University Press.

———. 1903. Lowell Lectures of 1903. Eighth Lecture. Abduction, MS 475.

Perin, Constance. 2005. *Shouldering Risks: The Culture of Control in the Nuclear Power Industry*. Princeton, N.J.: Princeton University Press.

Perrow, Charles. 1999. *Normal Accidents: Living with High-Risk Technologies*. Updated edition. Princeton, N.J.: Princeton University Press.

———. 1984. *Normal Accidents: Living with High-Risk Technologies*. New York: Basic Books.

Pfeffer, Jeffrey, and Gerald R. Salancik.1978. *The External Control of Organizations*. New York: Harper & Row.

Plato. [1968] 1991. *The Republic of Plato*. 2nd edition. Trans. Allan Bloom. New York: Basic Books.

Podolny, Joel M. 2003. "A Picture Is Worth a Thousand Symbols: A Sociologist's View of the Economic Pursuit of Truth," *American Economic Review* 93(2): 169–74.

Polanyi, Michael. 1966. *The Tacit Dimension*. Chicago: University of Chicago Press.

———. [1946] 1964. *Science, Faith and Society*. Chicago: University of Chicago Press.

———. 1963. *The Study of Man*. Chicago: University of Chicago Press.

Popper, Karl [1974] 1985. *Unended Quest: The Autobiography of Karl Popper*. La Salle, Ill.: Open Court.

———. 1959. *The Logic of Scientific Discovery*. London: Hutchinson.

———. 1935. *Logik der Forschung*. Vienna: Julius Springer.

Posner, Michael I., Albrecht W. Inhoff, Frances J. Friedrich, and Asher Cohen. 1987. "Isolating Attentional Systems: A Cognitive-Anatomical Analysis," *Psychobiology* 15: 107–21.

Powell, Walter W., and Paul J. DiMaggio, eds. 1991. *The New Institutionalism in Organizational Analysis*. Chicago: University of Chicago Press.

Power, Michael. 1996. "Habermas and the Counterfactual Imagination," *Cardozo Law Review*. 17(4/5–1): 1005.

Presidential Commission on the Space Shuttle Accident. 1986. *Report of the Presidential Commission on the Space Shuttle Accident*. 5 vols. Washington, D.C.: U.S. Government Printing Office.

Prus, Robert C. 1987. "Generic Social Processes," *Journal of Contemporary Ethnography* 16: 250–93.

Quiggin, John. 2007. "Why Should We Care What Klein and Romero Say about the *Journal of Economic Theory?*" *Econ Journal Watch* 4(3): 359–360.

———. 2004. "Invariant Risk Attitudes." *Journal of Economic Theory* 117(1): 96–118.

Radkau, Joachim. 2009. *Max Weber: A Biography*. Cambridge, U.K.: Polity Press.

Rafter, Nicole. 2011. "What Does It Mean to Say That Genocide Is a Crime?" Unpublished manuscript, School of Criminal Justice, Northeastern University.

Rancière, Jacques. 2010. "Introducing Disagreement," *Angelaki: Journal of the Theoretical Humanities* 9(3): 3–9.

Rapoport, Anatol, Melvin Guyer, and David Gordon. 1976. *The 2 x 2 Game*. Ann Arbor: University of Michigan Press.

Raz, Amir, and Jason Buhle. 2006. "Typologies of Attentional Networks," *Nature Reviews Neuroscience* 7: 367–79.

Reason, Peter. 1996. "Reflections on the Purposes of Human Inquiry," *Qualitative Inquiry* 2(1): 15–28.

Reed, Isaac. 2011. *Interpretation and Social Knowledge: On the Use of Theory in the Human Sciences*. Chicago: University of Chicago Press.

Reichenbach, Hans. 1962. *The Rise of Scientific Philosophy*. Berkeley: University of California Press.

———. 1938. *Experience and Prediction: An Analysis of the Foundations and the Structure of Knowledge*. Chicago, Ill.: University of Chicago Press.

Ritzer, George. 1975a. *Sociology: A Multiple Paradigm Science*. Boston: Allyn and Bacon.

———. 1975b. "Sociology: A Multiple Paradigm Science," *American Sociologist* 10(3): 156–67.

Roberts, Karlene H. 1990. "Some Characteristics of High Reliability Organizations," *Organization Science* 1: 160–77.

Roe, Emery, and Paul S. Schulman. 2008. *High Reliability Management: Operating on the Edge*. Stanford, Calif.: Stanford Business Books.

Roy, William G. 2001. "Functional and Historical Logics in Explaining the Rise of the American Industrial Corporation." In *The Sociology of Economic Life*, ed. M. Granovetter and R. Swedberg, pp. 305–26. Boulder, Colo.: Westview Press.

Ryle, Gilbert. 1979. "Improvisation." In *On Thinking*, pp. 121–30. London: Blackwell.

Sandvik, Siv, and Oddvin Aune. 2011. "Terrorekspert Tror Al-Qaida Står Bak," *NRK* (Norway), July 22.

Sartre, Jean-Paul. [1960] 2004. *Critique of Dialectical Reason*. Vol. 1. London: Verso.

Schelling, Thomas C. 1984. *Choice and Consequence*. Cambridge, Mass.: Harvard University Press.

———. 1978a. *Micromotives and Macrobehavior*. New York: Norton.

———. 1978b. "Thermostats, Lemons, and Other Families of Models." In *Micromotives and Macrobehavior*, pp. 81–134. New York: W. W. Norton.

———. 1960. *The Strategy of Conflict*. Cambridge, Mass.: Harvard University Press.

Schickore, Jutta, and Friedrich Steinle, eds. 2006. *Revisiting Discovery and Justification: Historical and Philosophical perspectives on the Context Distinction*. Dordrecht: Springer.

Schutz, Alfred. 1945. "On Multiple Realities," *Philosophy and Phenomenological Research* 5(4): 533–76.

Seidman, Steven. 1991. "The End of Sociological Theory: The Postmodern Hope," *Sociological Theory* 9: 131–46.

———. 1983. "Beyond Presentism and Historicism: Understanding the History of Social Science," *Sociological Inquiry* 53(1): 79–91.

Seidman, Steven, and David G. Wagner. 1992. *Postmodernism and Social Theory: The Debate over General Theory*. New York: Wiley-Blackwell.

Shils, Edward. 2006. *A Fragment of a Sociological Autobiography: The History of My Pursuit of a Few Ideas*, ed. Steven Grosby. New Brunswick, N.J.: Transaction Press.

———. Shils, Edward. 1954. "Authoritarianism: 'Right' and 'Left'." In *Studies in the Scope and Method of "The Authoritarian Personality,"* ed. Christie and M. Jahoda, pp. 24–49. New York: Free Press.

Shomer, R. W., A. H. Davis, and H. H. Kelley. 1966. "Threats and the Development of Coordination," *Journal of Personality and Social Psychology* 4: 119–26.

Shwed, Uri, and Peter S. Bearman. 2010. "The Temporal Structure of Scientific Consensus Formation," *American Sociological Review* 75(6): 817–40.

Silber, Ilana. 1995. "Space, Fields, Boundaries: The Rise of Spatial Metaphors in Contemporary Sociological Theory," *Social Research* 62 (2): 323–56.

Simmel, Georg. [1907] 1997. "Sociology of the Senses."In *Simmel on Culture*, ed. David Frisby and Mike Featherstone, pp. 109–19. London: Sage, 1997.

———. 1950. *The Sociology of Georg Simmel*. Trans. K. Wolff. New York: Free Press.

Simon, Herbert. 1991. "The Scientist as Problem Solver." In *Models of My Life*, pp. 368–87. New York: Basic Books.

Skjervheim, Hans. 1971. *Deltagare och Åskådare: Sex Bidrag till Debatten om Människans Frihet i det Moderna Samhället*. Stockholm: Prisma.

Skocpol, Theda. 1979. *States and Social Revolutions: A Comparative Analysis of France, Russia, and China*. Cambridge, U.K.: Cambridge University Press.

Small, Albion. 1896. "Review of Arthur Fairbanks, *An Introduction to Sociology*," *American Journal of Sociology* 2(2): 305–10.

Smelser, Neil. J. 1997. "Sociology as Science, Humanism, and Art." In *Sociological Visions: With Essays from Leading Thinkers of Our Time*, ed. Kai Erikson, pp. 17–29. New York: Rowman & Littlefield.

Smith, Adam. 1977. *The Correspondence of Adam Smith*. Eds. E.C. Mossner and I.S. Ross. Oxford: Oxford University Press.

Smith, Adam. [1776] 1976. *An Inquiry into the Nature and Causes of the Wealth of Nations*. Oxford, U.K.: Oxford University Press.

———. [1790] 1982. *The Theory of Moral Sentiments*. Indianapolis: Liberty Fund.

Snow, David, Calvin Morrill, and Leon Anderson. 2003. "Elaborating Analytic Ethnography," *Ethnography* 4(2): 181–200.

Spence, A. Michael. 1974. *Market Signaling*. Cambridge, Mass.: Harvard University Press.

Steinbeck, John, and Edward F. Ricketts. 1941. *Sea of Cortez*. New York: Viking.

Stenner, Paul. 1998. "Heidegger and the Subject: Questioning Concerning Psychology," *Theory and Psychology* 8 (1): 59–77.

Stevens, Wallace. 1965. *The Necessary Angel: Essays on Reality and the Imagination*. New York: Vintage.

Stichweh, Rudolf. 2000. *Die Weltgesellschaft. Soziologische Analysen*. Frankfurt/Main: Suhrkamp.

Stinchcombe, Arthur L. 1978. *Theoretical Methods in Social History*. New York: Academic Press.

———. 1968. *Constructing Social Theories*. Chicago: University of Chicago Press.

Stock, Armin, and Claudia Stock. 2004. "A Short History of Ideo-Motor Action," *Psychological Research* 68: 176–88.

Strassmann, Diana. 1994. "Feminist Thought and Economics; Or, What Do the Visigoths Know?" *American Economic Review*, Papers and Proceedings 84(2): 153–58.

Strauss, Leo. 1953. *Natural Right and History*. Chicago: University of Chicago Press.

Sugden, Robert. 2002. "Credible Worlds: The Status of Theoretical Models in Economics." In *Fact and Fiction in Economics: Models, Realism and Social Construction*, ed. U. Maki, pp. 107–36. West Nyack, N.Y.: Cambridge University Press.

Sunstein, Cass. 1993. "On Analogical Reasoning," *Harvard Law Review* 106: 741–91.

Sutherland, Edwin H. 1949. *White-Collar Crime*. New York: Dryden Press.

Swedberg, Richard. 2013. "On C. S. Peirce's Lecture 'How to Theorize' 1903." Unpublished manuscript, Department of Sociology, Cornell University.

———. 2012a. "On Charles S. Peirce's *'How To Theorize'*(1903), " *Sociologica* 2: 1–26.

———. 2012b. "Theorizing in Sociology and Social Science: Turning to the Context of Discovery," *Theory and Society* 41(1): 1–40.

———. 2011. "Thinking and Sociology," *Journal of Classical Sociology* 11(1): 31–49.

———. 2010. "From Theory to Theorizing," *Perspectives: Newsletter of the ASA Theory Section* 32(2): 7–9.

———. 2009a. "The Craft of Theorizing," *Perspectives: Newsletter of the ASA Theory Section* 31(2): 1, 7.

———. 2009b. *Tocqueville's Political Economy*. Princeton, N.J.: Princeton University Press.

———. 2009c. "Tocqueville as an Empirical Researcher." In *Raymond Boudon: A Life in Sociology*, Vol. 1, ed. Mohammed Cherkaoui and Peter Hamilton, pp. 279–92. Oxford: Bardwell Press.

Swidler, Ann. 2001. *Talk of Love: How Culture Matters*. Chicago: University of Chicago Press.

Tavory, Iddo, and Stefan Timmermans. 2009. "Two Cases of Ethnography: Grounded Theory and the Extended Case Method," *Ethnography* 10, 3: 243–63.

Tawney, Richard H. [1912] 1967. *The Agrarian Problem in the Sixteenth Century*. New York: Harper & Row.

Tetlock, Philip E., Richard Ned Lebow, and Geoffrey Parker. 2006. *Unmaking the West: "What-If" Scenarios That Rewrite World History*. Ann Arbor: University of Michigan Press.

Thompson, E. P. [1978] 1995. *Poverty of Theory: Orrery of Errors*. London: Merlin Press.

Tilly, Charles. 1985. "War Making and State Making as Organized Crime." In *Bringing the State Back*, ed. P. Evans, D. Rueschemeyer, and T. Skocpol, pp. 169–87. Cambridge, U.K.: Cambridge University Press.

Timmermans, Stefan, and Iddo Tavory. 2012. "Theory Construction in Qualitative Research: From Grounded Theory to Abductive Analysis," *Sociological Theory* 30: 167–86.

Tocqueville, Alexis de. [1835–1840] 2004. *Democracy in America*. New York: Library of America.

———. 2003. *Lettres choisies, souvenirs, 1814–1859*. Paris : Gallimard.

Tsoukas, Henry 1993. "Analogical Reasoning and Knowledge Generation in Organization Theory," *Organization Studies* 14(3): 323–46.

Turner, Jonathan. 1985. "In Defense of Positivism," *Sociological Theory* 3 (Fall 1985): 24–30.

———. 1981. "Returning to Social Physics: Illustrations from George Herbert Mead," *Current Perspectives in Social Theory* 2: 187–208.

Turner, Stephen. 2008. "How Not to Do Science," *Sociological Quarterly* 49(2): 237–51.

———. 2007. "Public Sociology and Democratic Theory," *Sociology* 41(5): 785–98.

———. 1980. *Sociological Explanation as Translation*. New York: Cambridge University Press.

Tversky, Amos, and Daniel Kahneman. 1982. *Judgment under Uncertainty: Heuristics and Biases*. Cambridge, U.K.: Cambridge University Press.

———. 1974. "Judgment under Uncertainty: Heuristics and Biases," *Science* 185(4157): 1124–31.

Vaihinger, Hans. [1911] 2009. *The Philosophy 'As If'*. Mansfield Centre, Conn.: Martino Publishing.

Van Maanen, John. 1995. "Style as Theory," *Organization Science* 6: 133–43.

Varian, Hal. 1998. "How to Build an Economic Model in Your Spare Time." In *Passion and Craft: Economists at Work*, ed. Michael Szenberg, pp. 256–71. Ann Arbor: University of Michigan Press.

Vaughan, Diane. 2009. "Analytic Ethnography." In *The Oxford Handbook of Analytical Sociology*, ed. P. Hedström and P. Bearman, pp. 688–733. New York: Oxford University Press.

———. 2004. "Theorizing Disaster," *Ethnography* 5(3): 313–45.

———. 2002. "Signals and Interpretive Work." In *Culture in Mind*, ed. K. Cerulo, pp. 28–54. New York: Routledge.

———. 1999. "The Dark Side of Organizations," *Annual Review of Sociology* 25: 271–305.

———. 1998. "Rational Choice, Situated Action, and the Social Control of Organizations," *Law & Society Review* 32(1): 23–61.

———. 1996. *The Challenger Launch Decision: Risky Technology, Culture, and Deviance at NASA*. Chicago: University of Chicago Press.

———. 1992. "Theory Elaboration: The Heuristics of Case Analysis." In *What Is a Case?* ed. C. Ragin and H. S. Becker, pp. 173–202. Cambridge, U.K.: Cambridge University Press

———. 1986. *Uncoupling*. New York: Oxford University Press.

———. 1983. *Controlling Unlawful Organizational Behavior*. Chicago: University of Chicago Press.

Wagner, David G., and Joseph Berger. 1986. "Programs, Theory, and Metatheory," *American Journal of Sociology* 92(1): 168–82.

———. 1985. "Do Sociological Theories Grow?" *American Journal of Sociology* 90(4): 697–728.

Wang, Xiao-Tian. 2006. "Emotions within Reason: Resolving Conflicts in Risk Preference," *Cognition and Emotion* 20(8): 1132–52.

Weber, Max. [1919] 2012. "Science as a Profession and Vocation." In *Max Weber: Collected Methodological Writings*, pp. 335–53. Edited by Hans Henrik Bruun and Sam Whimster, translated by H. H. Bruun. London: Routledge.

———. [1909] 2008. *Max Weber's Complete Writings on Academic and Political Vocations*. New York, N.Y.: Algora.

———. 2001. *The Protestant Ethic Debate: Max Weber's Replies to His Critics, 1907–*

1910. Ed. David Chalcraft and Austin Harrington. Liverpool, U.K.: Liverpool University Press.

———. [1919] 1994. "The Profession and Vocation of Politics." In *Weber: Political Writings*, ed. Peter Lassman and Ronald Spiers, pp. 309–69. Trans. Ronald Spiers. Cambridge, U.K.: Cambridge University Press.

———. [1922] 1978. *Economy and Society: An Outline of Interpretive Sociology*. 3 vols. Ed. Guenther Roth and Claus Wittich. Berkeley: University of California Press.

———. [1922] 1972. *Wirtschaft und Gesellschaft. Grundriss der verstehenden Soziologie.* 5 ed. Tübingen: J.C.B. Mohr.

———. [1922] 1949. *The Methodology of the Social Sciences*. Glencoe, Ill.: Free Press.

———. 1946. *From Max Weber*. Ed. H. H. Gerth and C. Wright Mills. New York: Oxford University Press.

———. [1919] 1946. "Politics as a Vocation." In *From Max Weber: Essays in Sociology*, ed. and trans. H. H. Gerth and C. W. Mills, pp. 77–128. New York: Oxford University Press.

Weber, René, Ron Tamborini, Amber Westcott-Baker, and Benjamin Kantor. 2009. "Theorizing Flow and Media Enjoyment as Cognitive Synchronization of Attentional and Reward Networks," *Communication Theory* 19: 397–422.

Weick, Karl E. 2005. "Making Sense of Blurred Images: Mindful Organizing in Mission STS-107." In *Organization at the Limit: Lessons from the Columbia Disaster*, ed. W. H. Starbuck and M. Farjoun, pp. 159–78. Malden, Mass.: Blackwell.

———. 1995a. *Sensemaking in Organizations*. Thousand Oaks, Calif.: Sage Publications.

———. 1995b. "What Theory Is Not, Theorizing Is," *Administrative Science Quarterly* 40, 3: 385–90.

———. 1989. "Theory Construction as Disciplined Imagination," *Academy of Management Review* 14: 516–31.

———. 1976. "Education Organizations as Loosely Coupled Systems," *Administrative Science Quarterly* 21: 1–19.

Weick, Karl E., Kathleen M. Sutcliffe, and David Obstfeld. 1999. "Organizing for High Reliability: Processes of Collective Mindfulness," *Research in Organizational Behavior* 21: 81–123.

Weintraub, E. Roy. 2002. *How Economics Became a Mathematical Science*. Durham, N.C.: Duke University Press.

Weschler, Lawrence. 1982. *Seeing Is Forgetting the Name of the Thing One Sees: A Life of Contemporary Artist Robert Irwin*. Berkeley: University of California Press.

Whitehead, Alfred North. 1979. *Process and Reality (Gifford Lectures Delivered in the University of Edinburgh during the Session 1927–28)*. New York: Free Press.

Whitley, Richard. 2000. *The Intellectual and Social Organization of the Sciences*. New York: Oxford University Press.

Whyte, William F. 1943. *Street Corner Society*. Chicago: University of Chicago Press.

Wilcken, Patrick. 2010. *Claude Lévi-Strauss: The Poet in the Laboratory.* New York: Penguin.

Willer, David. 1996. "The Prominence of Formal Theory in Sociology," *Sociological Forum* 11(2): 319–31.

———. 1967. *Scientific Sociology: Theory and Method.* Englewood Cliffs, N.J.: Prentice-Hall.

Willis, Paul. 1977. *Learning to Labor: How Working Class Kids Get Working Class Jobs.* New York: Columbia University Press.

Wittgenstein, Ludwig. 1953. *Philosophical Investigations.* Trans. G. E. M. Anscombe. New York: Macmillan.

Wootton, Barbara. 1938. *Lament for Economics.* London: George Allen & Unwin.

Wright, Erik Olin. 2010. *Envisioning Real Utopias.* London: New York: Verso.

———. 1997. *Class Counts: Comparative Studies in Class Analysis.* Cambridge, U.K.: Cambridge University Press.

Zald, Mayer. 1995. "Progress and Cumulation in the Human Sciences after the Fall," *Sociological Forum* 10(3): 455–79.

———. 1991. "Sociology as a Discipline: Quasi-Science and Quasi-Humanities," *American Sociologist* 22(3/4): 165–87.

Zashin, Elliot, and Phillip Chapman. 1974. "The Uses of Metaphor and Analogy: Toward a Renewal of Political Language." *Journal of Politics* 36 (May): 290–326.

Zerubavel, Eviatar. 2007. "Generally Speaking," *Sociological Forum* 22(2): 131–45.

Zetterberg, Hans. 1963. *On Theory and Verification in Sociology.* Revised edition. Totowa, N.J.: Bedminster Press.

Zhao, Shanyang. 1996. "The Beginning of the End or the End of the Beginning? The Theory Construction Movement Revisited," *Sociological Forum* 11(2): 305–18.

Index